ULTIMATE
DOG
GROOMING

SECOND EDITION

ULTIMATE
DOG
GROOMING

Eileen Geeson

Additional material by Barbara Vetter & Lia Whitmore

FIREFLY BOOKS

A FIREFLY BOOK

Published by Firefly Books Ltd. 2015

First printing

Publisher Cataloging-in-Publication Data (U.S.)

Geeson, Eileen.
 Ultimate dog grooming / Eileen Geeson.
2nd ed.
[304] pages : color photographs ; cm.
Includes index.
Summary: "A step-by-step guide to grooming all major dog coat types, and on starting a dog grooming business." – from Publisher.
ISBN-13: 978-1-77085-517-5 (pbk.)
1. Dogs – Grooming. 2. Dog grooming industry. I. Title.
636.70833 dc23 SF427.5.G448 2015

Library and Archives Canada Cataloguing in Publication

Geeson, Eileen, author
        Ultimate dog grooming / Eileen Geeson ; additional material by Barbara Vetter & Lia Whitmore. — Second edition.
Includes index.
Originally published by Firefly Books, 2004.
ISBN 978-1-77085-517-5 (pbk.)
        1. Dogs—Grooming. I. Vetter, Barbara, author II. Whitmore, Lia, author III. Title.
SF427.5.G43 2015   636.7'0833   C2015-901668-1

Published in the United States by
Firefly Books (U.S.) Inc.
P.O. Box 1338, Ellicott Station
Buffalo, New York 14205

Published in Canada by
Firefly Books Ltd.
50 Staples Avenue, Unit 1
Richmond Hill, Ontario L4B 0A7

Designed by Sarah Williams
Cover design by Erin R. Holmes/Soplari Design.

Printed in China

Conceived, designed, and produced by
Interpet Publishing,
Vincent Lane, Dorking,
Surrey RH4 3YX

Author Eileen Geeson with her dogs.

DEDICATION

This is dedicated to Jeanne Beady, who gave me my first grooming job. I thank her for her kindness to dogs and for her expert, caring knowledge. Also to Gigi, the first Poodle I clipped.

ACKNOWLEDGMENTS

Special thanks to Carol and Mandy at DeZynaDog for their help and encouragement, and for allowing me to use their salon and up-to-the minute equipment and products in the preparation of the dogs profiled. Thanks to the dogs and their owners who patiently sat through hours of grooming and photography, namely Pippa Clare, Barbara Thornley, Martin Butler, Kevin Dodds, Ron Ellery, Leslie Curry, Molly Jones, and Cathy Browne.

I thank the following for their help with the breed profiles: Val Watkins of Valsett (English Setter), Carol Ritchie (Griffon), Linda Mayne (Italian Spinone), Terry Spencer (Welsh Terrier), Gael Stenton and Ann Kemp (Lagotto Romagnolo), Gael Stenton (Italian Spinone diagrams and additional information), Violet Slade (Black Russian Terrier), Jan Wakerley (Irish Water Spaniel), and Marita Bott of Bardonhill (Irish Setter). Thank you to all the groomers who contributed expertise and photographs including Lisa Rendall, Barbara Turnball and Lesley Garratt. Many thanks to all the breed clubs and advisors who checked or gave advice on their breed profiles. If you would like further information on a breed, or its grooming requirements, contact the relevant breed club (your national kennel club will have details). Photography: Sally Anne Thompson and R. Willbie. Line drawings: Viv Rainsbury.

$\mathcal{C}$ONTENTS

(Smooth and Wire); Dalmatian; Dobermann; Foxhound; French Bulldog; German Shorthaired Pointer; Great Dane; Hamiltonstövare; Ibizan Hound; Italian Greyhound; Labrador; Lancashire Heeler; Manchester Terrier; Manchester Terrier (Toy); Mastiff; Miniature Pinscher; Neapolitan Mastiff; Pharaoh Hound; Pointer; Pug; Rhodesian Ridgeback; Rottweiler; Sloughi; Staffordshire Bull Terrier; Swedish Vallhund; Vizsla; Weimaraner; Welsh Corgi (Cardigan and Pembroke); Whippet.

1 COAT TYPES

M any people think grooming is all about clipping Poodles, but it is much more than that. Grooming is the act of keeping the skin and coat in a healthy, clean, balanced state. It also involves the maintenance of teeth, ears and nails.

Grooming is an integral part of dog care. Not only does it keep the animal clean and looking good, but it is also a social act that strengthens the relationship between handler and dog.

How you groom a dog depends on the breed, coat type and the owner's personal preferences. Anyone can put a dog on a table and brush its coat up and down for a few moments, but with a little thought and hard work, both dog and owner can enjoy the experience and, who knows, you may be a future Groomer of the Year as a result!

BUYING A DOG: COAT CONSIDERATIONS

Among the many breeds of dog, there is a tremendous difference in the types of coat. Certainly, one should take this into serious consideration before taking on a breed of dog.

- Can you cope with the hair?
- Will the dog require professional grooming help? (See Chapter Four.)
- Can you afford the outlay of regular trips to the grooming parlor?
- Are you, or any of your family, asthmatic or allergic to shedding dog hair or dandruff, or both?
- Could you cope with all those long curls that get covered with mud during a wet walk?

You may be attracted to a breed with a luxurious coat (left), but can you cope with the reality of keeping it clean and well groomed?

These are just a few questions that need to be considered before deciding on the right breed for your family. It is wise to speak to owners of your shortlisted breeds before making your final choice.

Your national kennel club will be able to put you in contact with breed clubs of those types of dogs you might be interested in. The club representatives can tell you how demanding the coat care is for their particular breed so you will know exactly what you will be taking on.

It is a good idea to consult a groomer to inquire about the cost of grooming sessions before making a final decision on which breed is right for your family. Additionally, groomers, who have worked with dogs of many breeds for many years, often have valuable knowledge to impart about the characteristics of different breeds.

For full information on grooming different coat types and the equipment needed, see Part Three.

PUPPY COATS

Puppies of all breeds have a softer coat than they will have on gaining maturity, and it is easy to underestimate the grooming that is required as the dog matures.

Poodles, for instance, have a soft, fluffy wool coat that is easy to keep until they are about 7 months of age, when the coat will thicken. Unless it is properly groomed, the coat will mat or felt against the skin, especially if the coat gets wet and is left to its own devices to dry.

The Bearded Collie coat is quite manageable at the puppy stage (left) but the adult below requires regular attention.

BASIC COAT TYPES

There are many different types of coat. Part Three of this book is organized into the following categories.

The short coat: the Whippet

The long coat: the Yorkshire Terrier

The corded/curly coat: the Curly-Coated Retriever

The medium/silky coat: the Irish Setter

The thick coat: the Finnish Lapphund

The stripped coat: the Airedale Terrier

The trimmed/clipped coat: the Bichon Frise

2 THE HEALTHY COAT

The condition of a dog's coat is influenced by many factors. Genetically, a dog can inherit coat quality from its predecessors, but there are many other influences, such as diet, exercise, the dog's housing and bedding, as well as its grooming regime. All coats can be improved with just a little effort and consideration of the dog's individual needs.

FEEDING

What you feed your dog counts. When considering feeding, it is always advisable to listen to your breeder's advice.

Most reputable breeders have worked out a diet that suits their breed of dog and are careful to give new puppy owners a diet sheet

to follow through from puppyhood to adult age. Certainly, good breeders are keen to support the new puppy owner and will provide after-sales advice throughout the dog's lifetime.

As no two dogs are alike, it is possible for two pups from the same litter to have completely different dietary needs. Though this is unusual, as dogs are basically scavengers, some dogs will have special needs, and your breeder may be able to suggest a suitable alternative diet.

NATURAL DIET

We all try to do the best we can for our dogs, and this includes giving them the best food. Many people believe that the more they spend, the better the results, which is not necessarily the case.

We are what we eat, and dogs are no exception. Feeding the dog is important to skin and coat care, but it is essential to point out that the needs of individual dogs can differ; not all dogs suit the same diet, no matter what their owners' preferences. However, if a natural diet is fed, then there is far less likelihood of adverse reactions and the coat of the dog is a shining example of what goes inside the dog.

A diet of raw lamb and beef bones, tripe, lamb, chicken and beef with organic

SCAVENGERS

Dogs still retain many of their original characteristics from when they were living in the wild. Natural scavengers, they are resilient and largely resistant to food poisoning. They have dentition for carnivorous activity, with large teeth for cutting meat and tearing tough tissue. Even small dogs relish a good meaty bone or a chunk of chewy meat.

You are what you eat – a glossy, healthy coat is proof of good nutrition.

The raw, meaty bones diet is popular with many owners.

vegetables and, two or three days a week, a meal made from brown rice and chicken is a healthy, natural diet for a dog.

Additives are not generally required with this diet, but some dogs may benefit from evening primrose oil, flaxseed oil or starflower oil, at a dose of 500 mg daily. This is especially beneficial when the coat is poor from a previous diet, if the dog has a flea allergy problem or has suffered inherited or environmental effects that leave the coat looking far from good (dogs fed on raw natural food very rarely attract fleas, as their skin is less pleasant for parasites).

Raw, natural diets need consideration to ensure a variety of vitamins and minerals. Eggs are a good source of nutrients. Live yogurt has calcium. Cheese has many essential nutrients as well as being a good source of calcium, and most dogs love cheese. Meat can be varied, as tripe, beef, chicken, turkey and lamb are all easily available in wonderful little flat, easy-store freezer packs from most pet shops. Offal can be fed once a week.

Wheat is commonly used in dog food, but many dogs are allergic to this. Rice can be used along with lentils, peas, beans and chickpeas. Vegetables can be given to a dog with a free hand. Packs of mixed vegetables from the freezer at the supermarket are wonderful and easy to feed, and dogs love them – just give a handful a day to large dogs and a bit less to small dogs.

Dogs love fruit. Some like bananas, some like oranges. If the dog likes it, feed it – they usually know best. Certainly, they love blackberries and apples, and their mouth waters for raw cabbage and raw broccoli. However, it is best to avoid grapes, which are toxic to dogs.

Fats such as olive oil and peanut oil are nourishing, as are fish, brewer's yeast, kelp and dandelion. Fiber, such as oat bran, will help to prevent anal gland trouble. Cider vinegar is useful for the dog as well as us. It's good for arthritis and for helping the immune system. Extra vitamin C may be required where there is abnormal joint or bone development or weakness. Your veterinarian can advise you in this respect.

My dogs all look wonderful on a raw, natural diet and they have excellent coats.

COMPLETE FOOD

Dry, complete foods have a number of advantages. They are easily stored, quick and simple to feed, and clean. Most importantly, they provide a nutritionally complete diet, and so do all the hard work for you. Working out the dog's exact nutritional needs takes considerable research, and it is very easy to malnourish the dog accidentally.

There are several types of dry food on the market, but some are extremely high in protein, which does not suit all dogs. Indeed, excess protein has been known to make some dogs aggressive or hyperactive. Not all dogs of the same breed suit the same dry food, so take the advice of the breeder and/or your vet if you have any queries or concerns.

WORMING

If your dog has worms, its coat will suffer the consequences. Your breeder must supply you with details of when your new puppy was wormed and you must continue this process throughout your dog's life. Your vet will provide you with dosage details.

EXERCISE

Different breeds of dog vary enormously in their exercise requirement, but a fit and healthy dog will be recognized in an instant by the gleam of its jacket.

Healthy dogs obviously perform better than overweight or undernourished dogs. Young bones of the heavy breeds cannot take the strain of too much exercise and this is best kept to a minimum in such breeds as the Bernese or the Great Dane for instance, but moderate exercise will stimulate good health, which will show in the appearance of the coat. Exercise, walking, free-running and

Complete foods are quick and convenient, and provide all the nutrients a dog needs.

Regular exercise is essential for keeping a dog in peak fitness, and is reflected in its coat condition.

Where the dog is kept and what type of bed it has directly influences the appearance of its coat.

visits to new areas stimulate good health, and do the owner good too.

Do check your dog over carefully after a walk. Remove any burrs, grass seeds or other debris that may have accumulated. Check its feet too. In cold weather, check the pads for packed snow or ice, which can cause sores.

HOUSING

Where do you intend to keep your dog? This will depend largely on what breed you have. A Poodle, Cavalier King Charles Spaniel or Cocker Spaniel, for instance, will certainly live in the house at all times and probably sleep as near to you as possible, if not on the bed! A Bullmastiff, Bernese Mountain Dog, Newfoundland or Great Pyrenees may live in a utility room; an Alaskan Malamute may live in an outside kennel.

The bedding and housing you choose for your dog will have a bearing on the dog's coat. A dog that constantly lies on concrete will wear the hair off its elbows and elsewhere. A dog lying on grass all the time may get bitten by insects or parasites and may develop skin irritations from the damp. Scratching at insect bites can also destroy a beautiful coat overnight.

Bedding should be washed regularly and floors should be kept clean, but remember that too strong a disinfectant can be dangerous if it comes into contact with the dog's skin or coat, particularly if it is licked off by the dog.

EARLY DETECTION

When regular attention is paid to grooming, early detection of problems like runny eyes, bad breath, skin disorders and allergies can be recognized and nipped in the bud (see Chapter Eight).

One flea sighted means that many more are present. Recognizing the first signs of a parasite invasion will not only save the dog from considerable discomfort and pain, it will also save you a great deal of money and a lot of distress.

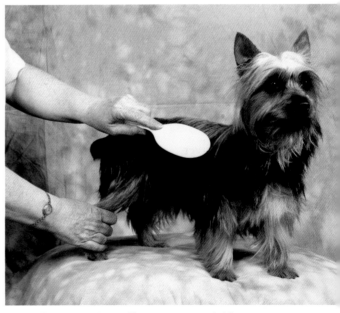

Regular grooming allows you to quickly spot any health problems.

3 *ROUTINE CARE*

When should you start a grooming regime? From day one is the simple answer. Choose a suitable brush for your dog or puppy's coat type (see Chapter Six and Part Three), and spend a little time each day getting the dog used to being brushed.

For most breeds of dog, it is a simple task to put the puppy on a table and brush it. Even with the heavier breeds, it is useful to put the dog on a table to begin with, while carrying out routine brushing, combing, checking ears, eyes and mouth, as well as ensuring the anal area is clean and completely free of foreign matter or feces. Be particularly vigilant with heavy-coated breeds as they tend to collect debris, such as twigs, which must be removed before more clutter collects,

and the anal area must be kept scrupulously clean.

HOW OFTEN?
With a new puppy, it is worth brushing it on a daily basis. This interaction will benefit the puppy and teach it to respond to you and to observe house rules and manners. Grooming interaction will also help the puppy to feel secure, while you will learn more about the character you have chosen to live with for the coming years.

With some breeds that don't need constant attention to their coats, grooming may later become a weekly occupation rather than a daily one. However, it is wise to brush your puppy every day in the early weeks so that it gets used to being handled and to accepting being groomed.

EARLY TRAINING
It is essential to train the pup to stand still and to be groomed. If you don't get it used to the routine when it is young, it will be even harder when the dog is a full-grown adult.

Take the puppy to your chosen grooming spot, stand it up, say "Stand," wait for just a couple of seconds, then give it a treat and praise it handsomely. Repeat a few times every day, until the pup learns what the word "Stand" means. The treats, praise and cuddles

PROFESSIONAL GROOMING

For the average pet owner of the numerous breeds that require specific attention to their coats (e.g., the Poodle, Cocker Spaniel or most of the terrier breeds), a visit to a professional groomer will be necessary at regular intervals, from the age of about 3 to 4 months. However, basic daily brushing is all that is required for the average young pup and the adult dog alike.

Puppies should get used to the routine of grooming from a young age. This is particularly important with high-maintenance breeds, such as the Shih Tzu (right).

will make the dog look forward to its grooming times.

It is also useful to teach your dog to lie on its side while being groomed, particularly with longcoated breeds. It is a safe and comfortable position, and the dog should feel at ease.

Most puppies are pleased to have the attention of daily grooming. They love the interaction, and handling will be beneficial to their growth and mentality. With only a few minutes a day spent on grooming, the dog will become accustomed to being handled and will be more responsive to its owner or family.

With very young puppies, don't prolong

PUPPY POWER

When grooming puppies, lay a thick towel on the grooming table. This will make it more comfortable for the pup, and it is less likely to become restless.

---

this session or the pup will become bored and will learn to hate the "boring" grooming sessions. Getting the pup used to being handled will prepare it for being handled by professional groomers, vets and show judges, and will mean it is generally happy and confident around all types of people.

One word of advice to the new puppy owner: check that your new young pup has relieved itself before grooming commences, so that it is not distracted. A pup that needs to urinate will object and whine all the time you are trying to brush it.

GETTING STARTED

Grooming incorporates the brushing, bathing, clipping or stripping of the dog's coat. The average dog owner rarely undertakes specialized or professional coat care. For the pet owner, it is sufficient to understand the rudiments of basic brushing and, depending on the breed of dog you have chosen, combing and bathing. This section is intended for the novice, or the new dog owner.

Brushing a dog on a table is far more convenient and less backbreaking than trying to see to its needs while kneeling on the floor. Dogs are usually far better behaved while on a table.

- Place the puppy on the grooming table, and stand close by, with a finger holding its collar to ensure that the dog does not fall or jump off the table.
- Tell the puppy to "Stand," and praise and reassure it when it stands quietly.
- Commence brushing with your free hand, starting from the head and working systematically down the body, legs and tail.
- Do this for a minute or two, then tell the pup to "Turn" as you turn the pup the opposite way round.
- Again, tell the pup to "Stand" and commence brushing this side, starting with the head and working across.
- Stroke the coat firmly but gently, and repeat the word "Stand" every now and

It is important to play with your puppy after grooming, so the dog learns to view it as a rewarding experience.

Grooming at waist height is far more comfortable for the handler.

then. Praise and reassure the pup intermittently.
- When you have finished brushing the coat, reward the pup with praise and its favorite tidbit.
- Then lift the pup down onto the floor, and play a game together.
- The puppy will soon look forward to its grooming sessions because they are so enjoyable.
- After a couple of days, when the pup is accustomed to being handled in this way, progress to using a comb after brushing where the coat necessitates this (see Part Three for details).

OTHER CHECKS
Your puppy should also get used to being checked all over – ears, teeth and nails need special attention (see Chapter Seven). Not only will this make your life easier in the long term (your adult will be more compliant), but your vet will thank you for not having a ticklish, nervous or aggressive dog.

Wrinkly breeds, such as the Chinese Shar-Pei or Bulldog (pictured), need regular skin care as part of their grooming routine.

WRINKLES

Wrinkly breeds, such as the Bulldog and the increasingly popular Chinese Shar-Pei, need special attention to keep their wrinkles dirt-free and dry, in order to ward off irritation and infection.

Wrinkly breeds should also be watched carefully to check that the facial wrinkles do not irritate the sensitive eye surface with constant rubbing.

- The skin must be parted and cleansed with warm water.
- Dry thoroughly.
- A light dusting of baby powder or cornstarch – first applied to cotton batting – may be necessary.
- This should be attended to weekly, as with all folds or wrinkles in the skin.

BATHING AND DRYING

All dogs benefit from a bath. Some breeders claim that show coats, on terrier breeds for instance, are made too soft if the coat is washed clean.

As far as a pet dog is concerned, it is up to the owner if they prefer a nice-smelling pet whose coat doesn't leave an odor or grease on the hands after stroking. Certainly, clean hair is easier to brush and comb than dirty hair.

For step-by-step instructions on bathing, see Chapter Seven.

SHAMPOOS AND CONDITIONERS

Ask your dog's breeder to recommend a shampoo that is suitable for your dog's coat type.

A mild, pH-balanced shampoo is usually all that is required. Insecticidal shampoos to treat fleas are available, but these tend to be strong and should not be used on a regular basis.

Some coats benefit from the application of a conditioner. This is the case with long coats (see Chapter Eleven) and "transition" coats (when the dog is midstage between the fluffy puppy coat and the mature adult coat).

4 THE GROOMING PARLOR

Many pet owners take their dogs to the grooming parlor or have a professional come to their own home (particularly useful if you do not have your own car). There is nothing quite like having your dog professionally groomed – you end up with a fabulous-looking dog, without having to lift a brush!

CHOOSING A PROFESSIONAL

Your groomer should be chosen with care, and you should start your quest before you purchase your dog. The vast majority of professional groomers are people who are devoted to dogs and will take every care of your pet. However, there are some that go it alone too soon. A minority go on a three-week course to learn the art of clipping, and then believe they are ready to trim any dog. They are not. Considerable experience is required to deal with the many ranges of coat textures and requirements, even more importantly, the varying temperaments of the numerous breeds of dog.

So how do you choose the right person to trust with your most precious puppy or adult dog? Perhaps the first question you should ask a groomer is not how long they have been trimming, but how long have they been involved with dogs in general. I have lived with dogs all my life and have had considerable experience with a wide variety

of breeds. Not all groomers can be this lucky, but at least two to three years of working at a kennel or at a grooming parlor would prove a great asset in learning about dog breeds, their characters and the different handling they require.

All dogs respond to kindness, but some need a firmer hand than others or a sterner voice. Dogs that appear to want to snap have to be analyzed to distinguish between fear and bad temper. I used to trim a Westie called William. The family moved away and the owner took William to another groomer. He bit her three times. I couldn't believe this at first, until I considered that William was

Knowing how to handle dogs is as important as the technicalities of grooming.

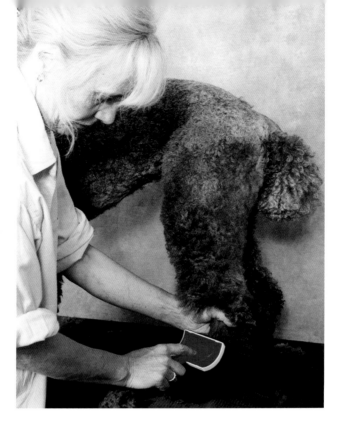

When choosing a groomer, ask to watch them at work before giving them your business.

very arthritic and I always trimmed him with this in mind. He never once attempted to snap at me.

You should ask the groomer if they have ever been bitten, and how often. I am always wary, for instance, when I talk to groomers at seminars and they say, "I hate doing Poodles, they are nasty, snappy things." If they can't get on with the tolerant Poodle, well...

However, we must not assume this is the norm; most groomers do care and are passionately devoted to their job, growing to love the dogs they trim on a regular basis.

In the U.S., you should ask if the groomer is licensed or certified. Some states require that the shop is licensed, not the groomer. Some require that the groomer is licensed to handle pesticides.

SEEING IS BELIEVING
If you are impressed by a groomer, ask to stay and watch some dogs being groomed. If you are pleased with what you see (i.e. that the dogs are happy and relaxed, and that the groomer is confident and skilled), make an appointment for your dog to be groomed, and ask if you can watch. No groomer with confidence in his or her own ability will

object to this request by the owner.

It has to be said that some dogs play up a bit to begin with if their owners are present. But if the owner ignores the dog and just sits quietly, the dog will soon settle.

Some groomers are happy for clients to watch their work, but are not keen on them being present when their own dogs are groomed – because of the time factor in getting the pet to settle. Consider your own dog's character and talk to your groomer to reach a compromise.

IMPORTANT INFORMATION
The groomer should request and record specific information from you. Besides your name and one or more phone numbers at which to reach you, they should ask your pet's age, the name and number of your veterinarian, and any specific health problems (e.g., moles or allergies).

SUCCESSFUL RELATIONSHIP
It is very important to take your puppy to see the groomer at the earliest possible date, even for a brush, so that the dog will become accustomed to being handled by the groomer at a young age. This will not only help the

groomer, it will help your dog and prevent it from getting into a neglected and matted state. The moment the coat becomes matted, the more uncomfortable it will be for the dog to be groomed – the dog will then associate the groomer with discomfort and will be less cooperative on future visits.

Often, problems occur because the owner doesn't think about taking the pup for professional grooming until it is more than a year old, or until the time comes when they can no longer cope with the mats that have formed in the coat. Of course, this makes the dog's first experience of being professionally trimmed less enjoyable than it should be, which can lead to problems later on.

ACCIDENTS HAPPEN

Do check that the groomer has adequate insurance coverage before you take your dog in to be groomed. Accidents rarely occur in the grooming parlor, but there will be the odd occasion where an accident will take place no matter how careful the groomer is.

Most pet owners' insurance covers such eventualities in the event of the groomer being personally uninsured, but it may be advisable to check this out with your own policy to be on the safe side. As well, you may injure your own dog and need veterinary help, so be sure that you are covered.

HOW MUCH WILL IT COST?

By the time this book is published, prices will have changed, but I can give you some helpful pointers. The cost of having a dog professionally groomed varies according to the breed and the work involved. For example, American Cockers take longer than English Cockers, as a rule. The following factors will also be taken into account:

- Whether the dog is clipped or stripped (hand-stripping takes far longer).
- Whether or not the dog is having a bath.
- The condition of the coat.
- The trim – all cut off, "Lamb," "Dutch," "Lion," etc.
- The geographical region (although this is now leveling out with the increasing membership of association bodies).

If you choose to own a coated breed of dog, such as a terrier, Afghan, Old English Sheepdog or Poodle, you will periodically have to take your pet to a groomer for a haircut, bath or professional groom. Hopefully, you will have considered professional coat care costs before purchasing your puppy.

Although they may look similar, the American Cocker Spaniel (below) takes longer to groom than the English Cocker (left) – something that should be reflected in your pricing structure.

5 *STARTING OUT*

The route to becoming a professional groomer is varied. Very often, people enter the profession through learning how to trim their own breed, and the interest grows from there.

There are those who have a romantic view of cuddly dogs that will look clean and fluffy with an imaginary wave of a wand, without understanding that such results are achieved only with effort and dedication. Such people usually fall by the wayside after a week or two of grooming neglected and filthy dogs, realizing that trimming the hair from the dog involves a lot more than using a pair of clippers in a slipshod manner. In fact, around 50 percent of those who actually complete their grooming schooling quit within a year of graduation, finding that the work is too hard.

GROOMING SEMINARS

For those contemplating a career in grooming, it is worthwhile to attend at least one of the seminars or roadshows that take place throughout the year (these are advertised in the weekly and monthly dog papers and magazines). At such seminars, qualified, highly experienced dog groomers from top establishments are on hand to offer advice and to give trimming demonstrations on many different breeds.

These seminars are very useful for picking up new tips and ideas, as well as professional hints on running a salon and turning out the best-dressed dogs. They are always extremely friendly and the comradeship between the groomers is strongly felt.

Trade (vendor) stands will also be present at these events with lots of special offers, some free samples and the very latest equipment. Much research has gone into the development of grooming equipment and there is now a specialized range of high-tech grooming tools designed to save time and

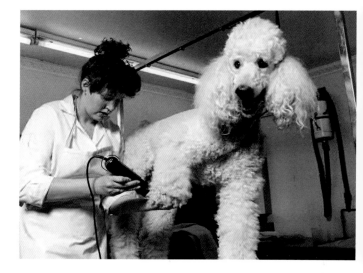

Grooming seminars are well worth attending – particularly if you are new to the profession.

money, making the life of the groomer less labor-intensive, less stressful and more cost-effective.

Various talks by veterinary surgeons feature throughout the day, and groomers share their experiences. Additionally, there are lots of demonstrations of trimming and styling, as well as mat-breaking. Invariably, there is a scissor clinic with special advice for those with problems, and demonstrations cover professional presentation for the groomer and preparing the dog for the show ring, as well as using professional grooming equipment.

If you are unsure about starting out as a trainee, then do make the effort to attend these informative occasions. Groomers love to chat and to tell you how they got started.

If available in your area, join a local groomers' association, which will afford you invaluable networking opportunities.

BASIC TRAINING

The initial and basic training for a groomer is tremendously important. The better the salon, by way of professionalism and a caring attitude to dogs, the more competent and successful the trainee groomer will eventually become. There are colleges that teach grooming, and courses are also available at kennels and grooming establishments; these are well advertised in the weekly dog papers.

Short courses offer only an introduction to grooming. It is impossible to learn the individual requirements of different breeds in a matter of weeks, let alone to get to grips with how to trim them all. It is possible to get some idea from these brief courses, but certainly no degree of experience. This can only be gained through an apprenticeship.

It is advised that you take a job with a grooming establishment of good reputation and spend at least a year gaining experience and expertise before setting up on your own. It is advisable to start as a bather and slowly work your way up to clipping. Rushing the process can be disastrous.

IMPROVING GROOMING SKILLS

Training in grooming can follow many paths, one being writing exams at various levels to achieve accreditation. The National Dog Grooming Association of America (www.nationaldoggroomers.com), the International Society of Canine Cosmetologists (www.petstylist.com) and International Professional Groomers, Inc. (www.ipgicmg.com) are three of the top sources of certification in the United States. Their websites provide details about courses, as well as accredited training locations where groomers can write their exams. All of these organizations base their criteria on the breed standards of the American Kennel Club.

International Professional Groomers, Inc., introduced the Salon Details Certificate program, the first of its kind in the world, in 2014. This certification essentially indicates that groomers who pass are highly knowledgeable about servicing dogs, with an emphasis on health and safety for pets and groomers. The program includes:

- professionalism and ethics
- shop safety practices
- canine first aid
- recognizing potential canine health issues
- how groomers can protect their own health
- legal permits and requirements
- skin and the effects of grooming
- canine behavior and handling tips, and more.

Grooming competitions are growing in popularity year by year, and groomers travel all over the world to compete. You need nerves of steel to get through, as the standard of grooming is usually extremely high. When I judged the British Dog Grooming Championship in 2010 at the Pet Care Trust's 30th anniversary the decisions were minutely close.

The association represents groomer members by providing training, education and support as well as organizing events for dog groomers. All members abide by the BDGA's Code of Professional Groomers' Charter. This is a code of practice designed to guarantee the highest possible standards for customer care and animal welfare.

Preparing a dog for competition takes some thought, not least regarding the temperament of the dog which has to cope with the fuss, noise and excitement. All aspects of the dog's comfort, not forgetting water, food, bed and toys, have to be planned. Dogs must be accustomed to standing on a grooming table and being groomed. Don't think of competing with a dog that is unsettled when being groomed.

Get to the venue in good time to allow you and the dog to relax and have a few friendly chats before getting started; this will set you at ease. Register as soon as possible after arrival. Don't be too disappointed if you do not get placed to begin with. Listen to the different judges' advice and opinions and see how you can improve your performance. It may be just a minor change that will get you the recognition you desire.

COST CONSIDERATIONS

Before you set up in business, it is important to consider all the costs you will incur. Firstly, where are you going to do it? Many groomers set up a business from home, even using a spare bedroom and their personal bathroom to wash dogs. This may suffice for a while, but can be impractical and does not give a professional impression. In the long term, you should consider either finding business premises or building an extension to the home where the facilities are more convenient and hygienic.

How much you charge for your services will have to take into account your expenses, or you will end up working extremely hard for nothing. All aspects must be considered, such as rent, electricity costs, insurance, equipment and your time. Also, setting up a business requires a certain amount of advertising, which can get expensive.

However, using your talent will help cut costs. If you or a friend has a computer, it is relatively easy to create a web page for your business, design a business card and/or flyers for distribution or create a Facebook page. These are all valuable ways of getting you exposure. Eventually, word-of-mouth recommendations should provide most of your business.

ASSESSING THE COMPETITION

Research how many groomers are covering your area. Realistically, is there room for another? What services do they offer? What prices do they charge?

Where groomers have set up business at home and have no major overheads, they can,

With time, word-of-mouth recommendations will help to build your reputation.

of course, charge less for what they are doing, or make a bigger profit. Cutting costs because others in the area are not charging enough may prove fatal for the groomer who has invested a large sum in equipment and needs to pay rent. There are only so many dogs any one person can do in a day and if you are breaking even or working at a loss, it's really not worth the effort.

Belonging to a professional trade body or association may be an added expense, but it does provide a guide to the prices charged throughout the country. Often, geographical location may determine price, and vary considerably.

Another way of finding out about prices in your area is to call local groomers and ask what they charge. Not all groomers are skilled on all breeds so they may well charge less for, say, a Poodle because they are better on terriers, or vice versa.

If your competitors are good at trimming, and cheap, you may have to consider if you will get enough business not only to survive, but to pay the mortgage. If the geographical area does not look viable, consider another.

Note: in the U.S., it is illegal to discuss pricing as a group.

INSURANCE

There are insurance companies that have specific packages for the groomer. Being self-employed, anything could happen. I once heard of a groomer who had a puppy hooked to the wall. She went away to answer the telephone, the dog tried to jump off the table, and strangled himself with his own leash. This would never have happened if the groomer had had proper training on safety.

Another groomer had a car accident and had to dissolve her business overnight when she was unable to work for six months. These may be extreme cases, but accidents can happen and for just a little expense a year, one can be covered for all eventualities.

ACCOUNTS

It is a good idea to start keeping a strict order of accounts from day one. If the new groomer does not have computer skills (there are some very simple accounting packages), it is relatively easy to keep two books in order:

- One book for your expenses (telephone expenses, gas, clothes, equipment).
- Another book for your income – any earnings you make.
- If you decide to venture into adding some retail to your business (selling grooming products), keeping an accurate inventory is essential.

It is also essential either to have a professional accountant, or to undertake self-assessment for tax purposes. Your local tax office will have details.

6 BUYING EQUIPMENT

At a recent seminar, I met a lady who spent thousands on equipment to start a grooming business from her own home. She only had one week of lessons with a breeder, and thought she was ready to start on her own. Good luck to her, I hope she succeeds. She certainly took my breath away, spending all that money when she hardly knows what being a groomer really entails.

When embarking on a grooming career, it is a good idea to do several months of training and an apprenticeship period before rushing out to purchase lots of equipment that is invariably unnecessary and very expensive. Instead, concentrate on the basics, and gradually add to your grooming kit along the way, as and when you consider that additional pieces are worth the outlay.

Always buy the best equipment you can afford, and upgrade whenever possible. Poorly designed equipment can lead to repetitive strain injuries, so spending a little more money on higher-quality equipment is well worth doing.

People like different things. Some groomers use nothing but Oster clippers, some have three types sitting on their wall hooks, ready to use on different coats. Certainly, it is recommended that you buy only the best-quality clippers. Small, vibrating clippers are cheap, but useless for a busy groomer, as well as causing many usually relaxed dogs to become unruly and more difficult to handle. Put the cheap clippers on your own face and see how you like it!

TOOLS OF THE TRADE
Here we will look at the many tools available to the groomer. The fundamental rule is that you only get what you pay for. Buying from an establishment where experienced people are on hand helps you to decide what, and what not, to buy. Remember, though, that these people are in business, and often the groomer who is starting out can be persuaded to buy items that are not strictly necessary.

Here is a selection of equipment that is readily available from shops selling grooming supplies.

PROTECTIVE CLOTHING
Getting your image right will help you to encourage clients to come back. Looking good should not only apply to the dog you are trimming. Grooming is sometimes a messy job with hairs getting everywhere, but a clean, smart pair of specially designed grooming overalls will keep you looking fresh and smart. The overalls will also allow you easy movement to make some of the intricate bends required to get around the dog.

A rubber-based grooming table gives the handler better control of the dog, and saves severe backache!

Nylon-type smocks are also popular. They can be cleaned easily, and shed dog hair with ease.

Comfortable shoes are a must. Soles should grip the floor easily (especially in the bathing area). You are likely to be on your feet all day, so the grooming salon is no place for high heels. Having a comfortable rubber or rubber-type mat to stand on is also a good idea.

GROOMING TABLE

The ideal grooming table is steady and strong. A rubber mat placed on top will stop the dog from slipping. The table should be a comfortable height for you so that you won't spend much of the day stooping over your canine customers. An adjustable (hydraulic) table is ideal, as you can alter the height at which you work according to the dog (a lower table height may be required for a Golden Retriever than for a Yorkshire Terrier).

BATHING

BATH

Every groomer needs access to a bath. Less backbreaking are those that are at waist level, but one person cannot lift heavy dogs into the raised bath alone. A low table or bench placed adjacent to the bath makes life easier so the dog can walk itself into the bath.

Some groomers have a ramp to assist them with this task.

If you prefer, you can buy a bath on wheels. This is an industrial plastic bath with high sides and back, and a low front. It is designed like this to prevent the pet from jumping out, to keep water in and to provide easy access at the front for washing the animal. It is on casters for mobility.

BATH BRUSH

A plastic brush for deep cleaning or distributing treatments in coat. (Tip: a firm hand will do.)

SHAMPOO

There are so many shampoos on the market: some are designed for certain coat colors, some are universal, some are antiflea, some are pro-skincare, some contain protein, some are superwhiteners ... the list is endless.

Most shampoos should be diluted with

A waist-high bath is another labor-saving option.

There are many shampoos and conditioners to suit all different coat types.

water before they are applied to the coat. It is always good policy to use a quality shampoo, and the milder the better. Most groomers have a selection of shampoos in the salon from which to choose the best one for each individual dog.

Some of the latest shampoos and conditioners are the "silver" and "diamond" types to make white dogs look sparkling, removing stains and discoloration from all or parts of the coat. Another recent trend is the special skin- and coat-purifying shampoos and masks that can be used occasionally for a healthier look and a superb finish.

"Sculpture rinses" for scissored and trimmed dogs are a must for the groomer who wishes to achieve an outstanding finish with both pet and show dogs.

CONDITIONERS

These are not necessary for all coats, but most (whether long, short, wiry or curly) will benefit from the use of oil-based enhancers to help to keep mats at bay.

Some conditioners are designed to improve the finish of scissored breeds; mostly, they are concentrated and should be diluted with water when required (always check the product label first).

Conditioners vary from a conditioning "sleek rinse" for long, lustrous coats to dematting cream rinses with anti-static properties, and "crinkle-beaters" (to straighten hair), which give a fantastic straight blow-dry.

Use oil-based conditioners sparingly or you may end up with a very greasy dog.

COLOR-ENHANCING

Another aspect of beautifying the dog is to have the coat color-enhanced. This is usually accomplished by using shampoos to bring out the natural coloring in the dog's coat – black for black dogs, blue for blue and silver dogs, extra-white shampoo for white coats (and parts of the coat, such as a Collie mane). There is no colorant in these shampoos – they simply emphasize the dog's existing color.

DRYERS

These are essential. It is always a good policy to have a hands-free, powerful, specially made dog dryer. There are several on the market. Because I love "one-to-one" interaction with the dog while I am grooming, I do not use cage-dryers (below), but they are readily available and a busy establishment may find these contraptions useful and maybe necessary.

There are also revolutionary dryers that are credited as being the ultimate in the drying experience, combining a tremendous airflow with heat for instant dying. They are thermostatically controlled and economical to use, and come with a stand for a hands-free operation. However, they do not appeal to all dogs – some hate the strong force of these dryers, and object.

AUTOMATIC DOG DRYER

An automatic dog dryer is a cabinet in which the dog is placed in warm air. It is sometimes described as a "cage-dryer." This dryer is thermostatically controlled and economical to use. The cage-dryer may be useful for German Shepherd Dogs and shorthaired breeds where blow-drying is not essential.

STAND DRYER

This is a powerful and robust dryer with a rotating nozzle – a favorite with exhibitors when presentation is a priority. It allows you to have both your hands free to brush and handle the dog.

HAND DRYERS

There are also several hand-held dryers available, and they are sometimes useful, especially for those groomers who trim dogs in their own home and do not want to haul a large dryer around with them.

POWER BLOWER/GROOMER

Modern methods and equipment will save the groomer from hours of work and from getting sore fingers. The power groomer is a highly effective blower that penetrates and separates every section of the hair, removing dust and tangles, and blowing the hair straight.

When the dog needs to be brushed prior to being bathed, the power blower can be used instead, provided the dog has no objection to the jet of air. Dogs soon get used to this piece of equipment and most dogs enjoy the invigorating action. Make sure dogs have cotton batting in their ears to protect from the noise.

Between baths, too, the power groomer can be used as a means of grooming the coat. Blow the hair away from the skin to remove dust and curls that may develop into tangles. This technique takes only a few minutes, and reduces the actual brushing time by many minutes. This is especially useful in breeds such as the Old English Sheepdog, which sometimes has a coat that mats by the minute!

Wetting a matted dog will severely exacerbate the problem because water tends to encourage hair to stick like glue to the mats; then, if the dog is not dried with great care, the situation gets worse as the coat shrinks into the mat and you end up with one big felt. (However, there is a three-stage grooming product that allows you to put even the most matted dog directly into the tub, and removes mats with ease. Contact your grooming supplier for information.)

A slicker brush is particularly useful for thick coats.

Novice groomers often get into a panic when trying to cope with a coat that has matted solid after a bath. The secret is to prevent this action by carefully analyzing the situation before you start grooming. Use the power blower, without heat, to separate each section of the coat, and also spray in detangle spray if the coat is dry.

TOWELS
Superabsorbent towels are a great asset for getting excess water from the dog before you start with the dryer. Consisting of a quality drying cloth that is hard-wearing, easy to clean and reusable, these superabsorbent towels soak up huge amounts of water and come in standard and large sizes.

COMBS
It would not be feasible to list every single comb, so a selection has been chosen.

COARSE
This comb has stainless steel teeth and a round handle for eliminating clogging (i.e., matting or felting).

MEDIUM
This is useful in eliminating clogging.

MEDIUM/COARSE
A chrome, all-metal comb with a rounded back for comfort.

UNTANGLE PET COMB
Features teeth that rotate 360 degrees and gently turn to remove tangles fast and without too much pain.

MOLTING COMBS
Coarse and medium combs, with stainless steel teeth, a white plastic handle and a round-shaped back. These combs virtually eliminate clogging.

BACK COMB
For styling and creating lift.

TAIL COMB
For separating and parting the coat.

FLEA COMB
Has very fine teeth to help remove parasites.

BRUSHES

PIN AND BRISTLE BRUSHES
Natural bristle brushes come in large, medium and small – with a cushioned pad.

A good pair of clippers and a variety of blades will be needed.

SLICKER BRUSH
These come in a variety of sizes and styles (universal, curved or with a straight back). Each brush has hooked steel pins to break up the tangles. Every groomer should have these.

CLIPPERS AND BLADES

AESCULAP FAVORITA II
A favorite with busy, professional groomers, this is cool-running and powerful when tackling neglected and felted coats. Blades range from GT703 1/10 mm as a surgical blade, GT712 1 mm for short precision work, GT742 2 mm for matted thick coats, GT758 5 mm for general purpose body, GT770 7 mm for winter, and up to GT784 16 mm for a very long coat (with a range of blades in between).

ANDIS CORDLESS
A professional cordless clipper with a battery, which can take Oster blades.

The Andis AG is a durable professional clipper that is easy to handle and quiet-running. Blades range from No. 50 for surgical, right through to No. 10 for face, No. 7 for body and up to No. 3.75 for very long.

OSTER
This two-speed clipper is a professional tool with Andis-compatible blades.

The Oster A5 clipper is a true friend of the trainee or student, as well as the experienced groomer because it is gentle on the dog. However, you must check it frequently to ensure the blade is not running hot.

Blades include:

- No. 40: surgical
- No. 30: used for clipping Poodle feet
- No. 15: a face blade
- No. 10: used where the skin is more delicate or where the hair is less thick on the face, such as on a white Poodle
- No. 5: summer body
- No. 4F: for a long finish.

BLADE BANK
A "blade bank" holds up to 15 blades, so they can each be identified easily.

CLIPPER OIL
Lubricant for blades and scissors is essential.

BLADE WASH
A degreasing, cleaning substance for blades.

GREASE
For clipper bearings.

COMB ATTACHMENTS
Check that they suit your type of clipper. Use for changing the size of the blade to leave a specific length of coat. Useful where owners like an inch or two of coat left on.

EAR CARE
Forceps, ear cleaner and ear powder are assets in the grooming room.
See page 51.

EYE CARE
Tear-stain remover and emollient are available

Scissors are needed not only for sculpturing the trimmed breeds, but also for general maintenance.

to aid a clean finish, and to help remove eye stains caused by tears (see page 60).

NAIL CARE

There are several types of nail clippers available, some of which include a safety guard to prevent too much nail being clipped off at a time. They come in small, medium and large sizes. The guillotine and scissor-types, with or without plastic-coated handles, are a matter of preference, but buy the best quality you can, as these tend to be smoother and easier to use. Some of the cheaper versions have ragged edges which can cut your fingers, so beware.

Permanganate crystals should also be on hand, should the quick of the nail be nicked. Tip a small amount into a saucer and dip some damp cotton batting into it. This should stop the bleeding (see page 50).

SCISSORS

There are literally hundreds of types of scissors on the market, ranging from the very expensive high-standard finishing scissors, which give a truly expert cut, to the more affordable, basic varieties.

The type of finish and the job at hand will determine which scissors are used. Generally, groomers use small scissors for clipping the hair between spaniels' feet, etc. Some people use the same pair of scissors for everything, even slicing through mats. I keep certain finishing scissors for show dogs, and use a different pair for general scissoring.

Some groomers prefer scissors with a finger guide – a rubber insert or a hook for the little finger, to prevent the scissors from moving or slipping while in use. Others prefer no finger guides.

At most shows, and at grooming seminars, it is possible to try out several different types of scissors, taking note of the job for which they are recommended. Remember, high price does not necessarily always mean a super finish.

Always try out any scissors you are considering purchasing – one pair may be a perfect fit for one person, but may slip in another's hand. In grooming school, you should be taught how to use scissors properly.

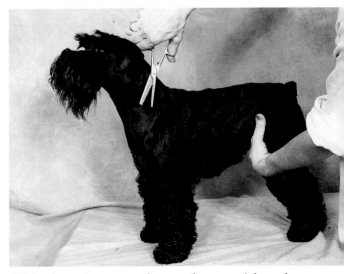

Thinning scissors are often used on spaniels and thick coats.

THINNING SCISSORS

Thinning scissors have a flat blade on one side and a blade with gaps on the other. They are used primarily on spaniels and thick coats that need thinning out rather than clipping off.

STRIPPING TOOLS

There are several tools available, used for various aspects of stripping different coats.

STRIPPING KNIFE

Left- and right-handed, the knife comes with a long, fine blade with a round, bobbled end. It can be used for carding (see page 48), and can be obtained in different sizes.

STRIPPING STONES

These are gray stones that some groomers use for stripping. They can be cut to size, and are used alongside – or instead of – the groomer's finger and thumb, or stripping knife.

DOG DRESSER

This is used for stripping, and comes with blades, as opposed to the "fixed knife" where the stripping blade is attached all in one.

A stripping stone helps to remove loose coats.

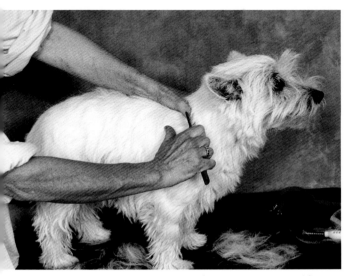

A stripping knife is useful for terrier coats if hand-stripping is not performed.

DEMATTING TOOLS

THE MAT-SPLITTER

This is an effective aid that cuts through mats and tangles with ease. It is simple to use, causing the dog very little distress, even with the toughest knots. The handle is shaped for comfort, has a tapered guide and has a honed steel cutting blade that penetrates the toughest of tangles.

MAT-BREAKER

This is scientifically designed for easy and efficient removal of mats and tangles with minimum hair loss. The stainless-steel blades are shaped for optimum effect, and the blades are replaceable.

DEMATTING RAKE

This comes in different sizes and can be reversed from right to left. This tool has replaceable serrated stainless-steel blades.

CLEANING PRODUCTS

You will also need some pet-safe disinfectants for cleaning your equipment, tools, floors, and so on. Your grooming supplier should have a good selection to choose from.

7 *TURNING OUT A DOG*

Turning out a dog (grooming and beautifying it) differs fractionally in some breeds and tremendously in others. Day-to-day care of the show dog often exceeds the grooming required in the pet dog, but the groomer has a responsibility to perform a work of art in both cases. Here is a detailed step-by-step look at exactly what is required when turning out a dog.

Most of the dogs that come into the grooming salon have mats and tangles, and some look quite neglected because their owners can't cope with the grooming commitments. These dogs may be hard work, but it is extremely satisfying to transform them.

Experienced groomers are respected for their ability to look at a photograph of any trimmed breed and to know instantly which bits of hair are clipped, scissored, thinned or hand-stripped. Training and experience will help a groomer to achieve this.

THE INITIAL BRUSH
Without a doubt, expert brushing is an art in itself. Many owners and inexperienced groomers will hand over a dog that they are sure has had every tangle removed from the coat, and are then quite shocked when a more experienced person gets a bin full of hair when complete brushing takes place.

- Put the dog on the table.
- Start on the bottom of the fore left leg. Using the correct brush (see breed profiles, Part Three), lift the hair above the section you are working on, and brush the section below.
- Then comb through the coat. Use a grooming spray if necessary. Continue all the way up the leg.
- With a full-coated breed (e.g., a Wheaten Terrier), continue the brushing and combing across the dog's quarters, along the back and neck, paying special attention to behind the ears and underneath the legs where matting is often more likely to occur.
- Brush the head, ears and whiskers, where applicable.
- Note: a mat-breaker, or slicing the mat with the aid of scissors, may be required to shift stubborn lumps. Splitting the hair with your fingers will also help to break apart the tangles. Always hold the dog's skin or the base of the mat when pulling; otherwise, you will be pulling at the dog's skin and causing great pain.

ROUTINE FOR BRUSHING

1. Start by grooming the bottom of one of the forelegs.

2. Brush up the leg, working your way to the chest.

3. Work your way methodically around the body.

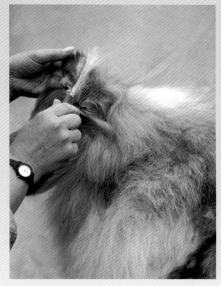

4. The hair at the base of the ears will need to be combed to remove tangles.

5. Lay the dog on its side. Pay particular attention to the armpits, where the hair can mat.

6. Brush the hair on the hindquarters. The coat often grows thickly here.

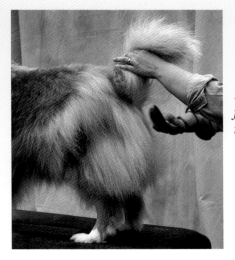

7. Don't forget the tail!

8. The finished result.

BENEATH THE COAT

Whether you merely intend to groom your own pet dog or you wish to become a top award-winning groomer, you should understand a little about the dog and its structure. The following diagram is of the canine skeleton. It doesn't matter if it is not correct for your breed (obviously it looks nothing like a Corgi or a Dachshund); the bones are all present in every dog we see, whatever the breed (the only exception being the Norwegian Lundehund, which has six toes on each of his four feet).

THE SKELETON
The skeleton of the dog is relevant to the groomer, especially when a dog's breed standard advises trimming to a certain point (such as the hock). Groomers who familiarize themselves with at least the more obvious points of the body (e.g., stifle) can follow grooming instructions with confidence.

The detailed breed profiles in Part Three sometimes refer to particular parts of the dog, and it will be useful if you refer back to this diagram when reading them.

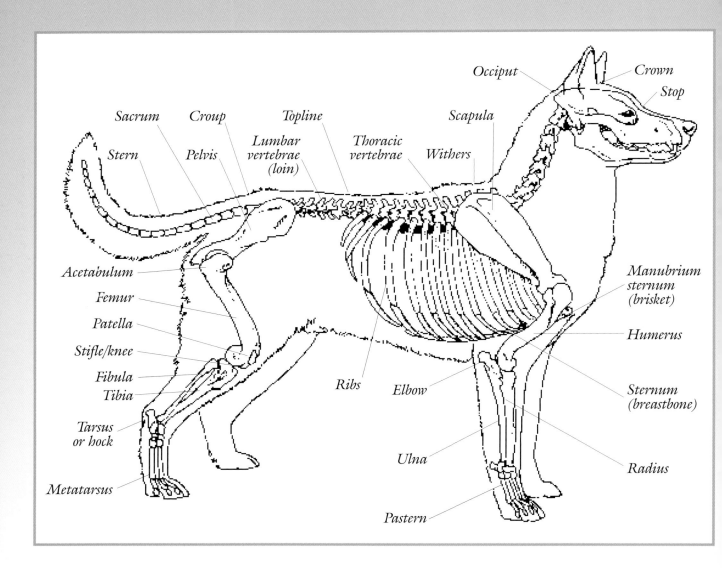

PET OR SHOW?

The professional groomer has to ascertain whether they are working on a pet dog or a show dog. There are many wonderful aids and coat-enhancing properties that are great for a pet, but which may be considered illegal substances in the show ring. The use of them may break the rules of some countries' national kennel clubs.

In North America, for instance, many breeds are prepared for the show ring by incorporating clipping and coat aids such as hair spray. That same technique may be classed as breaking the rules according, say, to the British Kennel Club.

However, preparation for the show ring or for conformation purposes does not, in general, fall to the average grooming salon to undertake, as most handlers prepare the dogs themselves. But, do ask the owner if the dog is likely to be shown. Remember – it is better to be safe than sorry.

Coat-enhancing materials, such as chalk or specialist shampoos, can be used on pet dogs, but show dogs should generally be kept natural.

Also, while clipping a pet terrier is perfectly permissible and saves hours of work, it is not the thing to do to a show dog, as it will take months and months before the dog can be shown again.

BEST TOOLS

Care should be taken to use the correct brush when brushing the dog. Even the skin of thick-coated breeds can be made red raw by a heavy-handed groomer who drags through the coat with too much vigor, scratching the skin. Don't use a slicker or steel pin brush on skin that has been clipped, especially on delicate parts, such as the face. It is inexcusable to graze the dog's skin in this way. Use a soft brush for these parts, if indeed they need to be brushed at all.

For more information on equipment, see Chapter Six.

MAT MATTERS

Undercoat, as seen in dogs like the Old English Sheepdog, can mat solid against the skin and become a horrendous task to remove. Inexperienced groomers have been known to bathe a dog full of matted undercoat or felted clogs of hair and then put the dog in a drying cabinet or cage. Once

dry, the top hair is then brushed to make the dog look fluffy. The dog looks good on the surface, but the full story beneath the topcoat is quite a different matter.

If the dog is bathed when matted, the shampoo will generally get clogged into the mats, making the situation even more disastrous. Many pet owners bathe their dogs between trims and leave them to dry, making the job of grooming far more difficult. The dog may be clean, but its coat is not in good condition and is certainly not free of tangles. Explaining the problem to the owner and how to avoid it can help to avert future problems.

No dog can look or feel its best unless all tangles, mats and felts are removed from the coat. When a dog has a badly matted coat, it is advisable to spray in a dematter or untangle lotion and leave it to soak for 10 minutes or so before using a slicker brush or mat-breaker to remove the offending sections.

Regular brushing will prevent mats, but if they are already established and cannot be removed, then clipping the dog is in its best interest.

If dematting the dog will be considered torturous to the animal, then the hair must be cut or clipped off. No groomer must be responsible for causing any dog severe distress. Discuss the problem with the owner, explaining that you have no wish to act in a cruel manner and that you will use clippers on the dog if necessary, rather than inflict needless pain. Saving some of the matting to show the owner can be effective.

PREBATH CLIPPING

Some dogs, such as a hairy Poodle or an Old English Sheepdog, can have a great deal of their thick coat clipped before a bath.

Admittedly, clipping clean hair is less wearing on clipper blades, but, with the use of an easy-clip lubricating spray and oil, there shouldn't be too much to worry about, and it will cut down washing and drying time by nearly half – less electricity, less time, less stress for the dog, more economy all around!

The clipping of some parts, such as the hairy feet of a spaniel, will shorten the drying time, but do clean your blades after clipping between feet or they will clog with debris, such as mud, sand and hair. Remember not to clip wet hair. Using a fine blade, it is relatively easy on the dog to clip the fiercely matted hair between some dogs' feet.

The same goes for dogs that are matted solid around the rear end. Clip over the anus area (but not the bulbous anus itself) with a medium-cut blade, being careful to hold the dog's genitals for protection. This will get rid of a lot of unwanted hair and debris that it is pointless bathing, drying or trying to comb out.

In hairy or matted pet dogs, it is often a good idea to clip out all the hair underneath the tummy, groin area and chest, right up to the dog's rib cage and sometimes between its front legs, underneath the arms. This procedure prevents matting and keeps the dog smelling fresher. When the dog is standing, the clipped hair is not noticeable and will only be seen when the dog rolls over onto its back to show you its nice clean stomach. Of course, this would never be done to a show dog.

Prebath clipping can save on washing and drying time.

BATHING

ESSENTIAL EQUIPMENT

Grooming techniques are getting ever more sophisticated, and we now have numerous coat aids, sprays, selective shampoos and incredible conditioners to help us turn out a first-class job.

Some aromatherapy shampoos, made from natural therapeutic organic compounds that nourish the coat and skin, are wonderful to use, and they produce a top-quality finish.

One essential for the bath is a long, secure rubber mat to prevent the dog from slipping. Also, it is impossible to cope without a decent hose spray to distribute the water evenly throughout.

PROCEDURE

Before we begin, remember that you should never leave a dog unattended. Some people think the dog is safe if it is restrained on a grooming table or in the bath, hooked on a frame or tied up. Dogs have hung themselves in a matter of seconds when groomers have made the horrendous mistake of leaving the dog unattended. Your customers are your responsibility and you should never leave them, even for a second.

When putting a large dog into a waist-high bath, it is a good idea to get assistance rather than break your back. Another way around the problem is to walk the dog up a ramp. Then place its front paws on the bath, lift up the back end and tip the dog in, or have the table placed next to the bath and encourage the dog to step into the bath from this height. Most dogs are fairly obliging, especially when they are used to visiting the groomer.

Posing more of a problem are the 100-pound (45 kg) heavyweights that are four years old and have never been on a table or had a bath in their life. These dogs tend to panic on initiation, but, with careful handling, they can be encouraged to respond and settle down – and may actually enjoy the experience!

Some people have hooks in the wall above the bath and clip the dog's leash to this in order to keep it still; however, some dogs react to this and are best left to stand of their own accord.

Sometimes, with a large breed that is not used to the bath, two people are better than one – one at the head, one at the other end. It makes the task twice as quick, so is economical in time.

WETTING THE COAT

The dog should be thoroughly wetted before a shampoo is applied. Lift long hair to be certain of getting right down to the roots. Anybody who has had a dreadful hairwash from an inexperienced junior hairdresser will know how itchy the scalp feels after hair has been insufficiently wetted.

It is not advisable to stand dogs in a pool of dirty water, so make sure the water drains away as it runs off the dog.

Use a decent water spray at all times, with the temperature set to warm. Test the water on the delicate underside of your arm, not on your hands, which are hardened to the elements.

Start with the head. The dog's ears may need to be protected with cotton batting to prevent water getting into them. Wet down the neck, along the back and down the left side (including the legs). Then repeat on the right side, turning the dog only if necessary (turning the dog at this stage will encourage it to jump out, so be warned). Lastly, wet the tail.

If the dog is very sensitive about having its head wet, then start with the tail and work up the body, wetting the head last.

APPLYING SHAMPOO

Now work the diluted shampoo through the

ROUTINE FOR BATHING

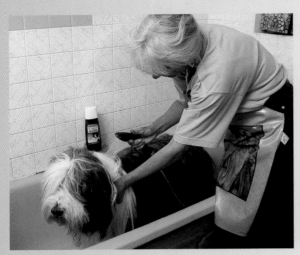

1. Wet the coat thoroughly with warm (not hot) water. Part the hair to check that the water has penetrated down to the skin.

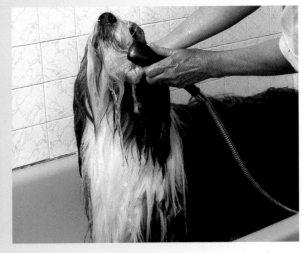

2. If a dog is sensitive about having its head wet, be particularly gentle around this area, and wet the head last – just before applying the shampoo.

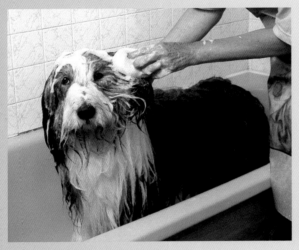

3. Apply the shampoo and lather down to the skin. Be careful not to get any soap into the dog's eyes.

4. Rinse thoroughly – any soap left in the coat will cause intense itchiness.

5. Dry the head first to make the dog comfortable.

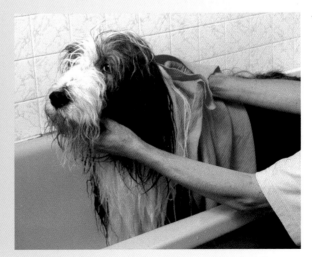

6. Work along the body, using a superabsorbent towel to remove most of the moisture.

coat with your hands. Shampoo is rarely put straight onto the dog without being mixed with a certain amount of water to help distribute it and prevent it from affecting the skin.

Massage the shampoo into the coat thoroughly, not forgetting the area underneath the chest and stomach, the anal area and the dog's feet. Make sure the shampoo gets down to the skin and is well lathered, adding water if required.

With the head area, you must be careful not to get shampoo in the dog's eyes. Rinse immediately if there is a suspicion of this happening. Do not put shampoo into the dog's ears at any time.

Rinse off the shampoo and use a second application if required. With experience, you will be able to feel when the coat is clean – it will "squeak" when clean, as human hair does.

RINSING

Rinsing should be thorough – rinse, rinse, rinse until the coat feels squeaky clean. Any shampoo left in the coat will cause flaking scurf, felting and intense itching. Some makes of shampoo claim to be mild, but are too strong for the dog's sensitive skin and may also cause the dog to itch. Use a very mild, natural-ingredient shampoo on particularly sensitive skin or with dogs suffering from an allergy.

With shortcoated dogs, such as the Dalmatian or Weimaraner, a thorough brushing with a hound glove when in the bath will remove a lot of dead and molting hair. The dog will dry smoother and quicker, and the owner will be delighted that far less hair comes out on their carpet.

DRYING

Water can be removed from the coat while the dog is still in the bath. Squeeze out the excess moisture with cotton towels or super-absorbent towels.

DEMATTING CONDITIONER

Dematting conditioners can be a godsend on some tangly coats. Brush them through the entire coat when the hair is wet, and the tangles unwind or loosen enough to be brushed and combed out. This is done before the drying commences, and most dematters should be rinsed out. Check the directions on the label.

Some breeds, like the St. Bernard and the heavy-coated spitz breeds, will benefit from having water blasted from the coat with a high-velocity dryer (see page 31). Do this by placing the dog on the grooming table and holding a superabsorbent towel behind the dog to catch the water. Then use a power blower on the coat before placing the dog in the drying cabinet or finishing off with the blow-dryer.

This method of removing excess water from the coat is not a good idea with dogs that need blow-drying, such as the show Poodle, as the hair would become dry too quickly and may crinkle and curl, hampering scissoring.

If a "stay-in-the-coat" spray conditioner is required, then apply this before drying commences, as recommended in the manufacturer's instructions. With coated dogs, such as the Poodle, it is essential to blow-dry the hair by separating the strands with the aid of a slicker or pin brush and using a power dryer to blow the hair.

Each small section must be parted, usually starting from the back foot and systematically working upwards. Be careful not to have the air blow directly onto the skin, as this would be too hot for the dog to endure, and it would react by trying to run away from the burning sensation. Blow the hair away from the skin, but do not blow the skin itself.

Most dogs hate the blower on their faces,

2. *Blow-dry the coat outdoors, or in a kitchen or utility room, which can be easily cleaned afterwards.*

3. *When the coat is damp – but not wet – start brushing and styling the coat as you dry it.*

1. *Once the worst of the wetness has been removed, let the dog out of the bath and towel-dry the coat once more.*

but do not object so much if the heat and ferocity of the dryer are turned down to a minimum.

Some breeds that require a flat look (such as a Flat-Coated Retriever or English Setter) will need to have their coat dried with the blower going with the growth of the hair, rather than being lifted, as with the Poodle.

Dogs with short hair, such as Whippets and Dalmatians, can be dried in a cage, or merely by using several superabsorbent towels and leaving them in a warm room. Do not leave wet dogs to dry on their own when it is not sufficiently warm, and never leave coated breeds, such as the Afghan, Poodle, Bearded Collie or Old English Sheepdog, to dry on their own; their hair needs brushing continuously while being blow-dried.

GROOMING METHODS

CLIPPING
SAFETY CONSIDERATIONS
Some groomers believe that the idea of clipping is to shave so close to the skin that it removes all the hair. It is cruel to do this. Clipping so closely can leave the skin red and grazed. Enough hair should be clipped away to create a clean, tidy appearance.

The point of having different-sized blades is to give the groomer the opportunity to predetermine the length of hair to be left. Dark faces can take a closer blade, while white faces can be severely grazed by a very fine blade, leaving horrific scalding which leads to weeping sores.

Clippers are designed to be maneuverable, and it is the job of the groomer to learn the art of twisting the wrist, and stretching and bending themselves to get into different parts, rather than twisting and contorting the dog. I have seen some groomers twisting a dog's feet in all sorts of directions in order to clip them. This is wrong. The clipper itself, in the groomer's hand, should be turned up, down, around, wherever, and the dog's foot should remain as still as possible.

Do be sure not to dig the clipper into the skin, but to run the blade over the top, as flat to the skin as possible. Be sure to tighten all wrinkles or loose flesh as you go, to prevent grazing and to obtain a neat finish.

Apart from when clipping Poodle feet, or unless you are experienced in what you are doing, always run the clipper with the grain of the hair. When attending to the face, you should always clip away from the eye, for safety's sake.

Good clipping is an art. Think of clipping as a caress. It should be done kindly, with consideration, and the finished procedure must give a clean, neat and comfortably appealing appearance.

TYPES OF CLIPPERS
There are several makes of clippers on the market (see page 33). Some will suit you more than others. I like one made for shearing thick-coated breeds, and another for clipping show Poodles and dogs with more delicate skin. Experience will help you to choose which ones you prefer.

SNAP-ON COMBS
These are plastic extensions that snap onto normal clipping blades to enable the groomer to leave more coat. They can be used on the body and legs to reduce scissoring time. Different sizes are available and are useful for giving puppy-type lengths on coats such as the Poodle, Lhasa Apso, Bichon Frise, Old English Sheepdog and many others.

Apply the attachment (size 1) to a No. 10 Oster, and experiment going with the grain and against the grain. Westies are often clipped with an attachment of a 1 on a No. 4 Oster blade. These are fun to try, but if you are a professional groomer don't experiment on a client's dog unless the coat is intended to be cut shorter to finish.

Note: snap-ons in the U.S. will leave the hair as short as a No. 7 blade or as long as three inches, depending on which setting is used. The blades usually used under the snap-on are: No. 50, No. 40, No. 30 or No. 10.

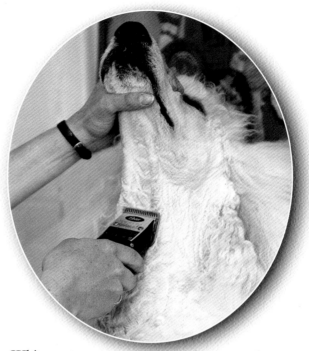

White coats are more prone to clipper grazing, so fine blades should be avoided.

HAND-STRIPPING
This is done before bathing (although some breeders with hand-stripped breeds claim that they do not bathe their show dogs at all).

Show dogs should always be hand-stripped, and some beautiful and elegant breeds, such as the English or Irish Setter, should never be clipped all over their body or it will encourage the hair to curl into a mass and destroy the wonderful slight waviness and sleek, silky appearance of the coat.

The required natural-looking coat, such as that of the Border Terrier, will be ruined by clipping because the softer undercoat takes over from the more coarse topcoat. It is essential to strip out this type of coat by hand twice a year, otherwise the dog develops a shapeless appearance. The dog will also feel hot, uncomfortable and itchy because the coat is full of dead undercoat. It is much better if the dog is hand-stripped every six to eight weeks. This way, there is less hair loss and the dog remains smart all of the time rather than just twice a year.

Stripping is done less and less in pet grooming salons. The use of thinning scissors

ROUTINE FOR STRIPPING

1. *A Parson Russell Terrier ready for stripping. Its coat is long and untidy.*

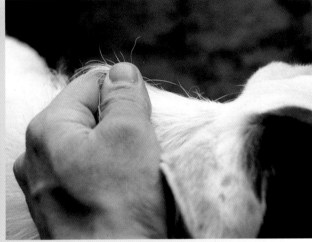

2. *Grasp a little hair at a time between your finger and thumb and pull.*

3. *Halfway there – the difference between the stripped and unstripped areas is clearly seen.*

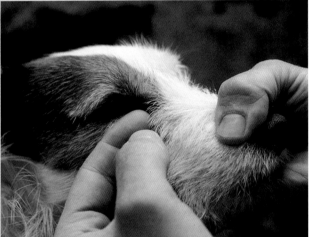

4. *A gentle approach is needed for delicate areas, such as around the eyes.*

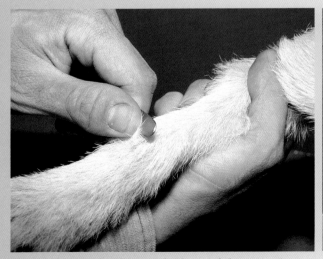

5. *A stripping knife can also be used for removing loose hair.*

6. *Fully stripped: the coat is close-fitting, showing a clean outline.*

and clever clipping has replaced this mode of grooming. It is a shame, and probably brought about by lack of good training and sheer laziness. However, the reluctance of the dog owner to pay for the time required to do a thorough job may also be responsible for hand-stripping's decline, particularly in the U.S., where most pet dogs are clipped rather than stripped.

HOW TO HAND-STRIP
- Lift a small section at a time, grasp a small amount of hair between your thumb and finger, and extract the loose hairs from each part with a quick, jerking movement.
- Be sure only to take a few hairs out at a time, as pulling large clumps will cause pain and distress.
- Always follow the direction in which the hair grows.
- Keep the skin taut as the hair is stripped out.

THE STRIPPING KNIFE
It is not difficult to learn how to hand-strip, but, because it is time-consuming, many groomers do not have the interest and patience required to undertake this task, and many owners do not want to pay an hourly rate for this work.

Many people find it easier to use a stripping knife, rather than the finger and thumb. The knife used is a blunt one (otherwise, the coat will be cut rather than pulled, so it may as well be clipped). It is advisable to use a serrated-edged knife. With a new knife, run it across a stone to blunt the edge before use.
Note: the knife and hair need to be pulled straight back and not flipped up at the wrist.

COAT GROWTH
Hand-stripped breeds will need attention to their coats from about the age of 3 months, when the coat begins to stand off in a frizz or

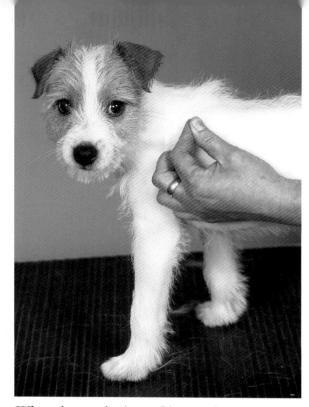

When the coat begins to frizz at about 12 weeks of age, the puppy can be gently stripped to get it used to the procedure.

halo. This fluff can be removed fairly easily by hand, using finger and thumb (see above).

Underneath this frizz there will be a new jacket, which will look tidy and which will last the pup until it is about 7 months old. When the long hair starts to form a natural parting and fall into clumps, the dog is again ready for stripping.

The adult coat will be seen around the third or fourth jacket. Unfortunately, many pet owners leave this type of coat until the pup is about a year old and then bring the dog into the grooming salon, which means a lot more work for the groomer, and far more for the dog to endure.

ADULT STRIPS
When hand-stripping is required in the adult dog, it is best done at natural shedding time (i.e., the spring and autumn molt).

Stripping with a blade is probably less tormenting for the dog, but still takes considerable skill, time and patience. Some dogs are most obliging about lying on their sides to be stripped and this does help to

A stripped terrier with an undocked tail.

make the task a little easier.

Before stripping the coat, the dog should be thoroughly brushed, and combed with a fine-toothed comb. Start the stripping from the head and work downwards, being careful not to strip out the soft undercoat. This is recognized, as it is a different color/texture to that of the top coat.

After stripping, the knife can be run through the coat to remove the loose undercoat. Scissors or clippers can be used on some breeds to trim close to the hair around the anus, and the feet are scissored to a neat appearance.

DOCKED TAILS

Now that docking dogs tails is banned in some parts of the world, it is essential to look at this area in a different light. As far as the Poodle is concerned, advice about dealing with an undocked tail will be found on page 274. The tail also needs to be properly finished in any stripped breeds that are no longer docked, such as the terriers.

Firstly, what breed is it, and how is the outline of the dog supposed to look? Leaving a tail undocked has caused many problems because this is one area where conformation has often been neglected. Consequently the variation in tail carriage is tremendous with tails incorporating everything from a pig-like curl to a full circle, a banana shape, or a Spitz-like version with the tail touching the body or back or the side of the rump.

Covering up tail faults is very difficult for the exhibitor. The general groomer does not have this worry. The best we can do is to make the dog look as neat as possible – and finished. Many a good-looking dog has walked out of the grooming salon with a tail spoiling the whole effect by being too long, or by not being in balance with the rest of the trimming. A short clip and a huge bushy

tail do not look right.

Perhaps the hand-stripping of an undocked tail is easier to balance. The section that is stripped can continue right to the end. The show person may prefer to strip more from one section underneath or on top to a desired effect. The groomer of pet dogs can simply continue the trimming with a blunt stripping knife, finger and thumb, clippers or scissors.

Some dogs hate being hand-stripped, especially on their tails. They can get distressed enough to misbehave or even snap. The dog is hand-stripped to retain its natural coat, but how important is this? Certainly not enough to stress the dog unduly. If dogs are distressed because of hand-stripping, it is best not to do this. Often parts of the dog, such as the back, can be hand-stripped while the tail is blended in with thinners or scissors, and maybe even clippers.

ROLLING

Show dogs frequently have their coats "rolled" to enable the exhibitor to keep the dog in tip-top condition all year round. Rolling – a type of hand-stripping – prevents a full molt. A full molt can result in the dog looking quite bald or "out of coat" in comparison, which thereby lessens the chance of the dog winning.

Rolling takes a few hours every 10 to 14 days, and it is much easier to keep the dog looking sharp at all times with this practice. Pet owners should be encouraged to consider the option of rolling, rather than putting the dog through the ordeal of hours and hours on the grooming table because the owner has left the coat for such a long time between trims.

When rolling, the skin is literally rolled between the fingers of one hand, while the other hand picks out the stand-off hairs (i.e., the longer, dead ones). Pet owners can sometimes be encouraged to have their dogs groomed this way on a regular basis, when the breeder has explained this procedure.

Unfortunately for the groomer, breeders often tell pet people only to have the dog's coat stripped once or twice a year. Re-educating in modern methods is the answer.

CARDING

To perform this, the clipper blade or blunt stripping knife is held in the hand and kept flat. It is used in much the same way as the stripping knife, to card through the coat and remove any thickened top coat. The undercoat, which is essential, can be kept in check by removing the excess with a blunt stripping knife; this process is called "scraping" or "carding" and allows the top coat to lie flat and neat at all times.

THINNING

Thinning shears thin the hair so it lies flat. They are used where the hair needs to be shortened but where it would be altered by using the clippers (and thereby destroying the typical appearance of a breed). For instance, clipping an English Setter down the neck may encourage thick, curly hairs to develop, which is undesirable. Using thinning shears will thin the hair to give a neat appearance, but they must be used correctly.

The shears are worked by taking two to three sections at a time, and combing or brushing out the loosened hairs. The shears must always be worked with the growth of the hair; they must never cut straight across the hair, as this will cause a doorstep effect.

GENERAL CHECKS AND PROCEDURES

ANAL GLANDS

These sacs or "scent glands" are situated on either side of the anus. They are inversions of skin where it joins the end of the digestive tract. The cavity formed is quite large and collects fluid. If it becomes blocked, the dog may show various signs of irritation:

- Rubbing his bottom along the floor
- Biting at the area
- Flying around in circles to bite his tail
- Snappy or oversensitive when you want to touch his quarters
- Hanging his tail, instead of carrying it high, sometimes tucking it well between his legs.

Other dogs seem not to show adverse signs, but are particularly smelly.

Where dogs are allowed frequently to chew raw bones, enough calcium deposit is expelled to harden the feces and the sac is emptied naturally. However, with today's trend of feeding less natural diets, more and more dogs need their glands emptied for them. If they are not emptied, abscesses can form. Bitches, after a season, usually benefit from having their anal glands emptied.

This is a job for the professional; not to be undertaken by a novice pet owner. Some vets claim this procedure should only be done by a vet; others feel groomers should handle it.

CHECKING

While the dog is in the bath, it is a good time to check his anal glands. If warm water is applied to the area, this tends to soften the skin and relax the dog, often making the emptying of the gland easier. With neglect of this procedure, an abscess may form, causing veterinary bills as well as severe discomfort for the dog. Squeezing the glands externally quickly performs this service.

PROCEDURE

Use a fine-rubber hygiene glove and absorbent paper towel, and place your finger and thumb on either side of the anus. You will be able to feel the hardened gland about 1 inch (2.5 cm) in. Press in, up and outwards to expel the vile-smelling fluid, which is sometimes almost as thick as toothpaste, and sometimes as liquid as water.

There is a knack to this and some dogs' glands are far easier to empty than others. If the area is very sensitive or smelly, or both, and nothing comes away, it is as well to advise the client to take the dog to the vet to have this area checked out in case something more sinister has developed.

NAILS

Once the dog is bathed (before or after drying the coat) and is sitting on the table, this is a good time to trim back your dog's nails, as they are softened by the water and are usually easier, and less brittle, to snip. Some dogs have long blood vessels in their nails because the nails have not been trimmed back on a regular basis since puppyhood, and very little nail can be cut. Using a large file or an electric file is often safer in these cases.

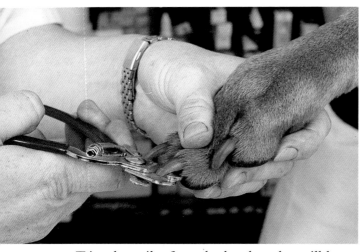

Trim the nails after a bath, when they will be softer and easier to cut.

However, electric filers often wind themselves up in long, loose coats. Breeds such as the Afghan or the American Cocker should be manually filed.

The "quick" is the nerve and blood supply in the nail. If this is cut, it will be very painful to the dog, and may become infected. Stop bleeding using a styptic pencil or permanganate crystals. Care should be taken with nails; it causes the dog severe pain when the quick is cut.

If the nails of a nervous or ticklish dog need cutting, then arrange for somebody to hold the dog and talk to it while you quickly carry out the task. Often, such dogs can have their nails filed without objection.

DEWCLAWS

Dewclaws are a problem in some active dogs because they can easily get torn away from the foot. Some dogs, such as the Poodle, have dewclaws removed at birth, while others, such as the Great Pyrenees, have a breed standard that requires these extra toes.

Dewclaws should be checked on a regular basis, as the nail can grow and grow, and may even grow back into the leg. This causes considerable pain to the dog and can result in infections, to the point where surgery is the only answer.

In the pet dog, dewclaws are not required at all. If they have been left on, they cannot be removed unless by a major operation. The nail of the dewclaw, however, can be clipped back with the rest of the nails. The less roadwork the dog does, the more likely it is that the nails will regularly need cutting or filing back (at least every three months).

Some dogs have poor feet, where the nails turn before they reach the ground. Such dogs will need their nails to be clipped back more often than others.

Check the dewclaws every week when you look at your dog's nails. Puppies that have

1. Brush the hair around the ears, and expose the ear opening.

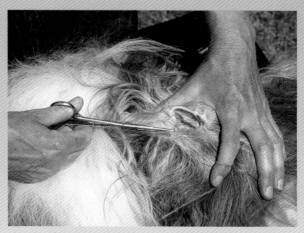

2. Use forceps to gently remove hair from the ear.

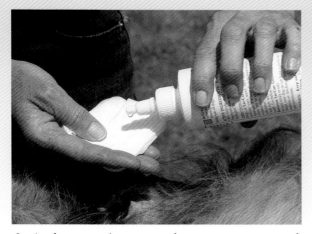

3. Apply a proprietary ear cleaner to a cotton pad.

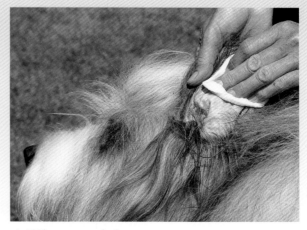

4. Wipe around the outer ear.

dewclaws need to have these clipped at the same time as you cut their sharp little needle-like nails.

EARS
Holding the ear flap back, clean the ears with alcohol or ear cleaner if necessary and apply ear powder to ensure the ear stays healthy and mite-free. After applying ear powder and leaving it in for a few minutes, use forceps to clean the hair from the ear, removing tiny bits of hair at a time. This will be less painful than using fingers.

Make sure that you clean the forceps with alcohol before and after each dog, to ensure that you do not spread infection or mites. See also page 59.

EYES
Keep the eyes clean, checking routinely for any sleep deposits or any weeping ducts. Use damp cotton batting to remove any accumulation or this will form a hard lump and could develop into a sore. See page 59.

TEETH
A dog's teeth should be routinely checked when visiting a professional groomer so early

problems, such as a decaying tooth, can be detected before they become advanced. Accumulation of tartar in dogs that have soft diets of processed food can create a problem. Left neglected, it can cause gum disease and tooth decay.

If your dog is not fed safe, raw bones, his teeth will need regular brushing to remove plaque.

If the mouth looks red and infected, or smells offensive, then a vet should be consulted.

TARTAR REMOVAL

If tartar has built up, this can be removed with a tooth scraper, provided that the problem has not accumulated out of control. The tooth scraper is a fine, long-handled tool with a flat edge rather like a miniature spade.

- Before use, the scraper is cleaned with peroxide.
- To scrape away plaque, hold the dog's muzzle in one hand, lift the flap of the mouth and chip away at the tartar. This can be difficult at first, but when the initial hard lump falls away, the rest usually comes away easily.
- Next apply an astringent. A solution of half peroxide and half water (or a purpose-made mouth astringent from the vet) to clean the gums before and after chipping

off the tartar is always advisable, to prevent infection.
- Dip a cotton pad into the solution and gently rub into the gums.

Do not undertake this procedure without first making sure that you are legally allowed to do so. In some places in the U.S., it can be illegal for professional pet groomers to scrape teeth, as it is considered the practice of veterinary medicine. In such places, groomers are allowed to brush teeth but not to scale them. If in doubt, contact your national grooming organization for advice.

TEETH STAINS

Rings of brown staining can appear on the teeth. Some believe these rings are a reaction to vaccines or to water quality. Whatever their cause – whether they are inherited or caused by illness – these stains will not be removed by any means. Often, the top of the tooth will also have a brown edge.

So, before you take a tartar descaler to your dog's teeth, check beforehand, as brown discoloration will not be removed. In fact, tartar accumulation is normally cream or beige in color, sometimes with a darker brown edge near to the gum.

TIME PER GROOM

There are many types of coat (as we will see in the following chapters), some of which are far easier and less time-consuming than others. Some need to be brushed, bathed, clipped, hand-stripped, carded, thinned, and so on, and many dogs, although shortcoated, will benefit from a bath and the removal of dead undercoat and molting hair on regular

A tooth scraper can shift built-up tartar.

occasions. The time spent on each breed, or even each dog, will vary according to its condition.

Here are some approximate times for the most frequently seen dogs in the grooming salon. The times apply to dogs in average condition (where extra time is not required to cope with nervous dogs and those in a badly matted state).

The times vary according to whether you clip or hand-strip. Hand-stripping can take up to three times as long, if not more, depending on coat condition and frequency of the application.

Unfortunately, because some breed books advocate a full strip twice a year, pet owners often leave the first trim until the dog is more than a year old. Then they have it done once a year and expect their dog to look as smart as the dog they have seen in books (where the dog is more than likely trimmed once every week or two – some are even stripped or rolled daily).

GROOMING TIMES

Airedale Terrier	2 to 3 hours
Bichon Frise	1 $1/2$ hours
Cocker Spaniel	2 $1/2$ hours
Lhasa Apso	1 $1/2$ hours
Miniature/Toy Poodle	1 $1/2$ hours
Old English Sheepdog	2 to 3 hours
Standard Poodle	2 $1/2$ hours
West Highland White	1 $1/2$ hours

Be realistic about the work involved for each breed. An Old English Sheepdog (left) will usually take twice the time of a Shih Tzu (below).

8 COAT AND SKIN PROBLEMS

Dog owners and groomers should be able to recognize when something is wrong with the dog's skin and coat, and to understand what action to take.

Often, these maladies are first detected by the groomer or owner and consequently dealt with before the dog is suffering unduly. Checking the dog on a regular basis will save valuable time and expense.

Coat problems and skin disorders come in many different forms, and are caused by a combination of factors, such as incorrect immune function, unsuitable diets and parasites.

Regular grooming, brushing and combing of a puppy or adult dog will help you to spot any skin disorders early on, so they can be dealt with promptly. You may need somebody more expert to help you with a diagnosis, so consult a professional groomer, vet, breeder or breed-club health officer at the first sign of detection.

ALLERGIES

FOOD INTOLERANCE
Many dogs suffer from food intolerances without their owners realizing. Digestive upsets are often symptomatic of a food allergy, though they can also be caused by a number of other conditions. Your vet should be your first port of call. Once it has been ascertained that a food allergy is causing the ill health, he or she will help you to investigate which ingredient is responsible.

Regular grooming enables you to keep an eye on your dog's health and to spot any potential problems in the early stages.

All breeds can suffer a low tolerance to gluten, found in most dog biscuits and complete, dry foods. Some manufacturers produce wheat-free food, but check that other glutens are also excluded.

A rice-based diet is often recommended for dogs with gluten intolerance, as rice is a grass, not a cereal.

CHEMICAL/CONTACT ALLERGIES
Some people go over the top with their ablutions and spray the dog with human perfume, not realizing that dogs can be highly allergic to the chemicals contained in it. So please, don't use your favorite Dior or Chanel on your pet. If your dog rolls in something that he finds wonderful but that makes you cringe, bathe the dog – don't try to cover up the smell with a perfume.

Some dogs are also allergic to household cleaning material, such as furniture polish. If you suspect this is the case with your dog, you must experiment with different types of polish until you find one that does not cause an allergic reaction, such as a skin rash.

Your vet will help you to discover the likely cause of your dog's contact allergy.

VACCINE REACTION
Some dogs develop skin problems after being vaccinated. Initially, the cause may not be obvious, but on inquiry one often discovers a booster shot or even a puppy's first jab will have been administered within three months of the dog developing skin problems. A homoeopathic vet may need to be sought to help calm the reaction.

ECZEMA
This can often be attributed to poor feeding or an allergic reaction to parasite invasion, such as mites, lice and fleas. In general terms, ectoparasites, which live on the skin, are the major cause of skin disease in dogs.

Any skin lesion or sign of irritation needs investigation by a veterinarian, but certainly the groomer must learn to recognize in an instant a dog suffering red, sore patches, sore spots or tiny blemishes that cause irritation, scratching and which sometimes weep. The skin will very often feel hot.

Treatment should be sought at once, as the eczema will be much more difficult to treat if it is left and gets worse.

ODORS

Dogs, like humans, have individual smells, and certain breeds have their own distinctive odors. Some oily-coated breeds, such as the Spinone Italiano, exude quite a strong odor that people either love or hate, and some spaniel breeds can smell very "doggie" when wet.

If you are concerned about doggie smells, consider sniffing the parents of the pup you intend to buy before taking the plunge, to make sure you are compatible.

If your dog smells unusual and you cannot identify the cause, it is worth consulting a vet, as odors can be symptomatic of underlying health problems.

PARASITES
Fleas, lice and mites are parasites that live on the dog, feeding from its blood. They can all cause the dog to become incredibly itchy, sometimes causing the dog to scratch so intensely that coat and hair loss leave the dog looking almost bald, with its skin red, raw and bleeding. With some invasions, such as the cheyletiella mite, the dog looks as though it has scurf. Unfortunately, this dandruff is of the walking, living kind, causing much distress. In some severe cases, it is necessary

to call in a pest control firm to treat the house.

Prevention and early treatment is the answer, and using the correct preparation is essential. Your vet's office is the best place to contact, as they will sell the safest, most effective products.

FLEAS

Fleas cause a huge number of skin allergies. The most common pest that invades the dog has a life that is completed off the dog. Eggs are laid in the dog's bed and around the house. Frontline (available from the vet) is probably the most effective treatment. As well as killing the fleas on the dog, it is essential that the entire home environment (including furniture and carpets) is also treated.

The secret is to analyze the problem as soon as the dog starts to itch. Fleas can be seen crawling across the skin when the hair is parted, though sometimes they have already hopped off the dog or cat to breed in the carpet. In this case, inspect the hair closely for tiny black particles (flea dirt).

A good way to determine if fleas are present is to comb along the skin with a very fine-toothed comb, lay the comb or its contents on a clean sheet of tissue and wet it. If fleas are present, invariably the tissue will show red spots, and this will show you the blood sucked from the skin by the parasite.

TICKS

Anyone who has seen ticks on dogs will shiver at the thought of these blood-sucking horrors. Dogs have died from disease-carrying ticks, though some countries suffer these parasites to a far worse degree than others. Dogs frequently pick up ticks from walking in woods and fields.

Ticks look a little like a wart to begin with, and get bigger as their sacs fill with blood

A good flea spray, available from your vet, will keep several types of parasites at bay.

For longcoated breeds, a pipette, applied to the back of the neck, may be more convenient.

sucked from their host. Surgical alcohol kills ticks and makes them easy to remove. There is also a tool (available from most pet shops) to aid this procedure.

MITES

If a dog appears rather itchy, you should inspect it closely. If there is nothing obvious lurking in the folds of the skin or under the belly and elsewhere (such as the base of the tail), it is quite possible that your dog has collected some mites. A very close inspection of the body (particularly the feet) could reveal tiny red spots. These are often early signs of harvest mites, and must be dealt with quickly.

Very often, immediately dousing three times daily for five days the red spots with cider vinegar will cure this problem. Alcohol also kills the red mite spots, and I have found that soaking the dog in a solution of half apple cider vinegar and half water is marvelous for eliminating the little horrors.

Otherwise, a trip to the vet will be necessary so you can be prescribed an adequate parasiticide before the situation gets much worse.

A yeast infection could also be responsible for itchy ears – your veterinarian will advise.

SKIN DISORDERS

SEBACEOUS ADENITIS

This is an uncommon skin disease. It may affect any breed of dog, but is seen more in some breeds than in others (see below). In its mild form, signs are limited to mild scaling, scurf and minimal hair loss. At its worst, however, it can be severe, leading to itching and considerable discomfort. In very bad cases, secondary bacterial infection may occur, with extreme hair loss. Sebaceous adenitis is seen in more than 30 breeds, including:
• Border Collie

Sebaceous adenitis can occur in many breeds, including the Border Collie, pictured above.

• Vizsla
• Old English Sheepdog
• Akita
• Lhasa Apso
• Samoyed
• Springer Spaniel
• Standard Poodle

This disease requires early attention and is not always readily recognized by vets. Dogs suspected of having this problem should be recommended for a skin biopsy, which is undertaken by most vets in conjunction with a specialist in the disease.

Professional groomers should be aware of this condition and should ensure that the owner consults a vet who has an under-standing of the problem. Treatments include waxing, oiling and antibacterial therapy. The administration of evening primrose oil and fish oils is being tested as an aid to treatment.

Hormone imbalances can cause bald patches, particularly on the sides, around the waist area. This is different from sebaceous adenitis and can be treated by a vet.

WARTS

These can cause severe discomfort, or else a dog can be covered with endless extrusions and not seem to feel a thing. Trying to clip a dog that has several warts hidden under a matted coat is a nightmare. The tops can be clipped off unintentionally and the bleeding can be quite worrying.

Some breeds seem to suffer more than others. Norwegian Elkhounds seem to have a particular problem with open cysts and wart extrusions, as do Cockers and Toy Poodles. Sometimes, these unwanted skin deformities are as hard as stone and grow in odd shapes to amazing lengths, when they may break off with no bleeding taking place. It is advisable to check thick and matted coats for warts and cysts – a groomer's worst headache.

Older dogs seem particularly prone to warts and can get quite touchy about being trimmed. It must be quite painful to have these extrusions cut or knocked off.

Treatment: Consult your vet if your dog develops warts – in some cases, the vet will remove them. Some people believe that banana skin, gently rubbed against the wart three times a day, is effective. Where the wart is inflamed or weeping, a vet should be consulted without delay.

COMMON PROBLEMS

ANAL SACS

The anal sacs, located under the skin near the anus, are two pouches that release fluid when the dog defecates; this fluid is used for identification among dogs.

If the sacs do not empty, they become blocked and may smell or become uncomfortable to the dog. The area around the anus may be swollen and puffy, indicating that the anal sacs require emptying.

Emptying anal sacs is a skilled job, and you are advised to seek help from a professional groomer or a vet. For more information, see page 49.

BEARDS

Bearded mouths cause many a headache. They collect debris with great ease, and woe to any owner who fails to remove twigs and general debris from a long beard. Once it is matted in, and this takes very little time, it is incredibly difficult to remove. Sometimes the only salvation is to cut the beard short, which is not an ideal option, particularly for owners of breeds like the Schnauzer, for whom the beard is a distinguishing characteristic.

Beards can collect everyday debris, such as food, and can stain easily.

EAR PROBLEMS

Erect-eared dogs (such as the German Shepherd Dog), and those with pendulous ears (such as the Basset Hound) are equally at risk of ear problems.

Ear infections seem to be ongoing and difficult to clear up. It is said that the ear is a perfect place for infection to flourish. As there is high humidity, the ear easily collects debris, moisture and dust, which provides the perfect environment for bacteria. No two dogs are alike, and a little bit of dust and hair in one ear can cause many ongoing problems, yet nothing at all in another ear.

It is a good idea to check the ears on a regular basis and to clean out the offending excess hair and wax (see page 51). Equally, overzealous ear cleaning can aggravate the situation, so it is a matter of getting the right balance. Ear problems should always initially be investigated by a veterinarian, as allergies are a prime cause of ear infections, and low thyroid levels can also be responsible for chronic problems.

Mites, which are very often carried unseen by cats, can invade a dog's ears. Early detection is best. There is frequently a brown, smelly discharge from the ear and sometimes red sores and inflammation are obvious. In cases of mite invasion, ask your vet for a suitable ear treatment.

Be extra vigilant in autumn when there is the danger of grass seeds working their way into the ear.

SNOODS

Pendulous ears get everywhere, as those with spaniels will confirm. Dogs love sniffing, and when their noses go down to pick up a scent, so do their long ears. Many owners wrap their dog's ears to prevent them getting too dirty. "Snoods" (home-knitted or made from old pantyhose) can be used to pull over the dog's head to keep its ears free of dirt while out walking, or to keep the ears from tipping into the dog's dinner while eating.

Snoods should not be used all the time, though, as they cover the ear canal and prevent fresh air from keeping the ear dry and healthy. They should be used only at meal and exercise times.

EYE PROBLEMS

Some dogs inherit eye abnormalities, which cause their eyes to water constantly, and which cause brown stains. A puppy's eyes often water during teething.

Entropion, where the eyelashes turn inwards, is a common cause of eye-watering, but sometimes infections are responsible. All cases should be seen by a vet to ascertain the cause.

Clean the eyes carefully with a wet cotton pad, using separate pads for each eye, and making sure any debris buildup in the corner of the eye is removed.

Some breeds are prone to weepy eyes and tear stains, and need regular eye care.

TEAR STAINS

Tear stains can rarely be completely removed. However, their appearance can be reduced by clipping the hair short; then staining will look less defined for a short period.

There are some preparations on the market that claim to make staining disappear. There is also a cream that will cover the staining on a temporary basis. Such products may be successful for short periods, but eyes that constantly water will produce stubborn tear stains.

Tears from sensitive eyes are a problem when it's windy or when the air is dusty. But most dogs cope very well, and it is only those with deeper-rooted problems, such as in-growing eyelashes, that have constant trouble; the vet should be consulted in such cases.

Some staining is caused by hair falling in the eyes and causing them to water, so topknots must be kept tidy to prevent this in such breeds as the show Poodle, Shih Tzu, Lhasa Apso and Bearded Collie.

- Take a ponytail band and secure the section of hair immediately over the eyes as soon as there is enough hair to clasp together. Do not use rubber elastic bands as they cling to the hair and make removal very difficult.
- In young puppies with just a little hair growth, this may need doing two or three times a day, but as the hair grows, once a day will suffice to keep the hair out of the eyes. With longer topknots, two or three bands may be required to restrain hair.
- Make sure you do not have the topknot pulled so tight that it pulls the eyes or the skin on the head. Anybody having their hair pulled back for the first time will know what a headache it can cause. If it is uncomfortable, your dog will soon scratch it out.

Keeping the head fall tied away from the face should reduce eye irritation.

GRASS SEEDS

The "dartlike" needles of grass seeds can find their way into paws or ear canals and can drive a poor dog mad by the burrowing seed, which causes intense irritation. If a grass seed has become lodged in the ear, the dog may continually shake its head, rub it against furniture and scratch at it to the point of bleeding.

The offending seed can be removed with a pair of forceps, but this needs to be done by a vet or at least by someone with past experience. Do not delay in seeking veterinary attention when this problem is suspected.

If the seed is in the paw, it can usually be removed with tweezers – provided it is removed promptly. If left untreated, it can burrow deep into the foot and will need veterinary attention for complete removal.

I have seen a dog with five nasty holes in the inside of its leg where a grass seed was attempting to escape. The seed was manually removed, and the leg took several months to heal; it took several more months for the sore bald spots to grow coat.

9 TROUBLE-SHOOTING

Some groomers experience difficulty when handling dogs. Often, this is because, although they have been trained to trim, they haven't necessarily had sufficient experience with dogs to understand fully why they act – or react – the way they do. A "doggie" background really helps – and working with dogs every day soon provides plenty of experience.

HANDLING SKILLS

Many groomers have asked me for advice on how to cope with vicious dogs. In more than 30 years of trimming, I can honestly say that I have met fewer than a handful of dogs that I would consider "vicious." Thoroughly nasty dogs that cannot be trimmed on their first visit to the groomer are rare. It is usually only nerves that cause them to react irrationally. An experienced groomer soon learns how to put a dog at ease.

The secret of success is to put the dog's welfare above the finish of a trim. This is certainly top of my list of priorities. Yes, I like a dog to look good when it walks away from my door, but I also like a happy dog that wags its tail when it sees me – rather than cowering or putting its tail between its legs. I will sacrifice a degree of presentation in order to achieve this. After a few visits, the dog will become increasingly confident about being groomed, and you will be able to groom it as you would any other dog.

Pet dogs who constantly have children and visitors around them are usually extremely cooperative, providing there is an incentive – a treat at the end of the session, a pat or a kind word.

Getting a dog used to being handled and groomed from an early age prevents many problems in later life.

Most dogs learn to accept grooming – and even enjoy the attention.

"DIFFICULT" DOGS

Unfortunately, through lack of time, skill or understanding, some groomers can make a dog react in a defensive way, which then means the dog is labeled as nasty. The only thing to blame here is the groomer's lack of training or experience. A spoiled brat of a dog is sometimes awkward to begin with, but dogs hate being ignored, so if you don't say much to them and don't take on their owners' "baby talk," the dogs soon pester you for attention.

Some dogs, who have been mistreated or misunderstood, will be difficult to trim for four or five visits to an experienced, flexible and well-trained groomer. Then they suddenly become angels. This is common, far more common than the dog that can't be won round by patience and kind handling.

Dogs with arthritis or puppies with growing pains should have their situation assessed and taken into consideration. Again, experience and good training allows the groomer to recognize these problems and act accordingly.

Dogs bite through self-defense and because they are worried or scared and feel vulnerable. Act confidently, treating the dog with respect and kindness at all times. If a dog is nervous, talk to it to reassure it.

Some dogs are aggressive because they consider themselves to be dominant over people. With such cases, the owner should enrole the dog at a good obedience class or seek specialist behavioral advice.

A new groomer, a lady with three weeks' training, proudly told me how she had fought with a 7-month-old Standard Poodle for more than an hour to clean the hair from its ears. I despair. Why put any dog through this sort of trauma? Trimming dogs is not a battle of strength or wits. If this lady had been a hairdresser and the dog a child, would she have still fought hand and fist with him?

Most dogs are far more ready to please you than children are. If you tie them up by neck and stomach, put a muzzle on them and fight them until they're subservient, what can you expect other than trouble?

This inexperienced person should have left the ears alone, and a vet or more experienced groomer should have been sought for consultation.

CLIPPER PHOBIAS

Electric clippers are greatly feared by some dogs. Why is it that a dog that is pleased to see you will sit on a table and be brushed, yet, the minute the clippers are turned on, it leaps six feet in the air?

Stop. Think. Why is the objection so acute?

• Does the dog have arthritis, which is fairly common, or some other bone or growth pain abnormality? If so, take this into

Elderly dogs are often clipped for their own comfort – but be aware that some golden oldies can be grouchy because of arthritis.

account when handling the dog (and check with the owner that the dog is receiving veterinary attention). For example, infected mouths with sore abscessed teeth and gums will cause some dogs to fight a clipper on their face due to pain.

• Has the dog been burned with hot clippers in the past? It is a good idea to use cool, lubricating clipper spray every five to 10 minutes to keep the blade free-running and cool. Test the blade on your own face every so often.

• Has the dog, perhaps even at the age of a few years old, never had a pair of clippers near it? If this is the case, the dog will need to be introduced to the sight, smell and sound of the clippers in a calm, controlled way. Have the clippers running nearby while brushing the dog so it gradually gets used to the sound. Only when the dog is comfortable with having the clippers nearby should you attempt to use them.

Most of the problems that occur during trimming can be attributed to lack of consideration by the owner and sometimes the groomer. Sometimes the owner causes the problem when brushing at home. Lack of patience, physically wrestling the dog into submission, hurting the dog without realizing it – these things must be recognized and overcome.

Often, owners tell me that their dog tries to bite them when they attempt to brush it, yet this same dog is as good as gold when it comes to the parlor. It is unlikely that the dog is behaving this way because it is spoiled and belligerent, but rather because the owner inadvertently hurts the dog, scraping his skin with too severe a brush, or twisting the dog's legs into awkward positions to achieve an objective. A little know-how goes a long way.

FIRST–TIMERS

Most dogs are nervous on their first visit to a new groomer, but they soon settle down, especially when you sing along to the radio or hold a conversation with the dog or somebody else. Your calm voice and casual manner will settle a dog quicker than anything.

Dogs very easily learn to sit, stand and stay on the grooming table without the aid of contraptions. A groomer takes on, as part of the job, the responsibility to teach the dog what is required of it in a calm and caring

Talking to the dog and acting in a calm, confident manner puts most first-timers at ease.

manner, without fuss and bother (page 17). Dogs of most breeds thoroughly enjoy going to the grooming salon. If you have more than your fair share of objecting dogs, then perhaps it is time you took more training or considered another career.

As a child growing up around horses, it was impressed upon me that I could never win a physical battle with anything that was more than twice my size and strength. The way forward was training with reward for response, gaining the animal's confidence and cleverly enticing it to respond and behave in an acceptable way.

Dogs have teeth that bite. They use them when they are confused, scared or cornered. It comes back to the fact that anyone can trim the hair off a stuffed dog, but it takes a special person to become a good groomer who understands dogs.

SOCIAL SKILLS

One would never believe how much diplomacy counts in the grooming game. Dealing with dogs is much easier than coping with nervous, neurotic, uncaring, overbearing and supercilious people, but it is all part of being a dog groomer.

Thankfully, on the whole, dog owners care about their dogs (sometimes too much). Only occasionally is there a time when tempers are so frayed that the dog owner gets a good taste of the whipping edge of my tongue. Neglect is one aspect that makes me livid. There is no need for it. There are so many groomers around that there is no need to visit a groomer only once a year, or when the dog is in a disgusting state.

There are occasions when the breeder is at fault, telling the new puppy owner that the dog should not be clipped until it is 6 months old (that's the story we are frequently told); this usually ends up with the owner leaving the dog until it is a year old. By this time, the coat is looking scruffy and out of control, with accumulated mats.

THE CUSTOMER IS ALWAYS RIGHT

Groomers do, from time to time, fall out with clients, usually because of the neglect of a dog, but sometimes because the groomer wants to trim a dog a certain way and the client prefers the dog all clipped off. It is as well to remember that the customer is always right. This may not be the case, of course, but as a groomer it is your job to give the customer what he or she wants.

Groomers that have a fetish for combing out knots and tangles and turning out a first-class trim may be admirable and deserve recognition, but sometimes it is more appropriate to opt for something simpler and easier to manage. For example, perhaps the dog leads a lifestyle whereby it is forever getting wet and muddy; perhaps the owner never puts a brush near the coat; or perhaps the owner just wants the dog to have a very short haircut for their own convenience. In such instances, there is nothing wrong with clipping the dog all over with a No. 5 Oster blade.

I know some groomers who will refuse to do this, but I don't understand why. If the dog is comfortable and the client is happy, where's the problem? The dog must come first. A matted dog is an unhappy dog. It will be much happier having its hair clipped short than enduring hours of having its mats and snarls ripped through with a brush.

NERVOUS OWNERS

Some owners are reluctant to leave their dogs. I don't see this as a problem. I invite the owner to stay and watch the proceedings, explaining that some dogs do act up with their owners present, but it won't bother me if it doesn't bother them. Once the owner is confident in your ability, they will happily leave the dog in your care.

Some owners are often shocked that I do not possess a muzzle – I never have – and I don't tie dogs to grooming contraptions or hooks on the wall. Dogs soon learn to sit or stand still and to be groomed, clipped, stripped, whatever. A little training goes a long way.

Putting people and their dogs at their ease is a gift and is incorporated into the training of any good groomer. It may take a bit longer to trim the dog this way for the first couple of visits, but the effort is worthwhile.

PART THREE: BREED PROFILES

The following chapters, split into coat types, give step-by-step instructions on grooming each breed of dog. Please note that, while the breed standards are touched upon, anyone wishing to know more about any particular breed is well advised to contact the relevant club or association for complete standard and comprehensive details. Contact your national kennel club for details.

The breeds are listed in alphabetical order, using their American Kennel Club names. To locate a breed according to its British Kennel Club name, refer to the index (pages 285–288) to find the correct page number.

10 CORDED AND CURLY COATS

CORDED COAT CARE

Dogs with long, corded coats are fairly rare, and are not breeds that usually frequent the grooming salon, although they are to be seen at most shows around the world in increasing numbers.

These dogs require specialist attention. The coat on corded breeds is totally unique and in other breeds would be considered as a bundle of tangles. Certainly, these dogs would be the inexperienced groomer's nightmare.

Trying to be objective about corded coats doesn't come easily to me. I have met and judged more unsavory-smelling corded dogs than clean ones. I cannot see how the dog can be happy and contented like this. Of course, there are some admirable, dedicated owners who keep these dogs in tiptop condition, and I wouldn't want to denounce them. Hopefully, as the breeds gain popularity, more attention will be paid to their coats.

Certainly, underneath the coat, most of these dogs are little charmers, although not necessarily easy living companions because of their working tendencies and the difficulty in keeping the coat.

CURLY COAT CARE

Curly coats are very attractive, and are shorter and easier to manage than the corded type. However, they still require attention and nurturing if the dog is to look good.

Tight curls are frequently rubbed and wetted, and the longer curled coat (such as the Bolognese) is combed through regularly; daily is best. If left, this type of long, curled coat will felt (just as the Poodle coat will), so the hair must be combed through from the skin down to remove all dead hairs and to prevent matting.

This procedure should start from puppyhood, continuing vigilantly through the change of coat, and into adulthood.

CURLY-COATED RETRIEVER

The featured Curly-Coated Retriever is Ch. Grenowood Hazey Idea at Lenellie.

COAT: The body, ears and tail (from the occiput to the tip of the tail) are covered with tight, crisp curls, lying close to the skin (without undercoat), while the face and muzzle are smooth-haired. The color is black or liver.

MAINTENANCE: This unique coat needs little preparation, but does require specialist treatment, sometimes on a weekly basis, to keep it at its best. It should not have bare patches when nurtured.

PROCEDURE

Equipment needed: A wide-toothed comb to remove dead hair.

Breed tip: The coat is not brushed, as this would make it fluffy.

- Rub over the curls with a wet hand to remove the dead hair. 1

- Bathe the dog in a protein pH-balanced shampoo. The coat comes up beautifully when washed in tea-tree oil and lavender, as our show star (right) illustrates. Of course, you must make sure that these oils are kept away from the eyes, as they can both cause extreme eye irritation. 2

- Apply a nourishing conditioner or a purifying shampoo and mask conditioning finish, a couple of times a year, and rinse. This breed is often bathed in a shampoo mixed with oil (leading grooming supply shops should stock a suitable product). 3

- Dry with an absorbent towel by pressing it against the coat, rather than rubbing it. Pat the curls and allow them to dry naturally in a warm room or cage-dryer. 4

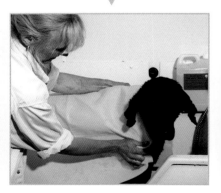

- Check the dog's nails 5, ears 6 and teeth. 7

- Spray the coat with an oil-enhanced conditioner and finger-touch in. Any hairs on the body that are straying from their curls, and which can't be encouraged in, can be snipped off with scissors. 8

- The ears are trimmed along the edge of the leather to give a neat look. Hold the leather, snipping the hair that is held at the end of your fingers for safety. 9

- The head is trimmed from the ear toward the throat. Hair can be trimmed with thinning scissors to prevent a topknot appearance. Trim the long hairs from the neck and the throat, to the brisket. 10

- The dog's forelegs can be trimmed round at the elbow and at the back of the leg to give a neat look. The foot hair is trimmed close to the foot for neatness. 11

- The underside of the tail is trimmed fairly short. Start at the root and work toward the tip, but not too close. 12

- The finished dog. 13

BERGAMASCO

COAT: The coat is the main feature of the breed, and the long mats are known as "broccoli."

The coat is abundant and long. It is harsh in texture on the front of the body, and softer on the head and limbs. There is a short dense undercoat which obscures the skin. The hair tends to form into strands or loose mats from the top of the body, rather than into cords. The coat is greasy to the touch.

The coat color is gray, solid or with white spots. Spots may be a shade of gray. Solid black is allowed, but should be dull and not at all shiny. Solid white is discouraged, but white markings are acceptable if not more than 20 percent.

MAINTENANCE: The mats are split by hand into manageable sizes while the dog is young – the coat is never brushed. The head hair can be combed. Think very seriously before taking on this responsibility.

PROCEDURE

Equipment needed: Wide-toothed comb.

Breed tip: The Bergamasco may look as if it has never received any grooming attention, but it actually requires quite intensive maintenance. It is wise to consider this before taking on the responsibility.

• Separate the mats (broccoli) by hand where required to prevent the hair from becoming one solid mass.

• If bathing is undertaken, shampoo in an easy-to-rinse natural application and rinse very thoroughly.

• Air- or cage-dry.

• Check the dog's nails, ears and teeth.

• Go through the coat to ensure the mats are well separated, and comb through the topknot with a wide-toothed comb.

• The dog is shown in a natural state. The pet dog and those that are no longer exhibited in the show ring are sometimes trimmed down to about 2 inches (5 cm) or more all over.

BERGAMASCO COAT CARE: THE EXPERT'S VIEW

The owner of the Albera Bergamasco kennel, Maria Andreoli, graduated in biological chemistry and then dedicated herself to university research. This scientific preparation was later an invaluable store of knowledge in the setting-up of the sheepdog kennels. She says that, after accurate and patient work, she was able to determine the genetic information of this breed, which had up to then been bred using disorganized and empirical methods. Here, Maria shares her expertise on effective grooming for this breed.

COAT CARE

When dealing with a Bergamasco for the first time, people are generally worried about taking care of the coat. They ask if it is true that a Bergamasco should never be brushed, and what they should do when large bunches of hair start to form.

In practice, the Bergamasco's coat needs little care, but it must be applied at the right moment. We can divide the coat care required into three periods.

FROM BIRTH TO 10 TO 12 MONTHS
During this period, the dogs have puppy coats that are soft and short. This coat shows no felting tendency, so occasional brushing with a steel-toothed brush is sufficient to keep it in order and to remove dirt among the hairs.

DURING THE SECOND YEAR OF LIFE
Around the 10th to 12th month (individual variations and seasonal variations are very common), the formation of hair with different texture begins, together with molting of the puppy hair. The first visible sign of this is that the coat seems to rise, as if it were blown up due to the growth of the fine, abundant undercoat which blends with the puppy hair that is gradually molting.

Starting at the rear of the body, on the croup and back legs, the woolly hair makes its appearance, while, first on the tail and later in the withers zone, the "goat hair" starts to form. From the withers, it will successively extend over the whole saddle and, in slightly smaller proportions, over the rest of the body, mixing with the woolly hair.

This is the period during which the coat requires the most careful and concentrated attention. The soft puppy hair, while molting, mixes with the undercoat and with the woolly and "goat hair" in formation. This creates shapeless clumps, often tangled. Be very careful not to let the clumps felt, as this makes it much more difficult for the adult coat to grow properly.

On the other hand – and against your natural instincts – limit brushing to a minimum, substituting a process of opening up the clumps by hand. Great care must be taken not to open up the clumps completely because this period coincides with the initial formation of the typical maps (i.e., mats).

During this manual operation, it is necessary to part the clumps right down to the skin, but not to divide them up too radically at the base of the future maps, which need to be quite large and consistent. You should, therefore, divide the coat into strands of 2 to 2³⁄₄ inches (5 to 7 cm) in width. Only at this point should you use the brush on hairs that stick out and that would otherwise tangle with the maps.

If felting has already started, it could be difficult or even impossible to open up the clumps using only your hands. In this case, you can use a pair of scissors, but only in the direction of the maps, i.e., from top to bottom. This operation should, however, be limited to a minimum.

This work should be carried out all over the body, except on the saddle. Since only "goat hair" is present there, the whole saddle requires brushing. Here, it could be the case that puppy hair mixing with the undercoat and the "goat hair" forms clumps, but the absence of woolly hair in the zone makes them different from those that form on other parts of the body. They are easier to disentangle, by hand or

with the brush and, finally, the comb.

In any event, the clumps must be opened up completely in order to reveal the "goat hair," which should be flat and orderly.

The appearance of the Bergamasco may not be particularly attractive during this period. All the budding maps stick out in all directions, making the dog look messy and clumsy. We just have to be patient and wait for the maps to grow and assume their permanent form. Only around the age of 3 years will the coat be fully formed and, even if the maps are still relatively short, they will be capable of constituting a dignified "skirt."

AFTER 3 YEARS

After the adjustment period, the coat requires very little care. The saddle always needs combing, especially at the end of the spring molting period when the abundant winter undercoat falls out and causes clumps in the "goat hair." The maps on the rest of the body need periodic checking to make sure that they do not get too wide. In this case, they should be divided so that the coat maintains an orderly appearance.

For the sake of clarity, we shall indicate the various body zones where the three hair textures and their different distribution can be noted. On the saddle and the upper part of the neck, there is only undercoat and "goat hair." The coat is smooth here and should be brushed regularly to remove dead undercoat hairs and keep the "goat hair" looking smooth and fresh. Under the saddle, at shoulder level and below on the underside of the neck and on the chest, the presence of woolly hair is evidenced by the formation of maps.

The woolly hair is not as plentiful as on the rear of the body, but is mixed with the "goat hair," which is abundant here. As a result, the maps in these areas are softer and thinner. On the forelegs there are also agglomerations of long, fine and soft hair. These are, however, so plentiful that they make the limbs look like solid, hairy columns emerging from the thick

coat over the body which mask the joints.

On the rear of the trunk, over the flanks and on the rear limbs, the woolly hair is extensive, so the maps are thicker and stiffer there due to felting of this hair in contrast to the "goat hair." These maps are also longer and tend to increase in length as the dog gets older. They grow down from the croup over the back legs, both sideways and to the rear, forming a wide "skirt'."

BRUSHING

Apart from keeping the saddle tidy, and dividing the maps that are too wide in order to keep the coat in top condition, regular brushing is required all over it, even where the maps are present. This should be done with a steel-toothed brush with fine, curved teeth, approximately twice a month.

Brushing is necessary in order to tidy the coat and to remove dirt. This cannot disturb the maps. Once these are properly formed, no amount of brushing can alter their internal structure.

BATHING

Frequent baths are detrimental to the Bergamasco's coat. The use of shampoo is not recommended as it dissolves the natural oils secreted by the skin for the purpose of creating a protective film around the hairs to make them waterproof and protect them from contact with any external agents. Without this protection, the coat would become very dirty and the skin would dry out. This is a danger to be avoided at all times in the Bergamasco, because drying the hairs that hold the maps together could cause them to fall out. In view of the length of time it takes for them to grow again, the dog would not resume its normal appearance for many months.

A good rule for Bergamascos is not to give a complete bath more than once or a maximum of twice a year. They should be washed in plenty of water with only a very small dose of detergent, if needed. If necessary, one can wash the parts of the body which tend to get dirty

The Bergamasco coat requires specialist attention but it is not a labor-intensive breed.

easily at more frequent intervals, i.e., the extremities, around the mouth to remove food remnants, etc. Again, use plenty of water and very little soap.

DRYING

Avoid the use of a hair-dryer unless it is absolutely essential. Whenever possible, choose a sunny day to wash your dog and let it dry naturally. If it is absolutely unavoidable to use a dryer, remember to add a good dose of cosmetic oil to the last rinsing water to minimize the damaging effect of drying out the hair.

CONCLUSION

From the above, I hope it is now clear that, despite its complexity and abundance, the Bergamasco's coat does not require a great deal of attention in comparison to the coats of many other breeds, which require constant grooming. The Bergamasco is a simple, uncomplicated dog that has remained close to nature; this is also reflected in its coat, which forms and develops spontaneously. All we need to do is check its development, intervening as little as possible and with the utmost caution when unavoidable.

With regard to the coat, as for everything else that concerns the breed, the Bergamasco is capable of fending for itself and finding the simplest and most natural solutions without assistance.

BOLOGNESE

COAT: The Bolognese has a distinctive non-shedding coat, rather like the Poodle's, which forms into flocks.

MAINTENANCE: The coat does not require trimming in the true sense, but needs care and attention, with regular combing to prevent tangles from forming. These dogs are shown in their natural state, but sometimes pet dogs are trimmed (scissored), as with the family pet Bichon Frise and Poodle. They are bathed and conditioned frequently, and sometimes put into a "lamb"-type clip (see Chapter Seventeen). Pet dogs are often trimmed with a snap-on comb for an allover uniform length (see bottom right).

PROCEDURE

Equipment needed: Wide-toothed comb.

Breed tip: Initial thorough combing will save you a lot of hard work.

- Comb the dog through from the roots to the ends with a wide-toothed comb. Then work through the coat with a medium comb to remove dead hair and tangles. All this should be done before you even start to contemplate bathing your Bolognese.

- Bathe the dog with a protein pH-balanced shampoo.

- Rinse thoroughly to ensure all traces of shampoo are removed from the flocks.

- Use a quality antimat conditioner, and rinse if the instructions advise.

- Cage- or lightly blow-dry, using a diffuser. Use your fingertips to help circulate air throughout the coat. Part any hair that may have matted onto the skin, forming a felt. This will not happen if the dog is thoroughly groomed beforehand.

- Check the dog's nails, ears and teeth.

- Check under the dog's pads, removing excess or clogged hair.

- Where the dog is trimmed down to a manageable length, use only a coarse blade (such as an Oster No. 7, or a No. 40 with $1/2$-inch/1.25-cm attachment).

Pet Bolognese are often given an allover trim.

BOLOGNESE ON THE MENU

Gina Taylor and Barbara Andrews are two devotees of the Bolognese. Here they share their expertise on this wonderful little newcomer with a big personality that is growing in popularity in North America.

GOLDEN RULES

The golden rule when grooming the Bolognese is never to bathe the dog without first giving the coat a thorough combing through, otherwise the coat will become very matted.

The dog is laid flat on its side on a table or towel spread across a lap. A long-toothed wide-spaced comb is worked through the coat, a small section at a time, and care must be taken to groom right down to the skin. The legs, feet, face and ears are groomed with a smaller shorter-toothed comb, as the hair here is shorter and of a finer texture. After thoroughly combing with a wide comb, follow with a finer comb to ensure all knots are removed. Done gently, dog and owner will enjoy the experience. The dog is now ready for bathing.

BATHING

Using a sprayer to ensure an even distribution of water, wet the dog thoroughly with warm water, and apply a shampoo especially designed for white dogs. To prevent unnecessary matting, try to keep the hand motion straight rather than rubbing in circles. Lather well, smoothing the shampoo through the coat. Rinse thoroughly and apply a conditioner to help stop the coat from knotting. After rinsing, towel-dry.

DRYING

The unique coat will now fall into very loose curls (rather like a shaggy perm). It can be left to dry naturally in a warm room or it can be lightly blow-dried using a hair-dryer with a diffuser.

WEEKLY CARE

The coat needs to be combed twice a week. Some tangles will require extra attention – a touch of hair-dressing cream can help to combat the static that causes this.

PUPPY COAT

A puppy coat needs more attention as it is of a finer texture and changes gradually to an adult coat by the time the dog is about 18 months old. The coat does not molt, but a little hair does come out each time you comb.

PET AND SHOW

No trimming is required for the show ring, but hair can be removed between the pads. Pet dogs are frequently cut down shorter.

CORDED POODLE

COAT: Cords can grow to an amazing length, sometimes longer than the dog.

A classic Champion from yesteryear was Champion Achilles who stood 23 inches (57.5 cm) high at the shoulder while his cords hung down for 30 inches (75 cm). He was described as a magnificent Poodle with much dignity and great carriage. His hair was never combed, but continually rolled and twisted.

MAINTENANCE: To create cords, the hair is never combed, but is continuously rolled and twisted with the fingertips, applying an oil to encourage the process if required. (Paraffin and Vaseline were used for this, once upon a time, but today we have special grooming oils that are nongreasy and serve the purpose very well, being less messy. Ask for details at your grooming supplies store.)

The cords are tremendously hard work to maintain, and most people find they look unattractive, preferring the Poodle to have a more popular fluffy, powderpuff appearance. However, where ringlets form, as opposed to matted plates, this can be quite attractive.

PROCEDURE

Equipment needed: Only fingers to separate the cords.

Breed tip: Brushing will destroy the cords.

- Separate any hair that has matted at the skin and encourage it into curls or cords.

- Bathe your Poodle in a protein shampoo.

- It is essential that you rinse the shampoo out very thoroughly. Any shampoo that is left in the coat, or an excessively strong shampoo, could cause the dog to itch and scratch.

- Again, check to ensure the ringlets are not matted at the skin, splitting them with your fingers where necessary and blending into cords.

- Pat the coat dry with superabsorbent towels, and finish off in warm air or a drying cage or cabinet. (Left to dry of its own accord, the coat could take up to 24 hours, which could cause the dog to catch a cold.)

- Check the Poodle's nails, ears and teeth.

- The face, the feet, the front of the neck and the base of tail are clipped as with the Poodle in all the other trims (see Chapter Seventeen).

- The hindquarters and legs can be shaved in the same way as for the "Continental Lion" clip (page 284), leaving a rosette on the hips, which is left to cord.

IRISH WATER SPANIEL

COAT: The coat is dark liver in color with a purplish tint or bloom peculiar to the breed and is referred to as puce-liver. The coat on the body is dense with tight, crisp ringlets, which cover all parts of its body except the muzzle, the front of the neck, and the first 2 to 3 inches (5 to 7.5 cm) of the tail.

Free from woolliness, the hair has natural oiliness. The forelegs are covered down to the feet with curls or ringlets, which form naturally. The skull has a covering of long curls forming a pronounced topknot, growing well into the well-defined peak to a point between the eyes. The ears have long, twisted curls, and the throat is smooth, as is the face.

MAINTENANCE: Brush and comb, separating the coat in layers at least once a week, and clean the ears. Bathe and trim with scissors every six to eight weeks.

PROCEDURE

Equipment needed: Wide-toothed comb, slicker brush, scissors.

Breed tip: Spray with rainwater to enhance the curls.

- Along the topline, flick the coat up with the comb so that it stands up and out, away from the back. Following the direction of the arrows on the diagram, trim a neat line.

- Now to the front legs. Sitting the dog in front of you, lift the leg and comb the coat towards the body. Then hold the paw, and shake the leg. Next decide what length you want the coat. Then, as before, follow the direction of the arrows and trim.

- For the rear legs, stand behind the dog. Comb out all the coat in the direction of the arrows, hold the paw and shake the leg. Trim as before. Now, stand to the side of the dog, and trim as before, but notice that the coat is left longer in front and shorter behind the stifle, then longer behind the hock and shorter in front.

- Next, the topknot. Comb the coat out from the crown, and trim out from the crown, shorter at the base of the skull and longer over the eyes.

- For the body of the dog, comb the coat in the direction of the arrows, and trim as before. Blend the sides and the chest so that they follow through from the legs to the topline – there should be no sudden changes of length in coat where the leg joins the body.

- Now comb all the coat down and trim under the belly. Let the dog have a shake to loosen any ends, then trim any long hairs that will now appear.

- Don't forget to check the dog's nails, ears and teeth.

KOMONDOR

COAT: The coat consists of long, coarse cords, which may be wavy or curly, with a softer undercoat. The hair tends to cling together like tassels to give the corded appearance. The color is always white, and the skin is gray, but pink skin is acceptable.

MAINTENANCE: If neglected, the coat forms into large, matted "plates." The cords are strong and heavy, and feltlike to touch. For the show ring, the Komondor is presented as corded.

PROCEDURE

Equipment needed: Scissors (to trim the adult coat, particularly the feet).

Breed tip: Do a lot of research before taking on this breed.

- Check through the cords and separate those that are matted at the skin.

- Bathe the Komondor in a shampoo, made from pure, natural, therapeutic ingredients of tea tree and lavender. When choosing a suitable shampoo, make sure it has easy-cleaning capabilities and is soothing and calming to the skin.

- Rinse the coat thoroughly, being careful that no trace of shampoo is left in, as it will be very itchy for the dog.

- Squeeze the excess water from the coat with superabsorbent towels.

- Air- or cage-dry.

- For pet (nonshow) dogs, the stomach can be clipped with Oster No. 4 for comfort and cleanliness, as can the anal area.

- Check the dog's nails, ears and teeth.

- Finish by checking all the cords to separate any clogs next to the skin.

LAGOTTO ROMAGNOLO

Photo: Kemp.

COAT: The coat of the Lagotto is its most important feature. Every part of this dog is covered with a thick, woolly-textured, double coat that forms tight, ring-shaped curls and is highly water-resistant. The coat on the head forms looser, more open curls.

LAGOTTO PUPPY COAT

From 7 weeks of age, the puppy should be groomed every few days, using a medium-toothed steel comb. Between 10 and 12 weeks, the coat on the head and body should be scissored to about ¾ inch (2 cm) in length. The hair on the tail is trimmed to ½ inch (1 cm).

At 5 months of age, a Lagotto is ready for its first clipping, which is undertaken with an Oster No. 10 or No. 8½, depending on the time of year. The development of the desirable curls can be greatly increased by frequent clipping in the first two years of a dog's life.

The color is off-white and solid; white with brown or orange markings; brown roan, brown (in different shades) with or without white; orange with or without white. Some dogs have a brown or dark brown mask. Tan coat markings (in different shades) are allowed.

MAINTENANCE: Given that the coat is nonshedding, it will, in time, felt and thus the coat must be clipped off at least once a year. The companion or working Lagotto is usually clipped two or three times a year, depending on the rate of hair growth. Show dogs are usually clipped 10 to 12 weeks before a major show and scissored between shows to maintain the outline.

Heads are not clipped, as the coat on the head is much slower-growing. Scissoring to maintain head shape is preferable.

When prepared for the show ring, the length of the coat should be about 1½ inches (4 cm), springing back to about ¾ inch (2 cm), and must evenly follow the line of the dog. It can be longer on the head, but must not obscure the eyes. It is permitted to remove hair in the genital/anal area.

A dog presented like a Poodle or Bichon Frise, clipped, sculptured or in any way glamorized, is highly undesirable. The correct coat presentation is functional and helps to maintain and enhance the rustic look that is typical of the breed.

The Lagotto is normally clipped using an Oster No. 10. If a midwinter clip is necessary, No. 8½ is more suitable.

The Lagotto also requires regular bathing, particularly its beard, and must always be allowed to dry naturally.

Remember, the coat must never be brushed or combed while it is wet.

PROCEDURE

Equipment needed: Good-quality medium-toothed steel comb. Plastic or composite combs are not strong enough. A steel de-matter, good-quality slicker, and wide-blade grooming scissors are also required.

Breed tip: When grooming – whether for a show, working or companion dog – it is important that the finished dog presents a thoroughly functional, appearance. Although of small size, the Lagotto is a working dog, not a large toy dog.

Three days before the show, comb and demat the coat, bathe and dry naturally. Two days before, scissor over any loose curls to maintain the outline. The morning of the show, spray the coat lightly with water to encourage it to curl.

- Before bathing, demat the coat. If the coat is very felted, it may be necessary to first reduce the length with scissors. Lagotto coats are very water-resistant, and dogs with coats longer than 2 inches (5 cm) will be very difficult to wet to the skin. Use a natural shampoo and rinse well. Follow with a conditioner if the dog is to be clipped.

- Before attempting to dry with towels, allow the dog time to shake. A couple of vigorous shakes will leave most Lagotto virtually dry. If in a hurry, superabsorbent towels can remove most of the remaining moisture from the topcoat, but the dog is best left in a warm place for 10 minutes or so to finish drying naturally. Cage-dryers are not recommended, as they tend to cause the coat to open and fluff and give a Bichon-like appearance to the dog.

- When dry, the coat should be a mass of curls. Scissor any loose curls on the body and legs to maintain the outline. For show dogs, the head coat should be lightly trimmed to enhance the width of the skull, but must never be sculptured like a Bichon. Eyebrows and beards should be trimmed to a functional length and very profuse ear hair shortened to show the shape of the ear. Companion and working dogs may have the coat on the skull and muzzle uniformly shortened.

- Many Lagotto have profuse hair inside the ear (to prevent water entering when diving after ducks). Unless the dog is to be used for duck hunting, the hair inside the ears should be regularly removed with finger and thumb. Grooming powder will help removal of this hair.

- Check the dog's nails and teeth.

- Check under the feet for excess hair and remove with scissors to prevent mats from forming.

- After clipping, grooming is a mere matter of combing the head hair and regularly removing seeds and burrs which lodge in the undercoat. A slicker is useful until the coat is about 3/4 inch (2 cm) and then a steel comb should be used instead.

- When it becomes too difficult to pass a comb through the coat, a steel de-matter should be used to periodically remove felted hairs and knots. Eventually, the entire coat starts to felt and it becomes difficult to pass even a de-matter through the undercoat. This indicates that the coat should once again be clipped off.

PULI

COAT: The corded coat is a natural formation. Over time, the weather-resistant topcoat becomes entwined with the softer undercoat, forming cords, of which there are various types.

The fully corded coat takes a long time to develop. For example, a floor-length coat can take up to five years to grow. Therefore, it is a must to remember that the first part of the cord will be there for a considerable time!

The Puli coat colors are black, sometimes with a rusty appearance, white and shades of apricot and gray.

The cords fall into various types: tight, narrow, round cords; looser, thicker, round cords; wide, flatter, ribbon cords; and narrow, flatter, ribbon cords. The main thing is that the cords are of similar type all over the Puli, with slightly thinner, shorter cords on the head and ears.

MAINTENANCE: A floor-length show coat will require a great deal of regular grooming and much care to ensure that the cords are preserved.

It should be remembered that the dog's coat has developed for a reason – a Puli working in a natural environment has a corded coat to protect it from extreme weather as well as hazards.

PROCEDURE

Equipment needed: Basic grooming is done with the thumb and fingers, but a good pair of scissors, a brush, a comb and a hair-dryer will be useful.

Breed tip: Make sure the cords are separated regularly and that the coat does not gather too much debris, which can cause irritation to the dog.

- Care is required from a young age, when a soft (baby) hairbrush can be used, both to get the puppy used to being handled and also to massage the skin.

- Once cord formation is seen to start in a young dog, the brush is put to one side, but it is a good idea to continue massaging the skin with your fingers. Tufts close to the skin (or small "rat tails") are the first sign of cording. From the onset of cording until the cords have become firmer and reasonably tight is undoubtedly the worst period of time to care for the coat. Grooming depends on the type

of coat – especially the amount of undercoat there is, as it is this that can cause bad felting in the cords. It is important to ensure that the cords are separated to the skin and that there is a good amount of air circulation. Separate the cords using a spray of baby oil and water.

- The coat should be bathed regularly using a good canine shampoo. It should be rinsed and rinsed again to ensure that all residues have been removed.

- Natural drying will take considerable time. A cage is a must, as are numerous towels. A canine hair-dryer helps to speed things along, but the drying process can still take a considerable period of time as the cords are quite spongelike.

- After the coat is dry, a mixture of one-third baby oil to two-thirds water can be finely sprayed, directly onto the coat. This spray can be used between baths to help tighten up the coat.

- Check the dog's nails, ears and teeth. The ears can become very matted with the coat, inside and on the leathers. Care must be taken to make sure this is not allowed to become a solid mat.

- Check the beard, around the mouth and the eyes. Often, food can get caught in the beard – sometimes it is possible to get this out by using a comb, or the beard can be short-trimmed.

- Check the paws, including between the pads Trim to remove any mats found on the feet, as well as any excess coat or long cords that might cause the dog to trip when walking or running.

- A long coat may well require trimming if it becomes too long.

SOFT COATED WHEATEN TERRIER

COAT: The coat, when natural, is soft and silky. It is neither woolly nor wiry, and is loosely waved or curly. If curly, the coat has large, light and loose curls. The coat should not standoff, but flow and fall naturally. The coat is abundant all over the body and equally profuse on the head and legs. The length of leg coat should be sufficient to give good balance to the length of coat on the head and body. The color is wheaten, but youngsters may have dark markings, which should clear with maturity.

MAINTENANCE: The coat is non-shedding so requires regular attention to remove dead hair and to prevent matting. Overtrimming or styling is considered wrong. For the show ring, it is permissible to tidy the coat to give a neat outline.

In Britain, this breed is shown in full coat, and in Ireland and elsewhere it is more heavily trimmed, but never to the extent of the Kerry Blue.

The Soft Coated Wheaten Terrier is a natural dog, and should appear as such. However, for the purpose of the show ring, the coat may be tidied up to present a neat outline, but the breed should not be clipped, stripped or styled.

The main differences between the U.K. and U.S. Wheatens are in the finish. The coat on the ears, for instance, may be left natural or the fringe trimmed off to accentuate their smallness, but they are not clipped so short as to appear shaved.

Secondly, thinning scissors are used to "tip" the coat (i.e., trim off the ends of the hair), as well as to thin it and to make the hair lie flat.

All trimming should create a balanced look, so that no one part of the body is accentuated.

PROCEDURE

Equipment needed: Wide-toothed comb, straight scissors and thinning scissors.

Breed tip: A wide-toothed metal comb is recommended for the Wheaten coat when it comes to daily grooming, as a slicker or pin brush tends to split the coat ends and strips out new hair growth.

- Comb through with a wide-toothed comb to remove dead hairs and to ensure no tangles are present.

- Mats and tangles can be removed by parting them with the finger and thumb, and then teasing them with the end of the comb. If necessary, use a mat-splitter – with care. Alternatively, spray the coat with conditioner to ease combing.

- Bathe the dog in a quality natural shampoo, such as tea tree and lavender.

AMERICAN METHOD

There is a great deal of variance in this breed in the United States. The Soft Coated Wheaten Terrier can look completely different on the East Coast as opposed to the West Coast. This applies to both pets and show dogs.

The pet dog is often clipped with a coarse blade or attachment blade to leave about one 1 inch (2.5 cm) of coat, or it is scissored shorter for the convenience of the owner and for the comfort of the dog.

The show dog, however, is groomed quite differently to its British show cousins – the differences are noted in the

following profile. As with any breed, you must study the breed club's recommendations and breed standard regarding coat presentation before entering any shows.

- Rinse well.

- Apply a quality conditioner to enhance the texture of the coat.

- Comb through, after thoroughly towelling the coat, and leave it to dry naturally. Or, separate the hair and gently blow-dry to assist drying. Do not overblow, as this will destroy the natural wave of the coat. Make sure you blow-dry the coat in the direction it should lie, so the coat lies nicely and doesn't appear overly fluffy.

- Comb through the coat once more with a wide-toothed comb.

- The head is trimmed with thinners from the back of the eye to the neck, and from the top of the ear to the throat, leaving the beard forward-facing, and giving the head a rectangular shape. The top of the skull is slightly domed in the U.S.

- Eyelashes should remain intact as these help to hold the hair away from the eyes.

- The head is not clipped short for general purposes, but this is sometimes requested by pet owners.

- The ears are trimmed to a V-shape, following the contours of the ears.

1

- Thinning scissors can be used on the flap going upwards from the bottom of the ear to the head, leaving longer hair toward the head and shorter at the tips.

- Excess hair under the ears should be trimmed away with thinning scissors.

- Where trimmed, scissor the coat to the dog's contours following the outline of the neck, body and legs, and keeping to a moderate length. Tipping the hair should be sufficient ("tipping" involves a light scissoring of the ends of the hair). Otherwise, use thinning scissors to remove unwanted hair. This hair should appear natural, rather than sculptured. 2

- The tuck-up line of the coat under the body is level at the elbow, sloping gently upwards towards the loin.

- Blend the leg hair to give a natural balance by snipping straggly hairs, following the contours of the stifle and hock. The front legs should look like columns.

- Check under the feet for excess hair and remove with scissors.

- Neaten around each foot.

- Tidy the tail to a neat outline. Trim underneath the tail to keep it clean and hygienic.

- The underside, belly and groin can be clipped with a No. 10 Oster on all pet dogs, for hygiene reasons.

- Check the dog's nails, ears and teeth.

SPANISH WATER DOG

COAT: The quality of its coat is a leading characteristic, which qualifies this dog as a shepherd and auxiliary to hunters of wild fowl and fisherman in the Iberian Peninsula (a similar history to the Poodle). The coat is always curly and of a woolly texture, forming fine cords when long.

The color is solid white, black and brown

in their different shades, parti-colored, and tricolored.

MAINTENANCE: Trimmed subjects are admitted in the show ring, but the clipping must always be complete and even; the dog must never become an "aesthetic" example of grooming.

PROCEDURE

Equipment needed: In Spain, combs and brushes are used, but in the U.K. these tools should never be employed. An Oster No. 40, with a half-inch attachment, is needed for pet dogs.

Breed tip: Dogs are usually clipped once a year, but if you require a short coat, two clips will be required.

- With the corded coat, these spirals are not combed out, but left in their natural state. Encourage the hair to separate at the body, and use water or coat-enhancer to encourage the cords to form.

- Bathe the dog in a natural shampoo (one that doesn't lather).

- Rinse well in cold or lukewarm water.

- Press the coat with an absorbent towel to take away the excess moisture. Never rub the coat.

- Dry the coat with warm air or cage-dry.

- Check the dog's nails, ears and teeth, and tidy up the ears if necessary. Scissor around the shape of the ears, but make sure you don't go too short.

- Check under the pads for clogged hair, and remove if found.

- Occasionally, the chin area can be tidied up because some dogs seem to grow beards, which spoils the look of the head.

- Dogs should only ever be clipped (with an Oster No. 40 with a $^{1}/_{2}$-inch/1.25-cm attachment) – never scissored. The Spanish Water Dog is a natural-looking breed, not a sculptured one, and should not be groomed like a Poodle.

COAT CORDS

The Spanish Water Dog's coat has cords rather like a Puli's, although its coat does not touch the ground – it only falls halfway down. Dogs can be shown once the coat is about 1 inch (2.5 cm) long – i.e., when the coat is curly.

11 *LONGCOATED BREEDS*

COAT CARE

Most of the longcoated breeds do not molt in the way that the shorthaired types do. However, they still lose hair, and if it is not removed on a regular basis (at least a couple of times a week), then it will fall into the coat, tangle, mat and felt.

Some dogs have been neglected to the extent that they are completely covered in a felted mass, so that the skin cannot breathe. In such instances, it is necessary to put a fine clipper next to the skin to shave the offending mass away (like shearing a sheep).

Thorough brushing on a daily basis, or at least three times a week, is crucial. If a grooming conditioner or oil has been put into the coat, then it is essential to wash this out and start again every seven to 10 days. Exhibitors wishing to groom the coat to a good length for showing purposes often do this.

If conditioner is put into the coat after a bath, then the hair is less likely to mat between baths, and brushing the coat through should be made easier, or less necessary.

Spraying dry hair with an oily coat spray is essential for maintaining a quality coat. A treasured coat should not be groomed out when dirty, as this will drag out too much hair.

Many of the longhaired breeds have their coats parted in the middle from the skull to the tail; a good example of this can be seen in both the Lhasa Apso and the Skye Terrier.

The topknot is often put into a ponytail band to keep the hair away from the eyes, such as in the case of the Maltese, Shih Tzu and Yorkshire Terrier.

CLIPPING

It is quite in order to clip the stomach of most longcoated breeds that are not destined for the show ring, to keep a clean and healthy flow of air to the skin and to prevent mats on the stomach and around the genitals. This can be done using a medium blade, such as an Oster No. 10, and the clipper can be taken right through to the dog's chest to remove underarm hair, too. When the dog is standing, the clipped area should not be noticeable, as the outline coat will hide it from view.

Some owners can get overwhelmed when dealing with a long coat and decide to have the dog trimmed off altogether. However, they should not worry about this – it is far better to keep a dog in a healthy short coat than to let it get matted.

To trim the dog, use a coarse blade, such as a No. 5 Oster. I have seen an Afghan Hound clipped all off, apart from pompoms left from the hock down, with matching hair on its front legs (like the "Sporting," or "Utility" clip on the Poodle, page 279), and it looked gorgeous (it is sometimes referred to as a "Clydesdale" clip). This is far more comfortable and kind to the dog than a hideous matted coat.

AFGHAN HOUND

Featured is the Afghan Hound Ch. Tico Raphael, owned by Mrs. Leslie Curry.

COAT: The coat should always be allowed to develop naturally, and is long and very finely textured on the ribs, forequarters, hindquarters and flanks. In mature dogs, the short saddle hair along the back occurs naturally and should not be formed by clipping or trimming. The hair is long from the forehead backwards, with a distinct silky topknot. The hair on the foreface is short, but the ears are well coated. Pasterns can be bare. All colors are acceptable, but it should be noted that different colors produce different textured hair, some of which is easier to work with than others.

MAINTENANCE: The silky coat requires a great deal of experienced effort in grooming, and careful consideration should be given before buying a puppy. To keep an Afghan pristine, bathing and grooming is a weekly task, which must not be neglected. This is particularly vital when the animal goes through the coat change (starting from 14 months and continuing for a couple of years until the mature adult coat is established). Be warned that, during the coat change, it is possible, in some instances, that the dog may require bathing and grooming every other day to keep mats under control.

Advice on grooming the Afghan should be readily available from the breeder. However, if this is not forthcoming, then contact a breed club for advice.

PROCEDURE

Equipment needed: Pin brush (but not one with "nobbles" on the end).

Breed tip: A water spray with a little conditioner mixed in will make it easier to brush the coat and prevent the hair from breaking. Ideally, the coat should only be groomed following a weekly bath.

NEGLECTED COATS

Where the dog is beyond grooming, it is the kindest thing to clip off the coat completely and start again. This should only take place after consultation with the owner. With time, the coat will grow again.

With today's mat-breakers and untangle conditioners, many a coat can be saved where once there was no hope. However, neglected coats need considerable time to master, so check with the owner about the total cost before undertaking such a task, and clip off if necessary.

- Brush thoroughly with a pin brush, using a spray-in conditioner or dematter if necessary to help eliminate tangles and dead hair. 1

- Use a mat-breaker if required. 2

- Bathe the dog with a mild shampoo 3 and rinse thoroughly. 4

- Apply conditioner to enhance the silky coat and to help prevent matting.

- Towel-dry to remove most drips. 5

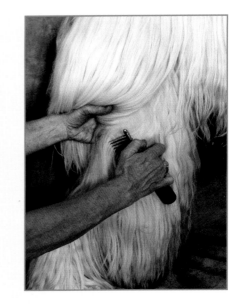

- Blow-dry using a pin brush. 6 While doing so, spray the coat with a fine mist of water and conditioner to reduce static electricity and to help reduce damage during drying. 7

- Check the dog's nails 8 , ears 9 and teeth. 10

- A properly exercised dog should never need its feet trimmed, and, in line with the rest of the body, the coat here should also develop naturally. However, care must be taken when brushing the feet. The Afghan can be particularly sensitive about having its feet touched.

- Give a final brush with the coat spray if required to enhance the chic appearance, and part the hair on the head and body, so it falls to the sides. However, if the dog has a natural saddle along its back, this will not be necessary. 11

- The finished dog. 12

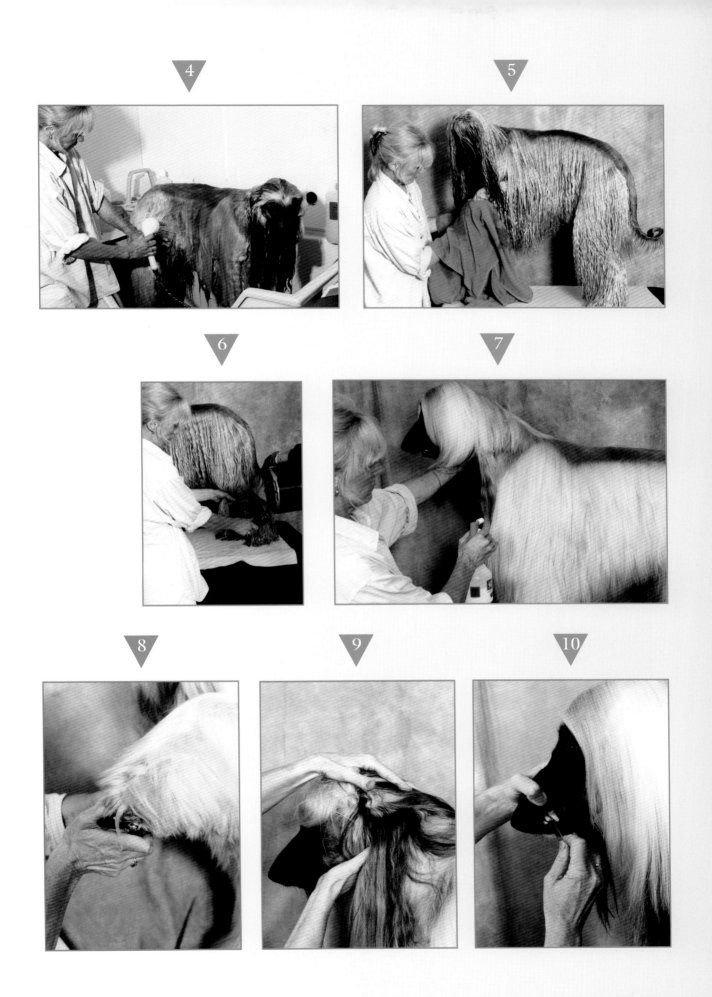

BEARDED COLLIE

COAT: The Beardie has a double coat. The undercoat is soft, furry and close-lying. The outercoat is flat, harsh, strong and shaggy, free from woolliness and curl, though a slight wave is permissible. There is long hair and a beard on the face (hence the breed's name).

MAINTENANCE: Needs constant attention to keep the coat free of tangles and looking good.

PROCEDURE

Equipment needed: A good-quality bristle brush, a pin brush, a large, wide-toothed wooden comb and a metal comb with wide teeth at one end and fine teeth at the other end.

Breed tip: A leave-in conditioner for brushing the dog when dry will make the job a little easier.

- Some people prefer to have the dog lying flat on its side when grooming; others prefer the dog to be standing. Do whatever works best for you.

- Start with the bristle brush, lifting the coat up and starting at the bottom and working through the coat in layers – this will ensure that the whole of the coat is reached. Brush in a coat-restorer or conditioner to ease the separation of the hair (use an untangle cream where necessary).

- Work through the coat again, this time using a pin brush. At this point, any mats will become apparent and can be worked on first with the brushes, then progressing to the wooden wide-toothed comb.

- A comb should only be used when the coat has been groomed with a brush first, otherwise any knots will pull a great deal and cause the dog discomfort. Do not bathe if the dog is matted – the coat must be tangle-free before you proceed.

- Bathe the Beardie in a protein pH-balanced shampoo, and use a quality conditioner.

- Blow-dry the coat, brushing continually using a pin brush. Use a lanolin lubricant to enhance texture and to prevent breaking or matting. Some people use a straightening conditioner, which is brushed or combed in after the shampoo and rinse (it should be rinsed out well). However, this is not really needed, as a Beardie coat is allowed to be wavy for the show ring – it does not need to be dead straight.

- The hair is parted along the spine by combing out the undercoat to leave it flat.

- Check the dog's nails, ears and teeth.

- In pet dogs, scissor the hair beneath the dog's feet and also under the tail (around the anus area) to prevent it becoming soiled with feces.

- Thinning scissors, or a de-matting thinner tool, can be used on an excessively profuse coat, taking care not to remove too much coat at a time.

BRIARD

COAT: The breed's flowing coat requires thorough and regular grooming, not forgetting the mustache, beard and eyebrows. The hair is about 2¾ inches (7 cm) long, slightly wavy and very dry, with a fine, dense undercoat. It is a picture to behold when given regular attention, but can look very bedraggled when neglected and left to mat and felt.

MAINTENANCE: Maintenance is fairly high as the coat will lose hairs into itself and

these will need to be removed regularly in order to prevent matting.

PROCEDURE

Equipment needed: A slicker brush, a wide-toothed comb, and a dematter, if necessary.

Breed tip: This is another breed that pet owners ask the groomer to clip no less than 2 inches (5 cm) all over. Use a No. 7 Oster, or scissor to the required length. Anything shorter and you will lose the correct overall breed shape.

- It is far easier to brush the entire coat through if you first apply a coat conditioner. Use a dematter or untangle product on matted areas. Where matting is bad, allow the untangle conditioner to soak in for several minutes before commencing grooming.

- Use a slicker brush and comb to work through the coat. All mats should be teased out by hand – using a pin brush will remove the undercoat. The Briard should be completely tangle-free before you attempt to bathe it.

- Bathe the dog in a protein shampoo and add body conditioner to enhance the coat.

- Dry the coat, using a power dryer to remove excess moisture from the coat, and then finish with the blower, while continuously brushing with a pin brush.

- Check the dog's nails, ears and teeth. Don't forget also to check the dog's dewclaws (double at the back – and part of the breed standard).

- Check between the toes and remove any clogged hair.

- Trim off hair around the anus in pet dogs.

CHINESE CRESTED

COAT: There are two distinct varieties: the Hairless and the Powderpuff. The Hairless has a crest of hair on its head, extending partway down the neck. There are socks covering its toes, as well as a plume on the tail. The rest of the body is hairless. The Powderpuff is covered entirely with long, soft hair (referred to as a "veil").

However, the "variable expressivity" of the hairless gene can mean that a dog can have no hair at all, excess body hair or anything in between.

MAINTENANCE: The Hairless requires the frequent use of moisturizers to keep the skin in good condition. The Powderpuff requires regular brushing and combing. The teeth need cleaning regularly.

PROCEDURE

Equipment needed: A good-quality bristle brush and a safety razor (to shave the face) for the Hairless variety. A good-quality bristle brush, a wide-toothed comb and clippers for the Powderpuff coat.

Breed tip: The skin of the Hairless type is frequently oiled by massaging baby oil or Nivea face cream into the hairless parts. This helps to keep the skin smooth and nicely moisturized.

HAIRLESS

- This dog needs to be kept clean with frequent baths, using a good shampoo followed by a moisturizer (e.g., baby oil or lotion).

POWDERPUFF

- The Powderpuff coat requires frequent brushing with a bristle or pin brush. This is particularly necessary as the puppy coat changes to the adult coat, at which time daily grooming may be needed.

- Any felting or mats should be teased out with your thumb and forefinger. Once all knots have been removed, work through the coat with a bristle or pin brush.

- Particular attention should be paid to the area between the front legs and the inside of the elbows. This is easier if the dog has been taught to lie on its side while having the tangles removed.

- Regular bathing with a good-quality dog shampoo, followed by blow-drying, will keep the coat in good condition. There are several shampoos to choose from, together with a variety of grooming preparations that are sprayed onto the coat while brushing to detangle and condition the coat.

- The coat should be brushed in layers with the lie of the coat. If you are using a pin brush, care must be taken not to cause the dog discomfort.

- The crest, socks and plume should be blow-dried and brushed with a good bristle brush.

- Due to the "variable expressivity" of the hairless gene, body hair can appear. If necessary, remove facial hair with a safety razor (or use an Oster No. 40 blade against the grain, which is safer). This can also be used to carefully remove excess body hair. In the show ring, any large patches of body hair are classed as a fault. Be very careful when using a razor. If you are at all uncertain, ask a groomer or breed expert to show you.

- Towel-dry and finish with a blower on the crest, socks and plume, brushing very carefully with a bristle brush only on the long hair, never on the skin. Check nails, ears and teeth.

- After bathing, grooming and blow-drying, the face should be shaved using clippers (10 mm blade), taking a line from the outer corner of the eye to the ear and in a gentle curve from the ear down to the "Adam's apple," similar to the face of a Poodle (see Chapter Seventeen). Note: in the U.S., the Powderpuff face is not shaved.

- It is important to check between the pads for any felting, which, if left, could cause discomfort to the dog when walking.

- After brushing and blow-drying is complete, finish off with a wide-toothed comb if desired. The comb will detect any remaining tangles in the coat and they should be teased out and brushed before proceeding with further combing of the veil.

- Check the dog's nails, ears and teeth. Note: the nails should be moderately long.

COTON DE TULEAR

COAT: A characteristic dry, flyaway coat, which is rather like cotton thread and is considered hypoallergenic. The hair is white (biscuit or cream included), black and white, or tricolor, and about 4 to 5 inches (10 to 12.5 cm) long. The coat is intended to protect the Coton from the equatorial sun in its native lands surrounding Tulear in Africa.

MAINTENANCE: The coat is long, dry and nearly straight, and requires brushing to remove an undercoat and to prevent matting. The Coton is a good candidate for the grooming salon, though pet dogs often have the coat cut to a more manageable length.

PROCEDURE

Equipment needed: Pin brush and a wide-toothed comb.

Breed tip: This breed can remain relatively clean without too many baths, provided the coat is groomed regularly. In addition to regular brushing at home, many owners take the dog to a professional groomer on a monthly basis.

- Brush the coat carefully. Do not bathe the dog with mats in the hair, as this will cause them to escalate.

- Bathe the dog in a natural, gentle shampoo.

- Add conditioner to aid brushing.

- Blow-dry the coat gently, brushing with a pin brush, and taking the hair away from the heat. Dry in small sections to prevent matting.

- If the dog is not being shown in the ring, it helps to mist the coat with a leave-in spray conditioner as you brush and dry.

- Check the Coton's nails, ears and teeth.

- Check underneath the dog's feet and between the pads for clogged hair, and remove with scissors, if necessary.

- Brush over the coat, using a fine grooming spray if required.

HAVANESE

COAT: The coat is soft and silky, wavy or slightly curled. The Havanese is full-coated with an undercoat. Any color (or color combination) is acceptable.

MAINTENANCE: The coat is not trimmed

for normal purposes or for the show ring, but regular brushing is required. Some pet dogs are either clipped or scissored down to a manageable length.

PROCEDURE

Equipment needed: Pin brush, and a wide-toothed comb. A slicker brush can be used on tough tangles, but otherwise avoid a slicker – it is generally too harsh.

Breed tip: It is important that a loose, natural look is achieved in this breed.

- Brush through the entire coat, removing any tangles, and then comb with a wide-toothed comb.

- Bathe the dog in a natural or protein shampoo.

- Rinse the long coat well.

- Apply a conditioner to enhance the coat texture and to aid grooming.

- Blow-dry gently with a pin brush, making sure you go away from the skin.

- Check the dog's nails, ears and teeth.

- Check the feet for hair that may have clogged between the pads, and remove if necessary.

- Brush along the back. The dog will generally shake the hair so it falls naturally in a parting. Do not use a comb to achieve a perfectly straight parting.

- The topknot can be tied up away from the eyes (but not in the show ring).

JAPANESE CHIN

COAT: The coat is profuse, long, soft, straight, of silky texture and absolutely free of curl or wave. Not too flat, it has a tendency to stand out, especially at the frill of the neck. The profuse coat is colored either black and white, or red and white.

MAINTENANCE: The coat sheds and mats, so regular brushing is required to remove dead hairs that will otherwise mat.

PROCEDURE

Equipment needed: Pin brush and a wide-toothed comb.

Breed tip: Enhance the coat with an occasional boost from a quality coat spray.

- Brush through with a pin brush then work

through with a wide-toothed comb.

- Bathe the dog in a tea tree and lavender or protein shampoo, making sure you rinse away the shampoo completely.

- Use a conditioner to enhance the coat quality.

- Blow-dry gently, brushing the coat away from the heat.

- Check the dog's nails, ears and teeth.

- Check under the feet for matted hair and trim away if necessary.

- Brush the coat once more. Start along the spine, and brush outwards from there.

- Keep the face clean!

LHASA APSO

COAT: This jaunty and proud little dog is an impressive sight when in full show coat, set off with a beautifully plumed tail. The coat is long, heavy, straight and hard, neither woolly nor silky. The undercoat is moderate. This breed has a parting down the middle.

MAINTENANCE: Grooming is required on a regular basis to keep the coat free from tangles and mats. The hair on the head falls down the sides of the face, but is usually tied up when not being shown.

PROCEDURE

Equipment needed: Pin brush, bristle brush and a wide-toothed comb.

Breed tip: Pets are frequently clipped short all over with a No. 4 or No. 5 Oster blade.

- Brush through the coat with a pin brush.

- Then comb with a wide-toothed comb, using a groom spray if necessary to remove tangles.

- Bathe the dog in a protein or suitable shampoo.

- Rinse thoroughly, and apply a quality conditioner to enhance the coat.

- Blow-dry the coat in sections with a pin brush.

- Check the dog's nails, ears and teeth.

- Lightly spray with a coat conditioner and brush with a bristle brush.

- Create a straight, precise parting down the back and brush the coat down either side.

LHASA FEVER

Sally Pointon has had a lifelong interest in dogs, and has been involved with Lhasa Apsos for more than 20 years.

DAILY CARE

According to Sally, getting the Lhasa in peak condition involves day-to-day care, both

*Sally Pointon and Ch.
Chethang Emogene at Ballito.*

mentally and physically. The coat, although an obvious part of the finished show dog, is just the icing on the cake, albeit an important one.

START EARLY

Start by table-training the puppy from day one of its coming into your care, and you will find that, by the time it needs daily care, the pup will be well behaved and accustomed to the methods you adopt. Remember, you can only obtain the best from the coat it was born with – for even the best coat care cannot make a poor coat into a good one.

NURTURING HEADFALL

To achieve a good headfall, start with banding a single topknot when the coat starts to flop over the eyes (at about 3 to 4 months), making sure that it does not pull. The band should always be cut out carefully to prevent damage and loss of hair. Once the hair gets too full or heavy, two bunches can be used (one each side), and eventually four (two each side). Face bands are also a good idea once the whiskers start getting long enough to get tangled up in the mouth.

FOOT CARE

Trimming out the hair between the pads (using a fairly blunt, small pair of scissors) is undertaken from an early age; and if you want your Lhasa to lie down quietly while you groom, this should be attempted slowly and when the puppy is feeling confident on the table, at around 3 to 5 months, depending on its temperament.

A pair of sharp, slightly curved scissors will achieve the best results on the feet and for the desired coat length; do this about a week before a show to give a neat but natural appearance.

WEEKLY BATH

Bathing and blow-drying once a week often produces better results than daily brushing – however, brushing out any obvious mats using a detangling spray may be necessary between bathing, saving time and coat in the long run.

Pulling knots apart by thumb and finger will help to separate the hair, but this should only be done if absolutely necessary. Knots often come out more easily on a wet coat during blow-drying. Brushing a dry coat can break the length or cause split ends.

Thorough rinsing after shampooing is essential, and using an absorbent towel or synthetic chamois to squeeze the excess water will cut down on drying time.

A brush should only be used initially, brushing the coat in layers from the skin to the end of the hair until the coat is tangle-free and dry. Use a pin brush and a bristle brush, choosing one of the many on the market to suit you, and depending on the coat texture. The wide-toothed steel comb is used for the whiskers and finishing off.

REGULAR REGIME

The key to achieving the best results is to work out a regime to suit the coat, and to stick to it, no matter how tired or busy you might be. Beautiful coats presented to perfection are not achieved the night before a show – they take hours of dedication throughout the year.

MALTESE

COAT: The coat is of good length, straight, silky, never woolly or crimped, and without an undercoat. It is always pure white, but slight lemon markings are permissible. The tail is well feathered.

MAINTENANCE: This breed needs a lot of attention to keep the long, silky coat in perfect order. The hair is parted along the middle from the skull to the tail and needs constant grooming. The topknot is tied back in one or two bows.

Sometimes these dogs come into the grooming parlor matted from top to bottom where the owners have frequently bathed them and left them to dry without brushing and combing out the tangles. In such cases, the only option is a short-back-and-sides clip all over.

Many pet owners have this breed clipped down to about 1 inch (2.5 cm) all over; use an Oster No. 5 to trim the hair before the bath. Condition, blow-dry and neaten any stray hairs with scissors. If clipped, this dog should look sweet and pretty – but still needs grooming.

PROCEDURE

Equipment needed: A pin brush, a bristle brush, a wide-toothed comb and an eye comb.

Breed tip: Use a light spray of water or grooming spray on the coat to aid daily brushing and to prevent breaking the hair.

- Brush through the entire coat using a pin brush.

- Spray in a little conditioning spray to aid grooming.

- Comb with a medium- or wide-toothed comb (depending on the thickness of the coat), and an eye comb. Always remember to do this before you bathe the dog, or matting will occur.

- Bathe the Maltese in a protein, pH-balanced or natural shampoo, ensuring that you rinse thoroughly.

- Apply conditioner and work through the coat. Again, rinse well.

- Next, blow-dry the coat, brushing the hair with a pin brush away from the skin (do not put the blower on the skin).

- Check the dog's nails, ears and teeth.

- Finish with a light spray of grooming conditioner, and groom in with a bristle brush.

OLD ENGLISH SHEEPDOG

COAT: The coat is of good, harsh texture, not straight, but shaggy and free from curl. The undercoat is of waterproof pile.

MAINTENANCE: The Old English Sheepdog needs a great deal of attention to keep its profuse coat even half-decent.

In ordinary circumstances, the coat is not scissored or clipped, but pet owners and breeders of retired show dogs frequently have the coat clipped to a more manageable length.

Dogs need regular attention and should be professionally or expertly groomed every four to six weeks.

PROCEDURE

Equipment needed: Slicker or pin brush, and a wide-toothed comb.

Breed tip: It is essential to keep on top of the grooming to prevent the coat from becoming one solid mat.

- Brush through the entire coat with a slicker or pin brush, working in sections from the back foot upward. Where excessive matting is present, use a mat-splitter to break through the matted felts.

- Comb with a wide-toothed comb.

- Bathe in a suitable tea tree and lavender shampoo (or similar), being vigilant about rinsing.

- White-enhancing shampoo can be used on the coat for that extra sparkle. It can also be used on the beard where saliva stains have formed (whitening cream washes are available from pet stores and grooming outlets).

- Apply a coat-enhancing conditioner.

- Blow-dry, lifting the hair with a pin brush. This separates the sections, avoiding tangles.

- Check the dog's nails, ears and teeth.

- Check under the feet for matted hair and remove carefully with scissors.

PET CLIP

With the pet dog, it is often required or requested that the entire coat of the adult Old English Sheepdog be cut off to about 2 inches (5 cm) in length. This can be done with scissors after bathing and drying is complete, or by clipping the dog, before bathing, with an Oster No. 40 with a $^3/_4$-inch (2 cm) attachment.

Some owners want the body hair left on, but are keen to have the hair thinned, and the coat clipped from underneath (stomach, under the arms and inside the groin area) for hygiene reasons and to keep the dog smelling sweet.

PEKINGESE

COAT: The Peke's coat is long and straight, and has a profuse mane extending beyond its shoulders, which forms a cape around the neck. The top coat is coarse, with a thick undercoat. Feathering on the ears is profuse, as on the legs and tail. All colors and markings are permissible.

MAINTENANCE: Brushing regularly is essential. On pet dogs, it is often as well to clip underneath the stomach and upward to the chest, as well as around the genital area. This will not be seen unless the dog rolls over on its back, and will aid comfort, keeping it cooler and cleaner. Do not do this to show dogs, however.

PROCEDURE

Equipment needed: Slicker or pin brush, and a wide-toothed comb.

Breed tip: Wrinkles and folds in the skin must receive regular attention.

- Brush through the entire coat, removing any tangles that may have formed, particularly underneath, with a slicker or a pin brush. Then work through the coat with a wide-toothed comb.

- Bathe in a natural-ingredient shampoo, being

vigilant about rinsing. Use a facecloth on the head, rather than spraying it with water.

- Blow-dry the hair in sections.

- Check the Peke's nails, ears and teeth.

- Also check under its feet for matted hair, and remove it with scissors.

- Clean the dog's eyes gently with a damp pad or cloth, and be sure that the folds or wrinkles on the face are free from moisture, drying this area carefully with cotton pads if necessary.

- Treat the coat with a coat dressing and brush over to finish. The coat is brushed away from the parting along the back.

POLISH LOWLAND SHEEPDOG

COAT: The coat of the Polish Lowland is long, dense, shaggy, thick and of harsh texture with a soft undercoat. Long hair covers the eyes. A slight wave in the coat is permissible. All colors are acceptable.

MAINTENANCE: Needs regular brushing at least three times a week.

PROCEDURE

Equipment needed: A slicker or pin brush, and a wide-toothed comb.

Breed tip: Not unlike the Bearded Collie (page 90), the Polish Lowland Sheepdog needs considerable coat care. Lift the hair, and brush and comb it in sections to remove all tangles.

- Brush through the coat using a slicker or pin brush, and comb through with a wide-toothed comb.

- Bathe in a natural shampoo to prevent the coat from drying. Rinse thoroughly.

- Apply a conditioner. Rub in well, and rinse.

- Comb again with a wide-toothed comb. Add a light spray of conditioning oil if required.

- Check the dog's nails, ears and teeth.

- Pet dogs can have their hair trimmed from underneath and between the pads.

- Note: the pet dog is sometimes trimmed to about 2 inches (5 cm) all over with an Oster No. 30/40 with a $^3/_4$-inch (2 cm) attachment.

SHIH TZU

COAT: The chrysanthemum look of the Shih Tzu's head is most attractive and is accentuated by the hair growing upwards on the bridge of the nose. The coat is long, dense, not curly, with a good undercoat. A slight wave is permitted.

MAINTENANCE: The hair on the head is tied up to keep it away from the eyes. This coat requires regular brushing, and some pet owners have this breed trimmed down to a manageable length of about 4 inches (10 cm).

PROCEDURE

Equipment needed: Pin brush and a wide-toothed comb.

Breed tip: Pet dogs are often seen clipped all over with a No. 4 or No. 5 Oster (No. 7 blades are usually used for matted dogs). The head is either trimmed shorter with scissors or clipped to the same length as the body, according to the owner's wishes and his or her capability to maintain the coat.

- Brush through the entire coat, removing dead hair.

- Comb with a wide-toothed comb, applying a spray of grooming conditioner where necessary.

- Bathe the dog in a suitable shampoo, rinse well and apply a coat-nourishing conditioner.

- Blow the hair dry, brushing with a pin brush in small sections.

- Check the dog's nails, ears and teeth.

- Check beneath the feet for matted hair and remove with scissors.

- Check any wrinkles or folds on the face.

- Clean them with a damp pad and thoroughly dry with cotton-wool (cotton) pads.

- Lightly spray with a finishing conditioner, and brush through with a bristle brush.

- The hair is parted and brushed away from the spine.

- The plumed tail hangs over the back to one side and is thoroughly brushed along with the entire coat.

SKYE TERRIER

COAT: The coat is long, profuse and glamorous. The undercoat is short, close, soft and woolly. The outercoat is long, hard, straight, flat and free from curl. The hair on the head is shorter and softer, and veils the forehead and eyes. The majority have pricked ears, but drop ears that lie flat are permissible.

The color is black, gray, fawn or cream with black points.

MAINTENANCE Coat needs regular weekly (or more frequent) brushing and combing.

PROCEDURE

Equipment needed: Pin brush, wide-toothed comb.

Breed tip: Prevent tangles by pressing the coat dry with a towel, rather than rubbing it.

- Brush the entire coat with a pin brush.

- Comb through with a wide-toothed comb.

- Bathe the dog in a natural-ingredient shampoo, using conditioner to enhance coat texture. Rinse thoroughly after each application.

- Towel off the excess water, without rubbing, to prevent the hair from tangling.

- Finish off the drying with a blower, while brushing lightly with a pin brush.

- Brush over the coat, parting the hair along the middle of the back to fall gracefully down the sides.

- Check the dog's nails, ears and teeth.

- This breed is often clipped all over with a No. 5 Oster if the dog is not exhibited, or if it has retired from the show ring.

TIBETAN TERRIER

COAT: The Tibetan Terrier has a double coat, consisting of undercoat and topcoat. The undercoat is fine and woolly. The topcoat is profuse and fine, but not silky nor woolly; it is long, either straight or waved, but never curled.

MAINTENANCE: This dog needs regular brushing and combing to keep it looking smart. Pet owners frequently have the coat trimmed back into the manageable length it was in puppyhood.

PROCEDURE

Equipment needed: Pin brush or slicker, and a wide-toothed comb.

Breed tip: When brushing the coat, lift and separate it in sections, and use a water or grooming spray to aid the removal of dead hair.

- Brush through the coat with a slicker, starting at the bottom of the back foot and working up in sections to remove dead and matting hair.

- For neglected coats, a mat-breaker will be required to slice through the felts.

- Work through the coat with a wide-toothed comb.

- Regularly bathe the Tibetan Terrier in a protein or suitable shampoo.

- Rinse thoroughly to remove all the shampoo and apply a quality conditioner to enhance the coat and to help prevent further tangles from forming.

- Blow-dry the hair in sections, brushing through with a pin brush.

- Check the Tibetan Terrier's nails, ears and teeth.

- Check under the feet, removing mats and excess hair with scissors, if necessary. However, leave the hair between the pads, because the hair here acts as protection for the pads.

- The coat is groomed away from the parting on the spine and the tail comes forward over the back.

- A pet dog can have its stomach, underarms and inside-thighs clipped with a No. 5 or No. 10 Oster, and the hair is trimmed around the anal area.

- The Tibetan Terrier often comes into the salon with a request from owners to clip the entire coat off to a length of about 1 inch (2.5 cm).

YORKSHIRE TERRIER

COAT: The coat on the Yorkie's body is said to be moderately long, but it is often seen hanging down to the ground in show dogs. It is perfectly straight (not wavy) and glossy, and has a fine, silky texture. The fall on the head is long, colored a rich golden tan.

MAINTENANCE: The glory of this dog in full coat is spectacular. A great deal of time and expertise is required to keep the coat of this tiny but hardy dog in such splendor. Often this breed is seen in the grooming parlor clipped down to about 1 inch (2.5 cm) all over because the owner really cannot cope with all the hair dragging on the ground.

PROCEDURE

Equipment needed: A stiff bristle brush and wide- to medium-toothed comb. Pet coats that are thick and woolly may require a pin brush. A slicker brush should never be used.

Breed tip: Keeping the dog in long coat is a full-time occupation.

- Brush through and remove all mats with a mat-breaker and a mat-removing anti-tangle cream, if required.

- Bathe the dog in a suitable shampoo for skin and coat quality. Apply a conditioner or balsam dematting conditioner to enhance the coat.

- Blow the hair dry, brushing continuously with a pin brush.

- Check the Yorkie's nails, ears and teeth.

- Spray with a conditioner, and brush through with a bristle brush.

- Where pet owners wish to have the hair clipped from this breed, and most do, clip off all over with a No. 5 or No. 7 blade before the bath. Or clip the body and leave the trousers like those seen on the "Lamb" clip of the Poodle (see Chapter Seventeen). The face is clipped or scissored to 1 inch (2.5 cm), leaving whiskers if desired. Many pet owners like their Yorkies trimmed like a Schnauzer.

- The show dog will have constant care applied to the coat, and wrappers or "crackers" will be placed around small sections of the hair, all over the dog, to prevent the hair from breaking, and to help it to grow to a glamorous length.

12 MEDIUM-LENGTH COATED BREEDS

MEDIUM-LENGTH COATED BREEDS IN THIS SECTION:

SHETLAND SHEEPDOG
- Australian Shepherd
- Australian Terrier
- Belgian Sheepdog and Belgian Tervuren
- Bernese Mountain Dog
- Border Collie
- Borzoi
- Cavalier King Charles Spaniel
- Chihuahua (Long Coat)
- Clumber Spaniel
- Dachshund (Longhaired)
- English Setter
- English Toy Spaniel (King Charles)
- Flat-Coated Retriever
- Glen of Imaal Terrier
- Golden Retriever
- Gordon Setter
- Grand Basset Griffon Vendéen
- Irish Red and White Setter
- Irish Setter
- Irish Wolfhound
- Kooikerhondje
- Large Munsterlander
- Nova Scotia Duck Tolling Retriever
- Otterhound
- Papillon
- Petit Basset Griffon Vendéen
- Pyrenean Sheepdog
- Saluki
- Scottish Deerhound
- Silky Terrier (Australian)
- Spinone Italiano (Italian Spinone)
- Sussex Spaniel
- Tibetan Spaniel
- Welsh Springer Spaniel

COAT CARE

Dogs that have this type of coat are usually attractive, elegant, even stunning looking when the hair is brushed and nurtured. They are relatively easy to work on, but still require regular attention if they are to be kept at their best.

Most of these breeds frequent the grooming parlor. For the groomer, these breeds are a joy to work on and look splendid when finished as a show dog or pet. Beautiful dogs deserve beautiful care.

The breeds in this category rarely mat, but some of the more active, working types collect burrs and other debris, which have to be removed. Odd bits of trimming are executed on some breeds (such as the Golden Retriever's tail), and thinning scissors are also used.

SILKY SMOOTH

This category contains several different coat types, such as harsh-coated breeds (e.g., Australian Terrier) and silky-coated breeds (e.g., Papillon).

Those breeds that do require a silky coat will need special consideration given during bathing and conditioning to use the correct preparation for the texture of the coat. Of course, conditioners and other coat softeners should be avoided for harsh-coated breeds.

SHETLAND SHEEPDOG

Featured is the Shetland Sheepdog Felthorn Holly Hobby, owned by Barbara Thornley.

COAT: A sturdy little dog with a double coat, the soft undercoat and harsh outercoat make the Sheltie able to withstand the winter elements. The mane and frill are very abundant, and the forelegs well feathered. The hindlegs above the hocks are profusely covered with hair; it is smooth below the hocks and on the face.

MAINTENANCE: Fairly straightforward. Simply requires a weekly brush, although more frequent brushing will be needed when the coat sheds. Do remember: frequent brushing gives you the opportunity to keep a close eye on your dog's skin condition.

PROCEDURE

Equipment needed: A nylon or nylon-and-bristle brush on a rubber cushion. A medium-toothed comb is needed for the front legs, behind the ears, and the hocks.

Breed tip: This breed likes to be on the go, so talk to the Sheltie when you groom it to keep it occupied.

- Brush the entire coat with a pin brush, removing the dead coat without stripping out the undercoat. 1

- Comb the coat through with a wide-toothed comb.

- If the hair is tangled and difficult, spray it with a grooming conditioner. Thick, neglected dense undercoat can be broken with the mat-splitter without ruining the coat too much, and it is better for coming out. The brushing/combing procedure of removing old coat can be arduous for dogs that do not have regular attention, and the mat-breaker may be required to strip some of this coat out. 2

- Bathe the Sheltie in protein pH-balanced shampoo or natural-ingredient shampoo, such as tea tree and lavender oil. 3 4

- Rinse thoroughly. 5

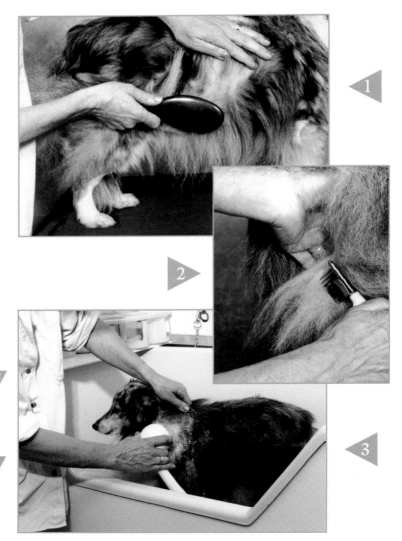

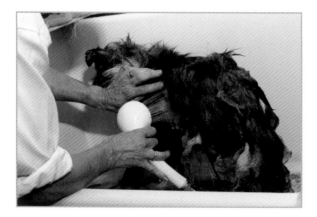

- Apply conditioner. Alternatively, use a purifying shampoo and mask as a toning treatment for the skin, and also to nourish the hair, three times a year.

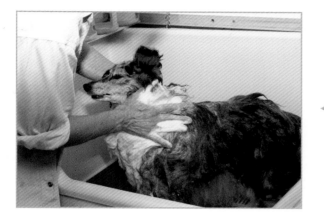

- Dry with a power blower after absorbing as much moisture as possible by towel-drying the coat. 6

- Brush the dog throughout the drying process with the pin brush. 7

- Comb with a wide-toothed comb. 8

- Check the dog's nails 9, ears 10 and teeth. 11

- Scissor-trim the Sheltie's hocks to a neat appearance. 12

- Trim under the pads, between the toes (only removing the tufts which stick up by using the scissor-points) 13, and around the foot to neaten to an oval shape. 14

- The finished dog. 15

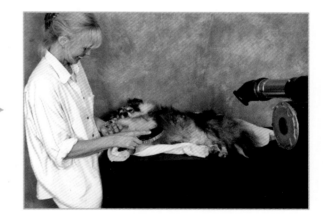

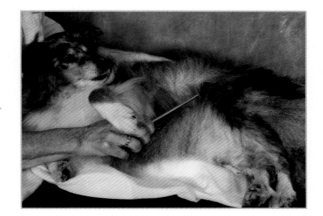

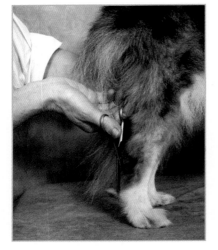

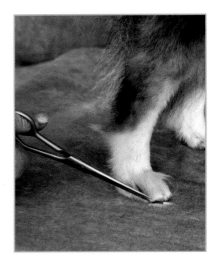

AUSTRALIAN SHEPHERD

COAT: The coat is of medium length and texture, straight to wavy, weather-resistant with undercoat.

The hair is short on the head, ears, front of the forelegs and below the hock joints. The backs of the legs are moderately feathered. The mane, described as moderate, is more pronounced in males than bitches.

MAINTENANCE: Relatively easy, with regular brushing.

PROCEDURE

Equipment needed: Slicker brush, comb.

Breed tip: Brush with a pin brush every week, from a young age.

- Brush the entire coat with a slicker to remove dead hairs.

- Catch any last dead hairs by combing the coat.

- Next, bathe the dog in a suitable pH-balanced shampoo, such as tea tree and lavender, which smells wonderful and brings the coat up beautifully.

- White parts of the coat may benefit from a whitening shampoo, which can be left in for a few minutes before rinsing. Bathing the white parts first, and then turning your attention to the rest of the coat, will save you time.

- Condition with a coat-nourishing finish.

- Use superabsorbent towels to remove as much of the moisture as possible.

- Next, blow-dry the coat, brushing with a pin brush to separate the hair and to assist the drying process.

- Check the dog's nails, ears and teeth.

- Trim the dog's hocks with thinning scissors or scissors to tidy, and clip away excess hair from between the dog's pads and around the anus.

AUSTRALIAN TERRIER

COAT: Harsh, straight, dense body coat with short, soft-textured undercoat and smooth ears. Lower legs are free from hair.

MAINTENANCE: This breed is trimmed to a greater or lesser degree in most countries for show purposes, and is thoroughly brushed, combed and conditioned. The pet dog is frequently clipped all over with a No. 7 blade, and sometimes clipped on the body with the trousers left on the legs, which are blended in with scissors.

PROCEDURE

Equipment needed: Bristle brush.

Breed tip: The Australian Terrier's coat will tangle underneath if it is not combed at least once or twice a week.

- Brush with a bristle brush, using a spray conditioner where the coat is dry (to prevent breaking).

- Comb with a wide-toothed metal comb.

- Bathe the dog in a pH-balanced shampoo and rinse well.

- Dry with a blower, or use a cage-dryer.

- Check the dog's nails, ears and teeth.

- Trim the hair out from under the feet.

- Strip out loose hair from the body with your finger and thumb, or a stripping knife, and blend straggly hair with scissors, leaving feathering on the back of legs.

- The tail is trimmed to neaten the outline.

- Neaten the dog's feet.

- Some people express a wish to have the hair clipped off to 1 inch (2.5 cm) in length all over. Those pets with body hair left can have their stomach and anal area clipped with an Oster No. 10 blade for hygienic convenience, or trimmed with scissors.

- Use thinning scissors from the dog's hock to the foot to give an even appearance.

- Clip or strip the back of the ears to a neat appearance.

BELGIAN SHEEPDOG AND BELGIAN TERVUREN

Belgian Sheepdog

Belgian Tervuren

COAT: The Belgian Sheepdog is longhaired with a harsh-textured black coat; the Belgian Tervuren has the same coloring as the Belgian Malinois (see page 153), but the outer coat is long, straight and abundant.

All varieties (Belgian Sheepdog, Belgian Malinois, Belgian Tervuren and Laekenois – see also page 153) have double-textured coats, with a harsh outercoat and a dense undercoat.

MAINTENANCE: Requires regular brushing at least once a week. Mature males tend to molt with the weather, but bitches lose their coats very dramatically about three months after they have been in season. They are likely to look quite dreadful at this point! The coat then takes about two months to grow back.

Puppies have a much thicker, bigger coat than adults, which they lose when they are about a year old.

PROCEDURE

Equipment needed: Slicker brush and a good-quality comb.

Breed tip: This is an active, working breed that will need regular brushing to remove from the coat any debris acquired after their energetic walks.

- Use a slicker to brush through the coat, after spraying lightly with a conditioner to protect the hair and to encourage growth. The coat should always be brushed when damp, not when dry. Misting with water is fine if no conditioner is available, and indeed is the correct thing to use for show preparation (as water is the only substance that is permitted).

- The coat should be brushed up the wrong way and then brushed right down to the roots with the slicker. Work in sections to take the coat back the right way again.

- Pay particular attention to the trousers and ruff. Long hairs here and on the undercarriage can get very matted between the back legs.

- Where the undercoat needs removing, use a rake or a twisting-teeth comb.

- If the dog is in molt, use a molting comb to remove all dead hairs.

- If the dog is neutered, the coat needs a lot more attention as the undercoat can become very dense and clumped. Daily attention is needed for spayed bitches and castrated dogs, using a twisting-teeth comb, particularly on the rump, flanks and back legs. Light trimming of the very long, wispy hairs that can grow in the neutered coat makes the dog much smarter-looking and more comfortable.

- Obviously, the Belgian Sheepdog and Belgian Tervuren coats, being longer, need more attention than those of the shorthaired Belgian Malinois or the rough-coated Laekenois (see page 153).

- Bathing these dogs is rarely necessary. If the dog is muddy, remove the worst with a bucket of cold water and a sponge (outside is best for this) or use a garden hose set at a gentle pressure. Dry the dog with an old towel and then, when it is nearly completely dry, gently brush out any remaining mud. The coat readily loses mud by using this method.

- Check the dog's nails, ears and teeth.

- Next, investigate under the dog's feet. If necessary, scissor out any excess hair and any build-up of debris.

- Finish with a light application of coat-enhancing spray.

- Note: the show dog may need a few days for the coat to settle after bathing.

BERNESE MOUNTAIN DOG

COAT: Of medium length, silky with a natural sheen and a fine undercoat. The coat should not curl, but may be slightly wavy.

MAINTENANCE: In general, brushing is required once or twice weekly after a major groom and bath – more if the coat is shedding. Bitches usually cast their coats twice a year; males cast once a year.

The Bernese is a naturally presented breed, apart from trimming around the outline of the feet and underneath the feet, as well as tidying the hair on the back pastern.

PROCEDURE

Equipment needed: Slicker or hard bristle brush, both a medium- and a wide-toothed steel comb, and round-ended scissors.

Breed tip: If mats have formed behind the ears, mane, tail, breeching and feathering, dab a drop of baby oil on the mat, work the oil into it, and then gently divide the mat into pieces and use the wide-toothed comb to break it up. Work in from the outside of the mat. Do take care not to pull on the dog's skin while doing this.

• A light spray of conditioner will aid brushing.

• Work from the head to the tail in small overlapping areas. Brush the outer hair first, then comb the same area to separate the hair to the skin, taking care not to scratch the skin and ensuring that all tangles are removed.

• Next, bathe the dog in warm water, using a good, low-lather shampoo. Be sure to rinse well. Let the dog shake itself before toweling, and comb the coat again before drying.

• Check the dog's nails, ears and teeth. Nails are not usually a problem in the breed, but, if dewclaws are present, these should be kept trimmed.

BORDER COLLIE

COAT: The Collie has two varieties of coat – moderately long, or smooth. The topcoat is dense and medium-textured, while the undercoat is soft and dense. In the longer variety, the abundant coat forms a mane, breeching and brush.

MAINTENANCE: Fairly easy, simply requiring a weekly brush.

PROCEDURE

Equipment needed: Soft slicker, and a medium-toothed comb.

Breed tip: The Border Collie coat looks easy to maintain – provided it is groomed regularly. Some coats can be quite profuse, and will mat terribly if neglected, so a groom at least once a week is vital.

• Brush through the coat with a soft slicker.

• Comb with a medium-toothed comb, removing any tangles and dead coat with the help of a dematter if necessary.

• Make sure you check the breeching and behind the ears for mats.

• Bathe the Collie in a protein shampoo, being careful to rinse thoroughly.

• Use a purifying shampoo and mask (used together) about three times a year, to nourish and enhance the coat and skin.

• Blow-dry or cage-dry the coat.

• Check the Collie's nails, ears and teeth.

• Scissor the hair to a tidy and smooth appearance from the back of the hock to the foot. This can be done to the show dog, as well as to the pet dog, as long as the trimming is not excessive.

• Scissor from the back of the pastern to the foot or front leg, to neaten the appearance.

• Finish by brushing in a light spray of coat conditioner, if required.

BORZOI

COAT: The long, silky coat has a slight wave and comes in numerous colors. Short and smooth on the head, ears and front legs, the coat is much longer on the body, with heavy feathering on the backs of the legs, the hindquarters, tail and chest. The neck carries a large, curly frill.

MAINTENANCE: Coat requires dedicated application from the groomer to prevent it from becoming tangled. These dogs look magnificent when regularly beautified.

PROCEDURE

Equipment needed: Slicker or pin brush on long hair; bristle brush on shorter hair; a comb.

Breed tip: A balsam conditioner will help to prevent static electricity in the coat.

- Thoroughly brush the entire coat with a slicker or pin brush. Remember never to use a slicker on parts that have short hair.

- Remove dead hair and mats with an untangle cream or comb, or both.

- Bathe the Borzoi in a good-quality shampoo and rinse thoroughly. Apply a balsam conditioner to enhance the coat and to lessen the effect of static electricity.

- Towel-dry or use absorbent towels to remove most of the water from the coat.

- Blow-dry while brushing the hair in the direction of its natural growth.

- The hair on the neck and top of body can be flicked forward to allow the blower to lift the hair, leaving a more accentuated topline.

- Check the dog's nails, ears and teeth.

- Trim the hair underneath and between the pads, and around the anus for good hygiene.

CAVALIER KING CHARLES SPANIEL

COAT: The coat is silky and free from curl; a slight wave is permissible. There is plenty of feathering, which should not be trimmed for the show ring.

MAINTENANCE: Although trimming is not permitted for show dogs, many pet owners like the feet to be trimmed of feathering, especially in winter. Some even advocate that all feathering is removed.

PROCEDURE

Equipment needed: Slicker brush and comb.

Breed tip: Pet or show dog, this is a delightful creature to groom.

- Brush the dog thoroughly with a slicker.

- Comb through the coat to ensure all tangles are removed, using an untangle spray if necessary.

- Bathe in a natural pH-balanced shampoo.

- About every four months, use a purifying shampoo and mask conditioner to enhance the coat and skin.

- Dry with a blower, making sure you go along with the hair growth, rather than against it. Alternatively, cage-dry after combing through the coat with a balsam conditioner.

- Check the dog's nails, ears and teeth.

- Many pet owners like the thicker-coated dogs to be thinned out. Use thinning scissors with the growth of the coat, and comb thoroughly before assessing whether more thinning is necessary.

CHIHUAHUA (LONG COAT)

COAT: The Long Coat has a soft texture, which is either flat or wavy. There is feathering on the ears, feet, legs and tail. Pants on the hindquarters and a large ruff on the neck are considered desirable. The tail should be long and full (plumed). The color is any mixture.

MAINTENANCE: Easy to maintain with weekly brushing. The Long Coat may need attention a couple of times a week.

PROCEDURE

Equipment needed: Cushioned bristle brush, medium-toothed comb.
  See page 159 for the Smooth Coat Chihuahua.

Breed tip: A companion breed, the Chi loves the attention of being groomed.

• Brush through the entire coat with a natural bristle brush and then comb to check that tangles have not formed.

• Bathe the Chihuahua in a suitable shampoo,

such as natural tea tree and lavender oil. Unless they get very dirty, a bath every three months should suffice. Rinse well.

• Condition the coat with a coat-enhancing cream.

• Blow-dry the coat, brushing the long hairs.

• Next, comb through the feathers.

• Check the dog's nails (they should be moderately short), ears and teeth.

CLUMBER SPANIEL

COAT: The Clumber Spaniel's coat is an abundant one. The coat is close, silky and straight, while the legs and chest are well feathered.

MAINTENANCE: The Clumber Spaniel is a breed that requires regular weekly brushing in order to keep the coat in the best condition.

PROCEDURE

Equipment needed: Slicker brush and a comb.

Breed tip: The Clumber Spaniel's eyes can be a problem, so do not forget to check them carefully as part of your regular grooming routine.

- Brush the coat with a slicker to remove dead hair and tangles.

- Bathe the Clumber in a suitable shampoo and thoroughly rinse.

- Apply a coat conditioner.

- Dry with a blower, ensuring you work along the hair growth to encourage the coat on the body to lie close.

- Check the dog's nails, ears and teeth. It is also advisable to clean the eyes (page 59), as the breed can suffer from tear stains.

- Tidy the hair from the back of the hocks with scissors, and trim off any hair that is obvious between toes.

- It may be necessary to thin the hair under the ears to allow them to lie flat.

- Excess hair on the skull can be smoothed with thinners.

DACHSHUND (LONGHAIRED)

COAT: The Longhaired Dachshund has a soft texture with straight or slightly wavy hair. The color is variable, but dapples should be evenly marked all over, and no white is permissible. There is red, black and tan, chocolate and dapple.

MAINTENANCE: The long coat, which is ideally flat and silky, needs little attention except for a regular comb-through to keep it free from tangles, and to help remove hair which is shed during a molt.

For details of the Smooth and Wirehaired Dachshunds, see page 161.

PROCEDURE

Equipment needed: Bristle brush, medium-toothed comb.

Breed tip: These hounds love following their noses, going down holes and sniffing in the undergrowth, and always end up with a great deal of the countryside in their coat! Consequently, a quick brush at the end of every walk is advisable.

- Brush the entire coat with a pin brush or slicker.

- Check for mats by combing through the coat with a medium-toothed comb.

- Dachshunds all benefit from an occasional bath, using a good dog shampoo. Rinse thoroughly, and dry with a blower or in warm air. Bathe the dog at least several days before a show to allow enough time for the coat's natural oils to be replenished.

- Check the dog's nails. The Dachshund's nails should be regularly trimmed for show and pet dogs, and must be done with great care since the quick (the nerves and blood supply) cannot be seen.

- The ears can be wiped with cotton batting, and the teeth should be kept clean by regular brushing.

- Check under the tail and remove excess hair from around the anus.

- Add sparkle to the coat by lightly spraying (or applying with your hand) some coat-finish lanolin. Of course, if you are showing your dog, no substances must be added to the coat.

ENGLISH SETTER

COAT: The coat is basically white, either lightly or heavily flecked with blue or orange (known as "belton"). The blue or orange can be of different shadings. Occasionally, lemon or liver beltons are seen. Blue beltons with tan around the muzzle and feet are known as tricolor.

The coat from the back of the head, in line with the ears, is slightly wavy (not curly) and, like the rest of the coat generally, is long and silky. The breeches and forelegs nearly down to the feet are well feathered.

MAINTENANCE: The coat is trimmed in parts to accentuate the dog's elegance and glamor. The art of trimming an English Setter is to make a clean and tidy outline, while maintaining a natural appearance. Thinning scissors should only be used for cutting up and into the lie of coat. This will mean that it is only the undercoat that is removed, allowing the topcoat to lie flat. Scissors are not used on the back or sides of the dog as, ultimately, the coat will be ruined – often permanently.

Clippers should not be used on the body, as this will ruin the gentle, flowing look of the

coat. Some Setters do have a thick and unruly coat, and the temptation is to clip this off. However, consultation with the owner is essential before performing this procedure.

PROCEDURE

Equipment needed: Slicker brush and fine-toothed comb.

Breed tip: It is advisable only to cut once or twice with the thinning scissors before brushing out the loose hair. This way, you can check if sufficient hair has been removed and will not accidentally overtrim.

Novice pet owners who decide to show their English Setters would be well advised to seek the advice of an experienced show exhibitor.

- Brush through, being careful to remove any tangles. Use untangle cream if necessary.

- Next, turn your attention to the head. The soft, tufty down that grows on the head is best removed by gently plucking with the thumb and finger, taking a little at a time. ▼

- The neck: the hair under the neck grows in an upside-down fan shape (down to the breastbone, curving out towards the shoulder and ears). With the thinning scissors, clean out this fan-shaped area until the hair on both sides of the neck blends in with the longer hair on the shoulders. ▼

- The ears: with the thinning scissors, cutting upwards into the long hair, repeat the cutting action until all the hair is short and lies flat. Leave the hair on the front edge of the ear longer, giving the desired soft expression. Remove the hair from under the ears so that the ears lie close to the neck.

- The tail: with the thinning scissors, remove the hair from under the base of the tail to about 1 inch (2.5 cm). Brush the tail feathers well. Then, holding the feathers firmly against the tail, measure against the top of the Setter's hock. The tail should stop at this level or slightly above. With the ordinary scissors, remove all the excess hair that falls past the end of the tail, or, if the fleshy part of the tail is short, cut a little further down. Once you let the tail-feathering loose, it will then fall in a scimitar shape.

- The back of the pastern: using the thinning scissors, trim off all the excess hair that can be found growing down the back of the hock to the foot. ▼

- The feet: with a pair of ordinary scissors, trim off the hair around the pads. Then, with the thinning scissors, trim the excess hair from between the toes. To do this, view the foot from the top. With your thumb, pull up all the excess hair from between the toes, cutting upwards from the nail toward the leg, using several cutting motions until all the protruding hair is removed. This method is applied to both front and back feet.

- Bathe the English Setter in a suitable shampoo.

- Rinse thoroughly and then apply conditioner.

- Towel-dry the dog, then blow-dry along the growth of the hair. Alternatively, cage-dry after combing through the entire coat.

- Check the Setter's nails, ears and teeth.

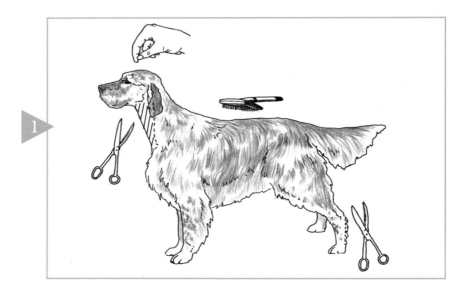

ENGLISH TOY SPANIEL (KING CHARLES)

COAT: The coat is long, silky and straight. Slight waves are allowed, but the coat should never be curly. The legs, ears and tail are feathered profusely.
Colors:
- Black and tan (rich, glossy black, with bright mahogany tan markings on the muzzle, legs, chest, linings of the ears, under the tail and spots over the eyes. White patches on the chest are undesirable).
- Tricolor (ground color pearly white, with well-distributed black patches, and brilliant tan markings on the cheeks, linings of the ears, under the tail, and spots over the eyes. There is a white blaze between the eyes and up the forehead).
- Blenheim (ground color pearly white, with well-distributed chestnut-red patches. There should be a wide, clear blaze, with a "spot" in the center of the skull – a clear chestnut-red mark about 3/4 inch (2 cm) across).
- Ruby (whole-colored a rich chestnut-red. A white patch on the chest is highly undesirable).

MAINTENANCE: Fairly easy to maintain with regular brushing.

PROCEDURE

Equipment needed: A pin brush and a medium-toothed comb.

Breed tip: Brush and comb your English Toy Spaniel every day, from early puppyhood. The coat should not be trimmed – any loose hair will be brushed or combed out easily if regular grooming is carried out.

- Brush through the coat using a pin brush.

- Comb through with a medium-toothed comb, making sure all tangles are removed.

- Next, check the dog's skin. If you notice dandruff, do not dismiss it as dry skin – a small mite could be responsible, which causes the skin to scale. If so, you will need a special veterinary-prescribed shampoo.

- Now, bathe and shampoo the dog (a protein-enriched or tea tree and lavender shampoo work wonders) and rinse well.

- Apply a complementary conditioner.

- Blow-dry the hair, brushing in the direction of the hair growth, not against it.

- Check the dog's eyes. If necessary, wipe with cotton batting soaked in an eye-cleansing solution.

- Check inside the dog's ears to ensure they are clean and free of wax. If necessary, apply a light dusting of canker powder.

- Check the nails and cut if necessary. Also check under the feet, and trim out any excess hair between the pads.

FLAT-COATED RETRIEVER

COAT: The coat is dense, and fine to medium in texture. It should be of good quality and lie as flat as possible. The legs and tail are well feathered, and full furnishing on maturity completes the elegance.

MAINTENANCE: Easy to maintain with regular weekly brushing.

PROCEDURE

Equipment needed: Stiff brush and a wide-toothed comb.

Breed tip: Frequent bathing destroys natural oils and lubricants in the coat, which are vital when the dog is working in water.

- Groom regularly, using a stiff brush and a wide-toothed comb. Pay particular attention to the feathering, especially the ears and under the elbows where the coat easily becomes matted.

- If a bath is absolutely necessary (for attendance at a show, or if your dog has rolled in something nasty), wet the coat thoroughly and use a good-quality dog shampoo.

- After toweling, blow-dry the coat along the direction of the growth of the hair to keep the coat as flat as possible.

- Check the dog's nails, ears and teeth.

- Remove any hair from between the pads on the bottom of the feet.

- Tidy the outer edge of the foot with scissors.

- Tidy hair from the hock to the heel of the foot, using thinning scissors.

- The ears should be close to the head, so a little thinning beneath the ear will assist this requirement. Any excess or dead hair on the ears should be gently removed by plucking it out with your thumb and finger.

GLEN OF IMAAL TERRIER

COAT: The coat is of medium length and of harsh texture, with a soft undercoat.

The Glen of Imaal color is blue, wheaten or brindle, and the hair looks fairly crinkly where it hangs longer on the legs and on the belly.

MAINTENANCE: A weekly comb-through is usually sufficient.

PROCEDURE

Equipment needed: Slicker brush and a comb.

Breed tip: The coat is tidied with thinning scissors to create a neat outline.

- Comb through with a medium- or wide-toothed metal comb, and then use a fine comb to remove all knots.

- Bathe the dog in a suitable shampoo, and rinse well. Do not use a conditioner on the coat – the hair must be harsh.

- Towel-dry and finish with a light blower or dry in warm air.

- Comb through.

- Use thinning scissors on the neck to enhance the outline and to define the length if required. This also makes the coat tidy on the body.

- The head hair is sometimes shortened with scissors on the pet dog, tidying around the eyes to keep them free of hair and debris.

- Tidy the hair beneath the tail, as previously described.

- Check the dog's nails, ears and teeth.

GOLDEN RETRIEVER

COAT: The Golden's coat is flat or wavy with good feathering, and a dense and water-resistant undercoat.

MAINTENANCE: The Golden Retriever is frequently seen in the grooming salon, although maintenance is relatively easy – simply brush through the entire coat on a weekly basis.

PROCEDURE

Equipment needed: Slicker brush, comb.

Breed tip: Brush daily – the Golden will love the attention, even though a weekly groom is usually sufficient. Goldens really love to get dirty, but also enjoy being spruced up.

- Brush through the entire coat with a slicker to remove molting or dead hair.

- Make sure you pay particular attention to the hair behind the ears, where the softer hairs frequently mat.

- Comb through the coat with a medium-toothed comb.

- Bathe the Golden in a suitable shampoo, rinsing thoroughly.

- Use a coat-nourishing conditioner or use a

purifying shampoo and mask, about three times a year.

- Towel-dry the coat and finish with a blower, going with the direction of growth.

- Check the dog's nails, ears and teeth.

- Trim any excessive hair from under the feet, around the pads, and the back of the hocks.

- Thin under the ears, if required, and carefully trim the edges of the ear, if necessary.

- This dog should look natural, but the tail is trimmed from the tip, tapering to form a plume. Place your finger and thumb at the end of the tail and cut a curve.

- Show dogs are groomed and trimmed regularly. Pet dogs need to be trimmed if the fringes get too long and bedraggled. In all dogs, really long fringes are impractical and untidy.

- Note: neutered or spayed dogs develop heavier coats and need more attention.

GORDON SETTER

COAT: The black-and-tan coat on the head, front of the legs and tips of the ears is short and fine. It is of moderate length, flat and as free as possible from curl or wave on all other parts of the body.

Feathering on the ears is long and silky. On the backs of the legs, it is long, fine, flat and straight. Fringes on the belly may extend to the chest and the throat.

MAINTENANCE: The coat is trimmed in parts to show off the dog to its best

advantage. The art of trimming a Gordon Setter is to make a clean and tidy outline, while maintaining a natural appearance. Thinning scissors should only be used for cutting up and into the lie of the coat. This will mean that it is only the undercoat that is removed, allowing the topcoat to lie flat.

Clippers should not be used on the body, as this will ruin the gentle, flowing look of the coat. Some Setters do have a thick and unruly coat, and the temptation is to clip it off. However, consultation with the owner is essential before performing this procedure.

PROCEDURE

Equipment needed: Slicker or pin/bristle brush, medium-toothed comb.

Breed tip: As with all Setters, this breed benefits from regular (daily) brushing to keep its coat dust-free and looking healthy. It is advisable to cut only once or twice with the thinning scissors before brushing out the loose hair. This way, you can check if sufficient hair has been removed and will not accidentally overtrim.

- Brush through the coat with a slicker or pin/bristle brush to remove any tangles.

- Next, turn your attention to the head. The soft, tufty down which grows on the head is best removed by gently plucking with the thumb and finger, taking a little at a time.

- The neck: the hair under the neck grows in an upside-down fan shape (down to the breastbone, curving out toward the shoulder and ears). With the thinning scissors, clean out this fan-shaped area until the hair on both sides of the neck blends in with the longer hair on the shoulders.

- The ears: at the top of the ear, with thinning scissors, go under and against the lie of the coat for approximately 2 inches (5 cm), blending in to lie flat, making a smooth, flowing look. Remove the hair from under the ears so that the ears lie close to the neck. The rest of the hair on the ears remains long and silky.

- The tail: brush the tail feathers well. Then, holding the feathers firmly against the tail, measure against the top of the Setter's hock. The tail should stop at this level or slightly above. With the ordinary scissors, remove all the excess hair which falls past the end of the tail or, if the fleshy part of the tail is short, cut a little further down. Once you let the tail-feathering loose, it will then fall in a scimitar shape. If any trimming is required to achieve this shape, this is best done with trimming scissors.

- The feet: with a pair of ordinary scissors, trim off the hair around the pads. Then, with trimming scissors, trim the excess hair from between the toes. To do this, view the foot from the top. With your thumb, pull up all the excess hair from between the toes, cutting upwards from the nail toward the leg, using several cutting motions until all the protruding hair is removed. This method is applied to both the front and back feet. On the front legs, with thinning scissors, from the back pads go up approximately 2 inches (5 cm), taking off excess hair. Finish with straight scissors for a neat appearance.

- The hocks: do not remove all hair off the back of the hocks. Thin and trim to the required shape.

- Bathe the dog in a suitable shampoo, rinsing well before applying conditioner.

- Towel-dry the dog, then blow-dry along the growth direction of the coat. Alternatively, cage-dry after combing through the entire coat with a medium-toothed comb.

- Check the dog's nails, ears and teeth.

GRAND BASSET GRIFFON VENDÉEN

COAT: The coat is rough and long without exaggeration, with a flat structure. It has a thick undercoat and should be neither silky nor woolly. Fringing is not too abundant.

The color is white with any combination of lemon, orange, tricolor or grizzle markings.

MAINTENANCE: The coat is not trimmed but needs regular grooming, brushing and combing to remove dead or matted hair and dirt, with some tidying around the head and feet.

PROCEDURE

Equipment needed: Pin or slicker brush, wide-toothed comb and stripping knife.

Breed tip: This dog will root through undergrowth, collecting brambles, thorns or tangles in the coat – check it over regularly.

- Brush or comb through the coat, removing debris and teasing out matted hair, especially under the body and armpits, and from the beard.

- Bathe the dog in a natural, mild-ingredient shampoo and rinse thoroughly.

- Towel-dry and finish in warm air, in a cage or with a blower.

- Brush the coat flat and strip away excess hair around the ears and feet.

- Clean and remove excess hair from the ear canal, clean the dog's teeth and check its nails (clipping or grinding if necessary).

IRISH RED AND WHITE SETTER

COAT: The coat is finely textured with good feathering, and a slight wave is permissible.

The color is clearly parti-color, with a base of pearl white with solid red patches. Mottling or flecking is permitted around the face and feet, up the forelegs to the elbow and up the hindlegs to the hock.

MAINTENANCE: Brushing on a regular, twice-a-week basis will keep the coat smart and remove dead hairs. Comb through the feathering with a medium-toothed comb.

This dog does not normally grow a profuse coat, but may benefit from added attention. It does not need a lot of trimming – the ears may be shaped around the bottom, the feet should be trimmed up to the stopper and the hock joint. The end of the tail may be trimmed, but not the feathering. The neck may be trimmed out.

- Brush through the entire coat, and comb the longer hairs thoroughly.

- Examine the ears. If necessary, remove the hair under the ears so the ears lie close to the neck.

- With scissors, remove all the excess hair that falls past the end of the tail (or, if the fleshy part of the tail is short, a little further down).

- Using thinning scissors, trim excess hair that grows down the back of the hock to the foot.

- Next, trim the hair around the pads. With thinning scissors, trim the excess hair from

PROCEDURE

Equipment needed: Good-quality brush, comb.

Breed tip: Be careful not to overtrim, as the Irish Red and White Setter's coat is one of its most attractive features.

between the dog's toes. (See English Setter profile, page 117.)

- Bathe the dog in a protein or natural shampoo, rinsing well.

- Apply a complementary conditioner to enhance the appearance and to nourish the coat.

- Towel-dry, removing excess moisture from the coat.

- Put the dog in warm air or a cage-dryer, or use a low setting on the dryer.

- Check the dog's nails, ears and teeth.

IRISH SETTER

COAT: The hair on the head, front of legs and tips of the ears is short and fine; on all other parts of the body and legs it is of moderate length, flat and as free as possible from curl or wave.

Feathering on the ears is long and silky. On the back of the forelegs and on the hindlegs, the hair is long and fine, with a fair amount of hair on the belly, forming a fringe which may extend to the chest and throat. The feet are well feathered between the toes of this dog, though generally these are trimmed round to neaten. The tail fringe is of moderate length, decreasing as it approaches the tip or point.

MAINTENANCE: Relatively easy to keep, exercise and groom.

PROCEDURE

Equipment needed: A good-quality bristle brush, a pin brush to use where necessary, a wide-toothed metal comb and a finer comb for finishing.

Breed tip: Overtrimming will spoil the classic look, so any hairdressing must be carefully executed.

- Brush thoroughly with a good-quality bristle brush. Long hair can be tackled with a pin brush where required, to remove tangles.

- Comb with a wide-toothed metal comb to remove dead hair. A finer comb can then be used if more hair needs to be removed.

- Bathe the dog in a suitable mild shampoo.

- Use conditioner after rinsing thoroughly. A purifying shampoo and mask can be applied three times a year to enhance the skin and coat.

- The coat is blow-dried with the growth of the hair to keep it flat and sleek, rather than lifted and flyaway. This can be achieved by pointing the blower downwards over the dog. Spray conditioner will assist this process and leave the coat gleaming.

- Check the dog's nails, ears and teeth.

- Trimming to enhance a natural appearance, while emphasizing angulation and the good points of the dog, is undertaken as follows. Groomers inexperienced in this breed would be well advised to take expert advice on trimming particular dogs for the show ring, as every dog is different, and too much or too little trimming can spoil the overall picture of the dog.

- Head: excess hair is plucked out with finger and thumb to give the head a smooth finish.

- Neck: using thinning scissors, thin from the

throat to just above the breastbone, with the growth or lie of the hair. Trim from the underside of the ear to the center of the breastbone. The surrounding hair is blended with thinning scissors or shears to give a smooth, clean, natural appearance. Do not use thinning scissors across the grain of the coat, as this will leave a cutting, doorstep effect; only trim in the direction that the coat grows. The chest feathering falls from the breastbone to the fall of hair on the upper part of the front legs.

- Ears: thinning scissors are used on the inside and outside of the leathers, working downwards with the hair growth, to shorten the hair to a very neat appearance, removing the excess coat on the neck beneath the ear to blend in and flatten the coat. Trim around the leather to finish.

- Body: thoroughly comb through the body hair, working down the fringe of the chest to remove dead hairs and give a smooth, sleek appearance. First, use a medium-toothed comb and then a finer one if required.

- Front feet: the feet are trimmed underneath to remove excess hair, working an inch or so up the leg. Tidy around the toes with thinning scissors to give a neat appearance. Between the toes, it is beneficial to thin the excess hair to prevent it from becoming clogged with mud, etc.

- Back feet and hock: trim the rear feet following the same procedure as for the front ones (see above), to give a neat appearance. Comb the hair from the point of the hock upwards to the toes. Using thinning scissors in a downward action, remove the hair to give a flat, clean finish.

- Tail: this is trimmed to a moderate length, with the hair decreasing in a taper to the tip or point.

- The use of clippers may be undertaken when the coat has blown, and becomes extremely thick and unmanageable, as with a neutered pet for example. Clipping the Irish Setter should only be carried out as a very last resort.

IRISH WOLFHOUND

COAT: The Irish Wolfhound has a rough, harsh coat that needs brushing at least three times a week, with some finger plucking to keep the coat in good condition and keep the dog comfortable.

MAINTENANCE: It is fairly easy to look after the coat. All that is needed is a thorough weekly brush.

PROCEDURE

Equipment needed: Slicker brush, comb.

Breed tip: Invest in a bath ramp or get help to put this giant in the bath – or you will break your back!

- Aim to brush and comb daily, and you will probably do it twice weekly. Occasionally, you can use Savlon (a mild, gentle antiseptic cream) on a cloth, then brush out well. This will keep the Irish Wolfhound clean and smelling fresh.

- Monthly, or when necessary, remove any unwanted bushy or long, dead hair from the neck and under the belly. Pluck it out with your finger and thumb. Scissors can be used for around the genitals, under the tail and the feet.

- Trim the hair flat to the pads but do not remove from between the pads.

- Check the dog's nails. If they do not wear down, then, every month, cut the excess away with good nail clippers. Alternatively, use a rasp weekly, filing each nail a couple of times in turn so that they do not get hot. Keep going around until the nails are the correct length. The best time to do this is when your Irish Wolfhound is asleep after a meal. If you get it used to the procedure from a young age, the dog won't mind you doing it.

- Check the ears and clean them with an appropriate cleaner once a week. Check the teeth once a week.

- Only bathe once a year, during the summer months, on a nice, hot day outside. Use warm water and a good-quality shampoo.

- Try not to remove the natural oils from the coat, rinse well, towel-dry and then allow the coat to dry naturally. Do this in the morning, so you have the rest of the day for the coat to dry off.

- Do not use conditioners, as they will soften the coat; this is not allowed in the show ring.

- A good-quality dry shampoo brushed through the coat at about three-month intervals removes some grease and grime, and smells sweet.

KOOIKERHONDJE

COAT: The coat is medium-long, slightly waved or straight, but not curled, close-fitting and not too fine. It has a well-developed undercoat.

MAINTENANCE: Brushing is undertaken on a regular, twice-a-week basis with a bristle brush, and a comb is used for the feathering and tail hair. This is a relatively easy dog to look after and it looks lovely when well cared for.

PROCEDURE

Equipment needed: Slicker brush and comb.

Breed tip: The Kooikerhondje is jaunty and full of zest.

- Brush the entire coat thoroughly and comb through to remove dead hairs.

- Bathe in a suitable, mild shampoo and rinse well.

- Condition with coat-enhancing cream and rinse thoroughly.

- Once the dog has been rinsed, towel-dry to remove the drips.

- Finish drying the coat in warm air, or lightly blow-dry, going in the direction of the growth of the hair.

- Comb through the coat.

- Check the dog's nails, ears and teeth.

LARGE MUNSTERLANDER

COAT: The coat is long and dense, but not curly or coarse. It is well feathered on the front and hindlegs, and on the tail, more so in males than in bitches. The hair must lie short and smooth on the head.

MAINTENANCE: Requires brushing once or twice a week, particularly on the ears and feathering to remove debris picked up from walks.

PROCEDURE

Equipment needed: Bristle brush and comb.

Breed tip: Keep a close eye on the feathering, which tangles easily. Trim excess hair between the toes and on the back of the hocks.

- Brush through the coat with a bristle brush.

- Comb with a wide-toothed comb, and then a medium-toothed one, to remove dead hairs and to check for tangles, especially behind the ears and in the long feathering.

- Bathe the dog in a suitable mild or natural shampoo.

- Rinse thoroughly.

- Conditioner can be used, if required, to enhance and nourish the coat. Be sure to rinse thoroughly.

- Remove excess moisture from the coat by towel-drying.

- Finish drying the coat by putting the dog in warm air or a cage-dryer, or use a blower.

- Remember to check the dog's nails, ears and teeth.

- Check the feet, making sure you look at the area under the pads. Carefully remove any matted hair with small scissors.

- Finally, finish by combing through the coat one more time.

NOVA SCOTIA DUCK TOLLING RETRIEVER

COAT: The coat is straight and water-repellent. It is a double coat of medium length and softness, with a softer, dense undercoat.

The Nova Scotia Duck Tolling Retriever is allowed a slight wave on the back and has feathering at the throat, behind the ears and at the back of the thighs. The forelegs are moderately feathered.

Color: shades of red or orange, with lighter feathering under the tail. White marks are desirable in at least one of the following places: on the tip of the tail, the feet and chest, or as a blaze.

MAINTENANCE: Brushing on a regular basis is usually all that is required to keep this breed in tiptop condition.

PROCEDURE

Equipment needed: Bristle brush and a pin brush.

Breed tip: This breed will enjoy the personal interaction of being groomed, so set aside a couple of times a week to groom and keep it looking smart. Do note that excessive use of a brush will remove or damage the undercoat.

- Brush through the coat with a bristle or pin brush.

- Use a pin brush on the tail or feathering.

- Then brush through the coat with a pin brush on the body and on the feathering. Don't forget to brush behind the ears.

- Bathing can be undertaken, if necessary. Make sure you use a gentle shampoo so you do not remove the natural oils from the coat. Rinse thoroughly.

- Towel-dry. Tollers are practically "drip-dry" and they dry off in seconds, so any other form of drying (e.g., a cage-dryer) is not advised.

- Check the nails, ears and teeth.

OTTERHOUND

COAT: The Otterhound has an oily, rough double coat, which is dense but not wiry. The hair on the head is softer, as is the hair on the legs.

MAINTENANCE: The presentation is natural, but this is a dog that loves a bath, and it seems a shame not to oblige it.

PROCEDURE

Equipment needed: Slicker or curry brush and comb.

Breed tip: Do not use too harsh a shampoo, or you will strip the coat's natural oils and remove a characteristic feature of the breed.

- Brush the entire coat with a slicker or pin brush.

- Comb through with a wide-toothed comb to remove dead hair and any tangles that may be present.

- Bathe using a suitable mild shampoo. Apply a conditioner that suits the coat condition,

adding a teaspoonful of oil to it where necessary.

- Blow the coat dry, taking care that you follow the direction of the growth of the hair, brushing with a pin brush.

- Do not forget to check the dog's nails, ears and teeth.

- Finally, check under the foot, paying careful attention to the area between the pads. Remove any matted hair with scissors.

PAPILLON

COAT: The coat is long, fine and silky, and requires regular brushing. It is abundant, flowing, but without undercoat. It falls flat on the back and sides with a profuse frill on the chest. It is short and close on the skull, muzzle and front legs. The rear of the forelegs to the pasterns, tail and thighs are covered with long hair.

MAINTENANCE: Easy to maintain with weekly brushing.

PROCEDURE

Equipment needed: Plastic pin brush or bristle brush, comb.

Breed tip: A special whitening shampoo will make the coat shine.

- Brush through with a pin brush, then comb with a medium-toothed comb to ensure the coat is free from tangles.

- Bathe in a pH-balanced shampoo.

- Use white-enhancing shampoo on the white parts for that extra-special glow.

- Apply conditioner to the coat.

- Towel- and blow-dry the coat.

- Check the dog's nails, ears and teeth. The teeth need cleaning once a week, as the breed is susceptible to dental problems.

- Check under the feet. Remove any excess hair.

PETIT BASSET GRIFFON VENDÉEN

COAT: The coat is rough, long without exaggeration and harsh to the touch. It has a thick undercoat and should be neither silky nor woolly.
The color is white with any combination of lemon, orange, tricolor or grizzle markings.

MAINTENANCE: The coat is not trimmed but needs regular grooming, brushing and combing to remove dirt and dead or matted hair, with some tidying around the head and feet.

PROCEDURE

Equipment needed: Pin or slicker brush, wide-toothed comb and a stripping knife.

Breed tip: This dog will root through undergrowth and may collect brambles, thorns or tangles in its coat, so check it over regularly.

- Brush or comb through the coat, removing any debris and teasing out any matted hair, especially under the body and armpits, and from the beard.

- Bathe in a natural, mild-ingredient or harsh-coat shampoo and rinse thoroughly.

- Towel-dry and finish in warm air or a cage, or with a blower.

- Brush the coat flat and strip away excess hair around the ears and feet.

- Clean and remove excess hair from the ear canal, clean the dog's teeth and check its nails (clipping or grinding them if necessary).

PYRENEAN SHEEPDOG

COAT: The coat is long, or semi-long. It is fairly harsh, dense and almost flat or slightly wavy. It is denser and more woolly on the rump and on the thighs. The hair on the muzzle is short, but it is longer on the face and cheeks. Acceptable coat colors include various shades of fawn, with or without black hairs, light to dark gray, blue merle, slate or brindle, black, or black and white. Large areas of white, black or tan are undesirable.

MAINTENANCE: Grooming entails brushing with a slicker and using a wide-toothed comb on a regular basis (once a week).

PROCEDURE

Equipment needed: Slicker brush or pin brush and a wide-toothed comb.

Breed tip: Never neglect underneath the feet – where the hair can form mats.

- Brush through the entire coat with a slicker or pin brush.

- Comb with a wide-toothed comb to remove dead hairs.

- This breed should only be bathed if it is absolutely necessary, and certainly not on a regular basis. If bathing is vital, a natural-ingredient shampoo should be used, and make sure you rinse well.

- Add conditioner to aid grooming.

- Towel-dry, patting the coat rather than rubbing it.

- Finish the drying process in warm air, a cage, or with a gentle blower.

- Check the dog's nails, ears and teeth. Also check the dewclaws and trim the rear ones if necessary to prevent them curling around.

- Check underneath the feet for excess hair or clogged hair, and remove with small scissors if necessary.

- Finally, complete by brushing the coat over with a bristle brush.

SALUKI

COAT: The coat is smooth, of silky texture, with feathering on the ears, tail, backs of the legs and between the toes. Puppies, and sometimes older dogs, may have a slight woolly feathering on the thigh and shoulder. The smooth variety has no feathering. All colors and combinations of colors are possible except for brindle.

MAINTENANCE: The main part of the coat is easy to maintain, requiring regular brushing with a bristle brush. The long hair on the ears, tail, and so on, needs regular (weekly) attention with a slicker brush to remove mats. If the Saluki is inclined to grow fluff on the flanks, it can be removed with a stripping stone.

PROCEDURE

Equipment needed: Bristle brush and slicker brush.

Breed tip: Use a snood while the dog is eating or chewing to save the long hair on the ears.

- Brush the long hair (particularly behind the ears) with a slicker brush and remove all mats.

- Brush the whole coat with a bristle brush to remove dead hairs.

- Bathe the Saluki in a good-quality shampoo and conditioner when necessary. The choice of shampoo is important, particularly on black-colored dogs, if the dog is inclined to shed dandruff.

- Dry the dog in warm air or with a gentle blower.

- Check the dog's nails, ears and teeth.

SCOTTISH DEERHOUND

COAT: The coat is shaggy, but not over-coated, and a woolly coat is considered unacceptable. The correct type of coat for this breed is thick, close-lying and harsh or crisp to the touch. The hair on the body, neck and quarters is required to be 2³/₄ inches (7 cm) to 4 inches (10 cm) long. The hair on the head, breast and belly is softer. A slight hairy fringe on the inside of the forelegs and on the hindlegs is typical.

The color is dark blue-gray, darker and lighter grays or brindles and yellow, sandy-red or red fawns with black points.

A white chest, white toes and a slight white tip on the stern are permissible, but the less white the better, as the Scottish Deerhound is a self-colored dog.

MAINTENANCE: The coat is relatively easy to maintain, needing merely a brush with a pin brush on a regular basis, and combing through with a wide-toothed comb to remove burrs, etc.

PROCEDURE

Equipment needed: Pin brush, comb.

Breed tip: The show dog must be bathed and groomed about a week before a show to allow the coat to settle.

• Brush through the coat with a pin brush.

• Bathe as little as possible. If the dog is very dirty and there is no avoiding it, bathe it using a suitable shampoo for coarse hair.

• Towel-dry and finish with warm air, a cage-dryer or a blower.

• Comb or brush through the coat once again.

• Check the dog's nails, ears and teeth.

• The Scottish Deerhound is presented as naturally as possible, though the ears can be trimmed to make them appear "mouselike."

SILKY TERRIER (AUSTRALIAN)

COAT: It has a glossy, silky coat. The color is blue and tan, gray-blue and tan; the richer these colors, the better.

MAINTENANCE: The coat is easy to look after with daily brushing with a pin brush.

Where the owner neglects this duty, tangles need to be groomed out, sometimes with the aid of a conditioning spray or a mat-breaker. Commence at the tip of the hair, working gradually toward the root. Only attempt a small amount at a time and hold the hair to prevent it being pulled and hurting the dog.

PROCEDURE

Equipment needed: Pin brush, a wide-toothed metal comb and a pure bristle brush to finish and to aid shine.

Breed tip: Brush and comb through on a regular basis, but don't get carried away or you may break the hair unnecessarily.

- Brush through the coat with a pin brush or slicker, then comb with a wide-toothed metal comb, paying attention to behind the ears and beard, as well as under the legs and belly.

- Bathe the dog in a protein or mild shampoo, rinsing well.

- Apply a good anti-tangle conditioner and comb through.

- After rinsing, pat dry with an absorbent towel and dry the hair in layers with a gentle blow from your hairdryer.

- Check nails, ears and teeth weekly.

- The hair is parted down the back, so finish off with a light brushing away from the spine, using a bristle brush.

SPINONE ITALIANO (ITALIAN SPINONE)

COAT: The coat is tough, thick, slightly wiry and close fitting with no undercoat. It is about 1$\frac{1}{2}$ to 2 inches (4 to 6 cm) on the body, shorter on the nasal bridge, ears and head. It is even shorter on the front of the legs and feet. The eyebrows consist of longer, stiffer hair. Even longer, softer hairs cover the cheeks and upper lips, forming a mustache and beard.

The color is white; white with orange or brown markings; white speckled with orange (orange roan) with or without orange markings; white speckled with brown (brown roan) with or without brown markings.

MAINTENANCE: This is not a glamorous breed. The Spinone Italiano is a rustic, functional dog and part of its attraction is its slightly disheveled look. Care must be taken not to overpresent this breed. Too frequent bathing softens the coat, and show dogs are best hosed down and dried naturally. Regular brushing with a slicker will remove burrs and seeds. A comb should be used on the head.

Beards need constant attention and regular washing. These dogs are very prone to ear infections – therefore, ears should be checked every day and cleaned twice a week. Hair inside the ear should be removed with a finger and thumb. Ear powder will help.

A Spinone Italiano born with the unique and very desirable "pigskin-like" skin will have the correct single coat, which needs little stripping other than to enhance the shape of the head. However, many dogs are born with longer, softer coats, and regular stripping will help to improve the coat and encourage a harsher texture.

Strictly speaking, this task is undertaken by hand, although most owners use a stripping comb (a Mars 99 M328 is excellent). A stripping block is useful for finishing and removing stray hairs.

Dogs born with soft double coats always have thin skin and these coats are almost impossible to strip. Rather than cause the dog distress, it is better to bathe and clip it.

PROCEDURE

Equipment needed: Slicker brush, bristle brush and comb.

Breed tip: Strip the coat out several weeks before a show, paying particular attention to the head and legs. Brush the body coat regularly as the coat grows in. Heads may be tidied a couple of days before a show.

- Comb with a medium-toothed comb. Comb through beard and mustache to ensure no mats or debris are present.

- Body: Strip the body and legs before the head. When stripping for the show ring, the golden rule is to strip the side nearest the

judge. Dead hair should be stripped out by hand. Start at the top of the neck and strip out the hair following the direction of the lie of the coat. Chalk powder will help.

- Work down the neck along the body and down the legs, removing all fringing. Softer hair in the anal and genital region can be shortened with scissors. Strip the feet and, if necessary, trim to enhance the shape. Strip the tail, removing all fringing.

- Head: the aim of stripping the head is to make it appear long and narrow, and to reveal the correct divergent side profiles of the skull and muzzle. The golden rule is never to strip the coat forward of a line vertical to the outside of the eye. Stripping in front of the eye gives a highly undesirable Schnauzer-like appearance.

- Starting behind the eyebrows, strip out the coat on top of the skull, over the occiput, and blend into the neck. Then strip out the sides of the skull from the corner of the eye backwards. Strip down the ears to give a clean outline. If the ears are too short, leave a little hair toward the lower part of the ear flap and trim the edges with scissors to give the illusion of slightly longer ears.

- Comb the beard and, using thinning scissors, shorten the beard to enhance the squareness and length of the muzzle. "Goat beards" should always be shortened.

- Finally, using thinning scissors, shorten the eyebrows to about 1 inch (2.5 cm). Care must be taken to avoid a hard line. The eyebrows must always look natural and must never be so long as to fall forward and obscure the characteristic "peeping expression." Spinone eyebrows should always be brushed backwards, never forwards like a German Wirehaired Pointer. Some Spinoni (said to be of ancient lineage) have a fan of

hair growing from the stop in front of their eyes. If this obscures the eyes, it should be shortened, using thinning scissors.

- Bathe the dog in a natural-ingredient shampoo, such as tea tree and lavender.

- Rinse thoroughly, making sure all the suds are removed.

- Remove excess moisture from the coat with superabsorbent towels.

- Comb the coat through and finish in warm air, a cage or with a gentle blower.

- Check the dog's nails, ears and teeth. Spinoni have dewclaws on both front and rear feet. These must be clipped more frequently than the other nails.

- Check between the pads and remove excess hair, or this will knot and become uncomfortable for the dog to walk on.

- Lightly spray with a finish conditioner to enhance the coat, and replenish natural oils where necessary.

- If the dog is to be clipped instead of hand-stripped, demat the coat, bathe and condition. Using an Oster No. 5 blade, starting from the top of the neck, clip the body and legs. Scissor the tail, around the dewclaws, and the hair between the pads, and trim the feet to show the shape. Trim the anal and genital region. Trim off the very long hair from the outside of the ears. Using an Oster No. 8 blade, clip the top and side of the skull backwards from the eyebrows, over the occiput, and blend into the neck. Clip down the ears, and finish the head as described above.

- Sometimes, the breed is stripped to enhance its outline (where necessary) and,

occasionally, pet dogs are seen trimmed down shorter.

- However, the hair is relatively easy to maintain and should not require clipping short except for health reasons, or where the skin is thin and a double coat exists, as stripping here would be difficult and miserable for the dog to endure. In such instances, demat the coat, bathe and dry, then clip the entire body with a medium blade, leaving the coat about one to ³/₄ inch (2 cm) in length.

- From the eyebrows back, clip the ears and the top of the side of the skull shorter (about ³/₄ inch / 2 cm). Finish the head as detailed above.

TALKING ITALIAN

After losing her first Great Dane at an early age, Linda Mayne decided to try a different breed as she felt nothing could replace him. After visiting a local Championship show, Linda fell in love with the Spinone Italiano.

Having always been interested in showing dogs, but with her experience limited to a short-coated breed, preparing a Spinone for the show ring was going to be quite different. It became apparent that it was essential to start well in advance, as the benefits of stripping are not seen straight away.

BEING HARSH

To encourage a harsh coat, Linda regularly strips out the dead hair by hand. This is not undertaken within three weeks of a show, other than to keep the coat tidy, as this gives the texture time to regain its harshness.

As bathing tends to soften the coat, to keep it clean, Linda relies on regular brushing with a slicker brush. Spinoni love to get dirty and roll, so the occasional "hose-down" removes the worst of the dirt.

HEAD AND BEARD

The beard does get washed as often as possible, as it tends to collect food/debris/saliva. A typical Italian Spinone grooming routine also includes the normal checks of eyes, ears, toenails and feet, especially between the pads (see pages 136–139).

Linda finds the hardest bit is the head, because part of the Italian Spinone appeal is his "hairy" face. This is also hand-stripped (see page 138), being cautious to take just a little bit of hair at a time so as not to overdo it and lose that wonderful expression.

SHOW PREPARATION

"Most of our show preparation takes place well beforehand," says Linda, "However, just before a show, I brush or comb the coat thoroughly and make sure the beard is clean.

"Then all I need to do before we go into the show ring is to give a quick brush-through followed by a not-so-quick drying of the beard. Once I've done that, then we're ready."

SUSSEX SPANIEL

COAT: The coat is abundant and flat, with no tendency to curl, and the ample undercoat is weather resistant. The ears are covered with soft, wavy hair, which may be frequently profuse. The forequarters and hindquarters are moderately well feathered, and the tail is thickly clothed with hair, which is feathered and therefore customarily trimmed.

MAINTENANCE: Regular brushing is essential. The natural look is required, but these dogs need attention to brushing, and look stunning when nurtured.

PROCEDURE

Equipment needed: Slicker brush, wide-toothed comb, scissors and rubber thimbles.

Breed tip: Pay special attention to the ears, and "armpit" and groin areas, where the long hair can mat very quickly if neglected for even a short time. It is also advisable to trim away the hair on the underside of the ear so that air can readily circulate. Clean the ears regularly to prevent problems from occurring.

- Brush the coat, paying special attention to the long hair on the chest, legs, inside and outside the ears, the "armpits" and groin.

- Comb with a wide-toothed comb.

- Remove dead hair on top of the head, back, flanks and hindquarters with finger and thumb.

- Check the dog's nails, ears and teeth.

- Check underneath its feet for matted hair, and remove with scissors where necessary.

- Sussex Spaniels are very clean dogs and are free of odor. Regular bathing will destroy the natural coat oils that help to nurture the wonderful golden, liver coat, which will become dull and malodorous. If the dog does roll in something smelly and a bath is unavoidable, plain water only should be used.

TIBETAN SPANIEL

COAT: The topcoat is silky in texture. It is smooth on the face and on the front legs, of moderate length on the body, but lying rather flat.

This dog has an undercoat that is fine and dense. The ears and back of the forelegs are nicely feathered, and the tail and buttocks are well furnished with longer hair.

This is not a dog that is overcoated, and bitches tend to carry less coat and mane than males. All colors and mixtures of colors are permissible.

MAINTENANCE: It is sometimes useful to brush the coat the wrong way before brushing and combing it back the correct way. This ensures a good, thorough, tangle-free coat.

PROCEDURE

Equipment needed: A good-quality bristle brush and a steel comb.

Breed tip: Lift the coat and groom in sections to be thorough and methodical.

- Brush through the body coat thoroughly, and follow this by combing through. Use the comb to groom the tail, skirts, feathering and ear fringes.

- A pet dog will need infrequent bathing as Tibetan Spaniels keep themselves very clean. A natural shampoo (such as tea tree and lavender oil) will help to bring the coat to a beautiful blossom. However, the dog's coat condition is very much dependent on the correct diet and exercise (see Chapter Two: The Healthy Coat). Dogs that are to be shown will normally be bathed the night before a show.

- Rinse the dog well.

- A conditioning cream can be used. However, use these products sparingly, as otherwise the soft, silky coat will become flyaway. Conditioning cream is not necessary if the correct diet and exercise routine are observed.

- Dry with a blower after toweling well (the blower should be introduced at the puppy stage; if the dog reacts badly, revert to thorough drying with towels).

- When dry, brush through the coat thoroughly, and then comb through for the finishing touch.

- Check underneath the feet and remove excessive hair, which may clog and become uncomfortable to walk on.

- Finally, remember to check the dog's nails, ears and teeth.

WELSH SPRINGER SPANIEL

COAT: The rich, dark-red coat on the white background is striking to say the least. The coat is straight or flat, silky in texture, dense and never wiry or wavy. The forelegs and hindlegs above the hocks are moderately feathered, and the ears and tail lightly feathered.

MAINTENANCE: Trimming should not

cause too many problems, as only light stripping or thinning is required. The look should appear natural, and only tufts of hair are removed, as with the Springer.

PROCEDURE

Equipment needed: Pin brush or slicker, and a medium-toothed comb.

Breed tip: Use a pin brush on the long hair, and a bristle brush on the short, body hair.

• Groom the coat with a pin, slicker or bristle brush, according to coat length (see above).

• Comb through to remove dead hair.

• Use thinning scissors to shorten the hair below the hock joint.

• Next, tidy the feet to a firm catlike appearance.

• Thin out any excessive hair on the dog's head to give a smooth appearance.

• Use thinning scissors to tidy any areas that look overdressed. It is vital that the dog appear trimmed, but has a natural look.

• Bathe the dog in a suitable shampoo (tea tree and lavender, or similar).

• Rinse thoroughly.

• Next, towel-dry the dog. Then, finish in warm air or a cage, or lightly blow-dry with the coat growth.

• Check the dog's nails, ears and teeth.

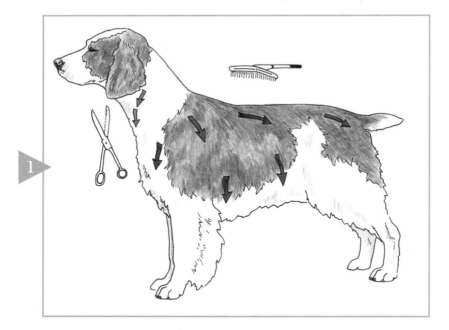

13 *SHORTHAIRED BREEDS*

SHORTHAIRED BREEDS FEATURED IN THIS SECTION:

GREYHOUND
- Affenpinscher
- Australian Cattle Dog
- Basenji
- Basset Fauve de Bretagne
- Basset Hound
- Beagle
- Beauceron
- Belgian Malinois and Laekenois
- Bloodhound
- Boston Terrier
- Boxer
- Bracco Italiano
- Bulldog
- Bullmastiff
- Bull Terrier
- Chesapeake Bay Retriever
- Chihuahua (Smooth Coat)
- Chinese Shar-Pei
- Collie (Smooth)
- Dachshund (Smooth and Wirehaired)
- Dalmatian
- Doberman Pinscher
- Foxhound (American and English)
- French Bulldog
- German Shorthaired Pointer
- Great Dane
- Hamiltonstövare
- Ibizan Hound
- Italian Greyhound
- Labrador
- Lancashire Heeler
- Manchester Terrier
- Manchester Terrier (Toy)
- Mastiff
- Miniature Pinscher
- Neapolitan Mastiff
- Pharaoh Hound
- Pointer
- Pug
- Rhodesian Ridgeback
- Rottweiler
- Sloughi
- Staffordshire Bull Terrier
- Swedish Vallhund
- Vizsla
- Weimaraner
- Welsh Corgi (Cardigan and Pembroke)
- Whippet

COAT CARE

One would think that this type of coat is the easiest to maintain. This is not necessarily true. Because the breeds molt, they must be groomed on a regular basis – otherwise their hair will get everywhere. Short, harsh, sticky hairs attach themselves to carpets, clothes, car seats, and so on, and are extremely obstinate about being dislodged.

The answer, or at least a great help in preventing this nuisance, is to brush regularly with a sisal or hound glove. You should also bathe the dog at hair-shedding time and remove much of the offending matter by scrubbing the jacket with the hound glove while the dog is in the bath.

As with all trimmed breeds, it is advisable to check whether the dog is going to be shown before tidying any hairs you may consider straggly, as the relevant breed standard may require it to be left natural. To keep a shorthaired dog looking fabulous, breeders run a stripping knife over the coat on a daily basis, and bathe them regularly. They usually allow a few days to pass before showing them to give time for the hair to settle.

GREYHOUND

Featured as an example for this group is the Greyhound Champion Porcelain of Springflite, owned by Martin Butler and Kevin Dodd.

COAT: The coat is fine and close. This breed comes in virtually every color of black, white, red, fawn, fallow, brindle or any of these colors broken with white.

MAINTENANCE: The coat is easy to maintain with a bristle brush and hound glove. It benefits from an occasional dust-over with chamois cloth.

PROCEDURE

Equipment needed: Hound glove, bristle brush, fine-toothed comb.

Breed tip: Brush with a hound glove while the coat is still wet to remove molting hairs more efficiently.

• The coat benefits from a thorough grooming with a hound glove to remove dead hair and to stimulate healthy growth. 1

• Bathe the dog in a 2 suitable shampoo, and rub the coat vigorously with the hound glove to remove molting and dead hair while the dog is in the bath. This will save a lot of molting hair from coming out onto the furniture later.

• Remove excess moisture with an absorbent towel 3 then finish off the drying process in warm air. 4

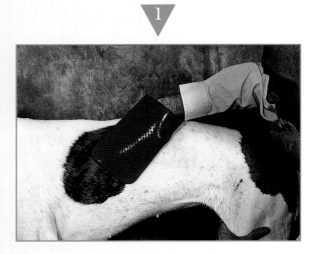

1

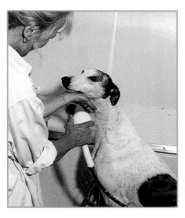

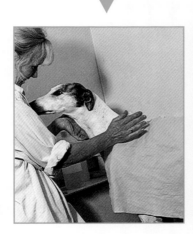

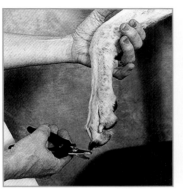

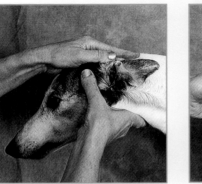

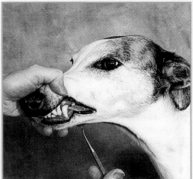

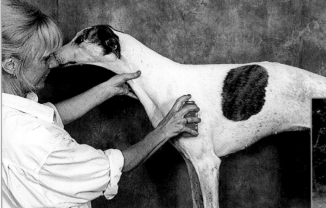

- Check the dog's nails ears and teeth.

- Finally, lightly spray the coat with a finishing conditioner and brush the dog with a polishing silky duster or pure bristle brush.

- The finished dog.

AFFENPINSCHER

COAT: The coat is harsh and rough-textured. The color is black, but gray shading is permissible.

According to the American Kennel Club, the standard is as follows:

"Dense, rough, harsh and about one inch in length on the shoulders and body. May be shorter on the rear and tail. Head, neck, chest, stomach and legs have longer, less harsh coat. The mature Affenpinscher has a mane or cape of strong hair which blends into the back coat at the withers area. The longer hair on the head, eyebrows and beard stands off and frames the face to emphasise the monkey-like expression. Hair on the ears is cut very short. A correct coat needs little grooming to blend the various lengths of hair to maintain a neat but shaggy appearance."

The KC, however, says:

"Correct coat needs no trimming, rough and harsh in texture, short and dense on some parts of the body and shaggy on others. In particular, longer on the shoulders, neck and head where loose shaggy hair stands away from the skull, framing eyes, nose and chin, giving the desired monkey-like appearance."

MAINTENANCE: Little coat care is required, but Affenpinschers should be combed on a regular basis to keep the coat in good condition.

Combing with a medium- or fine-toothed comb and then brushing with a nylon or bristle cushion hairbrush will remove loose hairs and keep the coat tidy and regular. A finer comb should be used on the face.

As the general appearance is somewhat shaggy, the pet dog can be left natural or trimmed to appear neat and smart, with the body coat thinned to give a smoother appearance.

The face is scissored to give a round shape when viewed from the front. The beard is left long for show purposes, but some pet owners like this cut shorter.

PROCEDURE

Equipment needed: A medium-toothed comb is required for general use, but you need a small, fine comb for the hair on the face, particularly around the eyes.

A small good-quality bristle nylon hairbrush (for ladies) is very good for Affenpinscher coats, but they tend to be expensive. Provided you do not let the dog chew them, they do last a very long time.

Breed tip: Don't attempt to make the dog too neat and tidy – a shaggy appearance is required.

In common with all breeds, make an effort to introduce grooming to the puppy from a young age. It is essential that they are taught that grooming is a pleasant experience. Grooming should also include general checks (i.e., teeth, nails and so on).

- Brush the coat with a slicker to remove dead hair.

- Comb the dog thoroughly, including the face furnishings.

- Use a finger and thumb to pluck out dead and loose hair, as the back half of the body should be "smoothed out." The shoulders should have longer hair, which forms the mane, the longer hair blending in to the smoother rump. Generally, frequent brushing suffices, and regularly tidying the hair will ensure the dog is kept looking perfect at all times.

- Bathe the dog in a natural shampoo and rinse thoroughly. A general coat-care conditioner that leaves a glorious gloss on both shorthaired and longhaired breeds, without leaving residue, can really enhance the appearance of these little dogs.

- Towel-dry and finish with a blow-dryer or cage-dryer.

- Check the dog's nails, ears and teeth.

- Use small, straight scissors or thinning scissors to trim the hair outside the ear leathers, from the base of the ear to the tip.

- The face is left quite natural (especially for the show ring), although some pet owners like the beard trimmed shorter.

- Shape down the chest and legs, and over the rump, with thinning scissors if required, blending the hair to give a natural look.

- Neaten under the tail hair.

- Affenpinscher feet should be neat like cat feet. If the feet get too hairy, they can look too big and flat. They should be neatened by trimming the excess hair from around the outside of the foot if necessary, so they do not look larger than they are. This is not essential for the pet dog, but it is for the show dog.

AFFABLE AFFENS

The following account is given by eminent breeders Wendy Boorer and the late Pat Patchen.

Most Affenpinscher coats require only the minimum amount of grooming to maintain a shaggy but neat appearance. The coat is rough and harsh in texture and needs little bathing. In particular, the dog should not be bathed before being shown, as this softens the coat. The hair is shorter and denser on the body, rear and tail, while being longer and shaggier on the head, neck, chest, stomach and legs.

The correct coat needs no trimming but Affenpinschers' natural coats do vary a great deal, from too short to too long, from very harsh to quite soft, and from straight to varying degrees of wavy. It is therefore necessary to concentrate on the overall outline when you are grooming, and always to keep in mind the end result you are trying to achieve – to enhance the monkeylike urchin look. Coats which show evidence of trimming (other than ears and tail) must be penalized as incorrect in the show ring.

HEAD

The monkey face of the Affenpinscher is enhanced by a wreath of loose, shaggy hair standing away from the skull and framing the eyes, nose and chin. If the owner prefers a slightly less shaggy appearance, the hair should be combed forwards all around the head from behind the ears, and then trimmed into a circle

The monkey-type head is typical of the breed.

before being brushed back. Hair on the ears should be smooth and trimmed close to the edges.

BODY

Hair should be longer on the shoulders than on the flanks, and dead hair can easily be removed with a fine-toothed comb or a stripping knife. Too long or too profuse a coat on the chest or the flanks can be thinned and shortened, remembering that the length of coat from the longer hair on the shoulders to the rather shorter hair on the hindquarters should be blended in for the neat but shaggy look.

LEGS AND FEET

The hair on the legs is longer at the top and feathery in appearance, but rarely needs tidying. The feet should be small, round and compact. On the correctly shaped foot, and where the dog has enough freedom, the nails should not need cutting until the dog's old age.

TAIL

Many tails, if left natural, resemble Christmas trees, and some pet owners like them like that. However, for the show ring, the tail should resemble a cigar; this is achieved by holding the tail up and combing the hair backwards before shaping. The tip should be slightly rounded and all the straggly ends cut off the tail hair with the scissors pointing downwards.

NOTE!

The Affenpinscher is a natural breed, with the correct coat needing little attention, other than ordinary brushing and combing.

AUSTRALIAN CATTLE DOG

COAT: The coat is smooth, double with a short, dense undercoat. The close topcoat is hard, straight and weather-resistant. Under the body and behind the legs, the coat becomes longer to form mild breeching near the thighs. The coat is short on the head, the front of the legs and the feet. It is thicker and longer on the neck. The color is blue, blue mottled or blue speckled, with or without other markings. Red speckled is also acceptable.

MAINTENANCE: The coat is easy to maintain, with only regular brushing required and combing to remove dead hairs.

PROCEDURE

Equipment needed: Bristle brush, comb.

Breed tip: The coat is longer underneath the body and behind the legs, so pay particular attention to these areas when brushing.

- Brush the coat thoroughly with a bristle brush.

- Next, use a medium-toothed metal comb to remove dead hairs.

- Bathe the dog in a pH-balanced or natural shampoo when necessary. Most show dogs are bathed only occasionally (once or twice a year) – a rub-over with a wet chamois before a show is usually all that is required.

- If you are a professional groomer, towel-dry and blow excess water from the coat with a power dryer if you have one. Finish drying the dog in warm air or with a blow-dryer, at the same time brushing the coat with a bristle brush.

- For nonprofessional groomers (pet and show dog owners) simply towel-drying and brushing the coat should suffice.

- Check the dog's nails, ears and teeth.

- Check between and underneath the toes, and trim unwanted hair.

- Show dogs should be presented naturally and do not require trimming.

BASENJI

COAT: The coat is short, sleek, close and fine.

The color is black and white; red and white; black, tan and white with tan spots over each eye ("melon pips") and mask; black; brindle (clear, red stripes on a black background); and tan and white. The white should be on the feet, chest and tail tips; white legs, blaze and white collar are optional. The tail is high-set and distinctively curled tightly over spine.

MAINTENANCE: The coat is easy to maintain with regular brushing with a sisal brush, bristle brush and hound glove.

PROCEDURE

Equipment needed: Hound glove, sisal brush, fine-toothed comb.

Breed tip: Use a hound glove to remove dead hairs when the dog is shedding.

- Brush with a hound glove or sisal brush, or both, to remove loose hair.

- Use a coat conditioner, such as lanolin, distributing it with the palm of your hands. Alternatively, use a spray conditioner for the purpose of enhancing the coat shine.

- Wash the coat two or three times a year with a protein shampoo or purifying shampoo, or both, and its complementary conditioner.

- Dry with an absorbent towel and cage-dry or lightly blow-dry.

- Check the dog's nails, ears and teeth.

- Give a final dressing with a cloth or sisal.

BASSET FAUVE DE BRETAGNE

COAT: The coat is wiry in texture, dense and flat. It should never be woolly, but may become so if clipped.

The Basset Fauve de Bretagne color is fawn, gold-wheaten or red-wheaten, and a white spot on the chest is permissible.

MAINTENANCE: The coat is easily maintained with a bristle brush and a hound glove for regular brushing a couple of times a week.

A pin brush or slicker brush will remove any extra hairs that are not required.

PROCEDURE

Equipment needed: Bristle brush, medium-toothed comb.

Breed tip: As this dog likes nothing more than exploring down holes for rabbits, it will need regular brushing with a bristle brush to keep it clean.

- Brush the coat thoroughly using a pin brush or a curry brush, taking care not to scrape the close hair parts. Use a hound glove to finish.

- Bathe the dog in a suitable shampoo to aid coat texture.

- Apply a rub-in or a spray conditioner if necessary.

- Cage- or blow-dry after removing the excess moisture from the coat with an absorbent towel.

- Remember to check the Basset's nails, ears and teeth.

- Give the dog a final brushover using a hound glove or chamois cloth. This will add a nice sheen to the coat.

BASSET HOUND

COAT: The coat is smooth, short and close, without being too fine. The outline is clean and free from feathering. The color is generally black, white and tan, or lemon and white, but any hound color is acceptable.

MAINTENANCE: This is a breed that is a regular and favorite in the grooming salon because it relishes the attention shown to it and enjoys looking spruce. Easy to maintain with regular brushing.

PROCEDURE

Equipment needed: Hound glove, bristle brush, fine-toothed comb.

Breed tip: Check the dog's wrinkles regularly to make sure the folded skin is clean and healthy.

- Brush the coat with a hound glove. Where the dog is molting, use a curry brush followed by a hound glove to remove any dead hairs.

- Bathe in a coat-protecting or protein shampoo, using white-enhancing shampoo on the white parts of the coat.

- Spray conditioner can be applied where necessary, or a lanolin conditioner can be applied with the hand.

- Cage- or blow-dry, after using a super-absorbent towel.

- Check the dog's nails, ears and teeth

- Finally, check the wrinkles to ensure they are free from wet patches or soreness.

BEAGLE

COAT: Very smart, the coat is short, dense and waterproof. The color is any recognized hound color other than liver. The tip of the stern is white.

MAINTENANCE: Maintenance is easy and requires daily brushing with a bristle brush and a hound glove. For a final shine, use a chamois cloth.

PROCEDURE

Equipment needed: Hound glove, bristle brush, fine-toothed comb.

Breed tip: Use a hound glove after bathing to remove loose hair.

- Brush the coat with a bristle brush, or lightly work through the coat with the hound glove to remove dead hair and to stimulate the skin.

- When required, bathe the Beagle in a suitable shampoo, using a superwhitening shampoo on white areas for extra brilliance.

- The body can be vigorously rubbed with the hound glove while in the bath to remove molting hairs.

- Use conditioner where required to heighten color and give a healthy gleam.

- Cage- or blow-dry after absorbing most of the moisture with a towel. Do not allow the dog to get cold.

- Check nails, ears and teeth weekly.

- Finally, brush all over with a hound glove or chamois cloth.

BEAUCERON

COAT: It comes in black and tan markings, or in a harlequin pattern where the base color is gray with black and rust torn patches.

MAINTENANCE: The Beauceron's coat is relatively easy to maintain, with regular brushing enhancing the natural, healthy appearance.

PROCEDURE

Equipment needed: Slicker brush, medium-toothed comb.

Breed tip: Brushing from an early age is essential to get the Beauceron acclimatized to handling.

- Brush through the coat thoroughly with a slicker brush to remove dead hair.

- Bathe in a natural coat-enhancing shampoo and rinse well.

- Towel-dry and finish with warm air, or a light blower.

- Check the dog's nails, ears and teeth, particularly the double hind dewclaws.

- Brush over with a hound glove or a cloth.

Belgian Malinois

Laekenois

BELGIAN MALINOIS AND LAEKENOIS

COAT: The Laekenois has a short, wiry coat; the Belgian Malinois coat is short with a firm texture. All varieties (see pages 110–111 for Belgian Sheepdog and Belgian Tervuren) have double-textured coats, with a harsh outer coat and a dense undercoat.

MAINTENANCE: Requires brushing at least once a week. Mature males tend to molt with the weather, but bitches lose their coats very dramatically about three months after their season. Regrowth takes about two months. Puppies have a thicker, bigger coat than adults; they lose it at about a year old.

PROCEDURE

Equipment needed: Slicker brush and a good-quality comb.

Breed tip: Needs regular brushing to remove any postwalk debris.

• Use a slicker to brush through the coat, after spraying lightly with a conditioner to protect the hair and to encourage growth. The coat should always be brushed when damp, not when dry. Misting with water is fine if no conditioner is available, and indeed is the correct thing to use for show preparation (as water is the only substance that is permitted).

• The coat should be brushed up the wrong way and then brushed right down to the roots with the slicker. Work in sections to take the coat back the right way again, paying particular attention to the trousers.

• Where the undercoat needs removing, use a rake or a twisting-teeth comb.

• Use a molting comb to remove dead hairs.

• If the dog is neutered, the coat needs a lot more attention. Daily attention is needed for neutered dogs, using a twisting-teeth comb, particularly on the rump, flanks and back legs.

• Bathing is rarely necessary. If the dog is muddy, remove the worst with a bucket of cold water and a sponge or a garden hose set at a gentle pressure. Dry the dog with an old towel and then, when nearly completely dry, gently brush out any remaining mud. The coat readily loses mud by using this method.

• Check the dog's nails, ears and teeth.

• If necessary, scissor out any excess hair and any build-up of debris under the dog's feet.

• Apply a light application of coat-enhancer.

• Note: the show dog may need a few days for the coat to settle after bathing.

BLOODHOUND

COAT: The smooth coat is short and weatherproof.

MAINTENANCE: Coat maintenance is light, requiring only regular brushing.

PROCEDURE

Equipment needed: Hound glove, bristle brush, fine-toothed comb.

Breed tip: Check the ears, eyes and facial folds every day.

- Brush the dog with a hound glove or a bristle brush to remove dead hair.

- When necessary, bathe the dog in a good-quality shampoo.

- Facial folds must be checked to ensure they are completely dry and free from soreness. Apply a skin treatment recommended by your vet or dog's breeder where soreness is obvious.

- Use a rough towel to dry the coat. No other form of drying is necessary.

- Check the dog's nails, ears and teeth.

- Coat-conditioning spray can be applied for a final finish, but should not be used for show dogs.

BOSTON TERRIER

COAT: The coat is short, smooth, lustrous and fine in texture. The color is brindle with white markings, or black with white markings. The white parts, such as the blaze over head, collar, breast, part or whole of forelegs, and hindlegs below hocks, look more defined when washed, and a bath and groom turns this dog into an attractive eye-catcher.

MAINTENANCE: It is easy to care for, but requires regular brushing with a bristle brush and hound glove.

PROCEDURE

Equipment needed: Hound glove, bristle brush, fine-toothed comb.

Breed tip: A good-quality dog shampoo will make the white patches sparkle.

- Brush through the entire coat thoroughly, using a bristle brush.

- Bathe with a good pH-alkaline shampoo.

- A vigorous rub with a hound glove, while in the bath, will remove a lot of dead hairs.

- Wrinkles or folds beneath the eyes should be cleaned and thoroughly dried.

- After rinsing, apply a light spray of conditioning gloss.

- Cage-dry the dog.

- Check that all the wrinkles are dry, and add a little powder.

- Finally, check the dog's nails, ears and teeth.

BOXER

COAT: The color is fawn, which varies from dark deer-red to light fawn; or brindle (i.e., black stripes on fawn shades). White markings should not exceed one-third of the ground color.

MAINTENANCE: Easy to maintain, the coat is short, glossy, smooth and tight to the body, and will look quite outstanding with a little application.

PROCEDURE

Equipment needed: Rubber curry and hound glove.

Breed tip: Puppyish and playful, most Boxers are a joy to groom – though they can be quite a handful!

- Brush the entire coat with a rubber curry and a hound glove.

- Bathe the dog in a good-quality shampoo and give extra sparkle to white parts with blue-rinse or superwhite.

- Use a hound glove vigorously while the dog is wet in order to remove molting or dead hair.

- Dry the coat with absorbent towels and finish in warm air or a cage.

- Check the Boxer's nails, ears and teeth.

- Spray the coat with a coat-gloss conditioner.

BRACCO ITALIANO

COAT: The coat is glossy, fine, dense and short. The color is a most attractive orange and white, orange roan, chestnut and white, or chestnut roan. The only solid color allowed is white. The size is up to 26 inches (65 cm).

MAINTENANCE: The coat is easy to clean.

PROCEDURE

Equipment needed: Hound glove, bristle brush, fine-toothed comb.

Breed tip: Don't bathe too frequently, or you can ruin the glossy coat.

- Brush regularly with a bristle brush and hound glove.

- Not regularly bathed, a natural shampoo should be used. Make sure you rinse well.

- Towel-dry the coat, and finish with warm air.

- Brush over the coat with a glove or a cloth.

- Check the dog's nails, ears and teeth.

BULLDOG

COAT: The coat is of fine texture, short, close and smooth, not wiry.

The Bulldog comes in various colors, including whole or smut (whole color with black muzzle) brindle; red in various shades; fawn; and fallow.

MAINTENANCE: The Bulldog is a breed that is easy to maintain with a bristle brush and hound glove.

PROCEDURE

Equipment needed: You will need a hound glove, a bristle brush and a fine-toothed comb.

Breed tip: Don't be fooled by their looks – the majority of Bulldogs are incredibly friendly, lovely dogs.

- Brush with a bristle brush or a hound glove, or both.

- Bathe the Bulldog in a protein shampoo, being careful to clean and then thoroughly dry the folds of the skin around the face, the legs and the body.

- Rinse thoroughly.

- Check the dog's feet for sores.

- Use a hound glove while the dog is still in the bath to remove dead hairs.

- Blow- or cage-dry.

- Powder the folds of the skin.

- Check the nails, ears and teeth.

- Brush a light spray of coat-enhancing or protein conditioner into the coat.

BULLMASTIFF

COAT: The Bullmastiff coat is short, hard and weather-resistant, lying flat to the body.

The Bullmastiff colors include any shade of brindle, fawn or red, and the color is pure and clear.

In accordance with the breed standard, a slight white marking on the chest is permissible but not desirable. The characteristic black muzzle, however, is essential.

MAINTENANCE: The Bullmastiff coat is generally easy to maintain.

However, as always with shorthaired breeds, the Bullmastiff will benefit from brushing and an occasional good bath – if you can get the dog in it!

PROCEDURE

Equipment needed: Hound glove, bristle brush, fine-toothed comb.

Breed tip: Start the grooming routine early, while the dog is still a puppy. An adult Bullmastiff unused to grooming can become too big and difficult to handle.

- Brush the coat very vigorously with a bristle brush or hound glove.

- Bathe in a suitable natural-ingredient shampoo, rinsing well.

- Towel-dry, and then dry the dog with warm air, in a cage-dryer or with a blow-dryer for a few minutes.

- Don't forget to check the Bullmastiff's nails, ears and teeth.

BULL TERRIER

COAT: The coat is short, flat, even and harsh to the touch with a fine gloss. A soft undercoat may be present in winter.

MAINTENANCE: Needs little maintenance, but adores a brushing with the bristle brush or hound glove.

PROCEDURE

Equipment needed: Hound glove, bristle brush, fine-toothed comb.

Breed tip: Many Bull Terriers are like powerful puppies – playful but strong! If the dog isn't well trained, bathtimes can be a two-person job.

- Brush the coat through.

- Next, bathe in a suitable shampoo and rinse thoroughly.

- Towel-dry well, and then air-, cage- or blow-dry the dog.

- Spray on a little conditioner to give the coat extra shine.

- Check the dog's nails, ears and teeth.

CHESAPEAKE BAY RETRIEVER

COAT: The Chesapeake coat is oily, thick and waterproof.

MAINTENANCE: Grooming is easy and elementary. The coat is best groomed with a stiff brush and a chamois cloth.

PROCEDURE

Equipment needed: Short-toothed zoom groom (rubber-type palm-held brush, which is very effective at removing loose hair), medium-toothed comb and a chamois cloth.

Breed tip: Just try to keep this dog out of the water if you can!

- Brush the entire coat.

- Bathe the Chesapeake in a suitable shampoo that does not strip too much oil from the coat. Only bathe if absolutely necessary, as excessive bathing can ruin the waterproof coat.

- After rinsing thoroughly, towel-dry the coat with a superabsorbent towel. Alternatively, you can use a chamois cloth to remove the excess moisture.

- Finish off by drying the Chesapeake with warm air.

- Check the dog's nails, ears and teeth (see pages 50–52).

CHIHUAHUA (SMOOTH COAT)

COAT: With the Smooth Coat, the hair should have a soft texture, close and glossy, with an undercoat and ruff permissible. The color is any mixture.

MAINTENANCE: Easy to maintain with weekly brushing.

PROCEDURE

Equipment needed: Cushioned bristle brush, medium-toothed comb.
   See page 115 for details of the Long Coat Chihuahua.

Breed tip: A companion breed, the Chihuahua loves the attention of being groomed.

- Brush through the entire coat with a natural bristle brush.

- Bathe the Chihuahua in a suitable shampoo, such as natural tea tree and lavender oil. Unless they get very dirty, a bath every three months should suffice.

- Rinse well, ensuring all the soap has been removed.

- Condition the coat with a coat-enhancing cream.

- Check the dog's nails (they should be moderately short)

- Also check the dog's ears and teeth.

- Use a chamois cloth to bring the coat up to shine.

CHINESE SHAR-PEI

COAT: The coat is extremely harsh, straight and offstanding on the body, but flatter on the limbs. There is no undercoat. The length varies from short and bristly (under $^1/_2$ inch/ 1.25 cm) to longer and thicker ($^1/_2$ inch to 1 inch/1.25 to 2.5 cm), but still offstanding and harsh to the touch.

All solid colors (except white) are acceptable. Frequently shaded with lighter color on the tail and backs of the thighs.

MAINTENANCE: No trimming is required and bathe infrequently. Care must be taken with the ears and nails.

PROCEDURE

Equipment needed: Rubber grooming mitt, stripping comb (e.g., Mars 628), large nail file.

Breed tip: Hot-spots on the coat can be treated with "flowers of sulfur" powder.

- Brush the coat with a rubber grooming mitt to remove dead hair, especially during molt.

- Bathe infrequently with a suitable shampoo.

- Rinse carefully, making sure that all the shampoo has been removed from the folds or wrinkles.

- Towel-dry.

- Check the dog's nails, teeth and ears (avoid probing too deeply with cotton swabs).

- Check the folds and wrinkled skin to ensure they are dry.

COLLIE (SMOOTH)

COAT: The Smooth Collie's short outercoat is water-resistant and the dense, warmer undercoat makes it totally weatherproof.

The color in this breed is frequently seen as blue merle, as opposed to the other two more frequently seen colors of the Rough Collie, which are sable and white, and tricolor.

MAINTENANCE: The Smooth Collie will easily be looked after with the minimum of fuss, only requiring a rub-down with a damp chamois cloth to turn it back into a clean, comfortable pet, even after a run in the muddiest weather. A weekly groom with a Mason Pearson type of bristle brush will remove all hair and debris, and the Smooth, which is noted for its fastidious cleanliness, will do the rest.

The Collie's coat casts twice a year and a firm daily brushing at this time is essential for two to three weeks to remove all the dead hair.

PROCEDURE

Equipment needed: Bristle brush, medium-toothed comb, natural shampoo and a complementary conditioner.

Breed tip: Trimming is not required, but the area under the feet may need attention. Trim away the long hair to prevent a buildup of debris, which will otherwise cause discomfort when it walks.

- Brush through the coat with a bristle brush to remove dead hair. Comb through with a medium- or fine-toothed comb.

- Bathe in a natural-ingredient shampoo and apply a good-quality conditioner for a sumptuous finish.

- A purifying mask and conditioner can be used on certain occasions to enhance the coat condition.

- Dry the coat with an absorbent towel and finish in warm air.

- Check the dog's nails. If necessary, the Smooth Collie's nails can be filed with a large workshop file.

- Also check the dog's ears and teeth.

- Brush over the coat once again with a bristle brush and a cloth.

- Check under the feet and remove any excess hair with scissors.

DACHSHUND (SMOOTH AND WIREHAIRED)

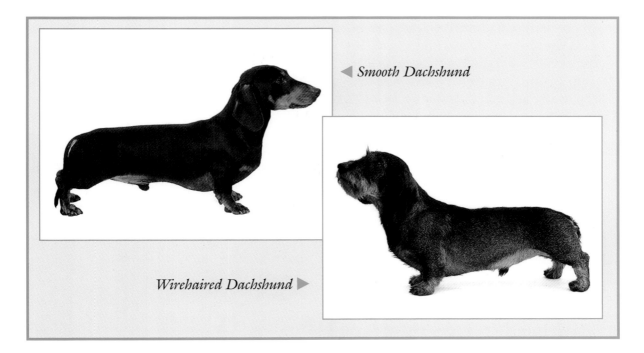

◀ *Smooth Dachshund*

Wirehaired Dachshund ▶

COAT: Smooth: dense, short coat. Wirehaired: short, straight, harsh hair, with a dense undercoat, bearded chin and bushy eyebrows. The color is variable, but dapples should be evenly marked all over, and no white is permissible. There is red, black and tan, chocolate, and dapple. See page 116 for details of the Longhaired Dachshund.

MAINTENANCE: The Smooth coat needs no maintenance other than a brush with a soft-bristled brush and a polish with a chamois cloth.

The Wirehaired variety is generally stripped twice a year. The wire coat consists of three types:

• The ideal pin-wire coat consists of a harsh topcoat with a soft, dense undercoat. It appears so flat that, from a distance, the dog has the appearance of a Smooth Dachshund, apart from some harsh whiskers and bushy eyebrows. This coat needs little attention, other than perhaps some tidying and thinning out on the neck with finger and thumb or by using a stripping knife about two weeks before a show.

• The more usual type of wire coat also consists of a double layer, but the top hair is more profuse and there will also be more beard, eyebrows and leg furnishings. This type of coat will need stripping with a stripping knife probably twice a year to keep it tidy, and certainly quite a lot of preparation and maintenance for show condition to give the desired smooth outline.

At least a month before a show, the hair on the neck, chest and back should be stripped right down, using a stripping knife, but only experience can be the guide to the time it takes for the new hair to grow through.

The hair under the dog must be tidy and the hair on the head should be neat and flat. Any long hair under the eyes and ears should be removed. The beard should be combed forward, and the hair behind it stripped flat. It is safer to use finger and thumb on the head area. Long hairs under the tail should be removed and just enough left at the end to cover the tip to a neat point. The hair around the Dachshund's feet should be trimmed, and the hair from the front of the forelegs should be removed. Strip away all the hair from the hocks to give a good, clean shape to the hindlegs.

• The softcoated Dachshund can be kept tidy only by stripping. Unfortunately, however, it can never be disguised. The hair on the legs, head and ears is always soft, and the harsh, even coat of the correct wirecoated Dachshund is completely lacking.

PROCEDURE

Equipment needed: Bristle brush, medium-toothed comb, stripping knife.

Breed tip: These hounds love following their noses, going down holes and sniffing in the undergrowth, and always end up with a great deal of the countryside in their coat! A quick brush at the end of every walk is highly recommended.

• Brush through the entire coat. A bristle brush or a sisal brush is the best choice for use on the Smooth and Wirehaired coat.

• Using finger and thumb, strip the Wire when required.

• Check for mats by combing through the coat with a medium-toothed comb.

- Dachshunds all benefit from an occasional bath, using a good dog shampoo. Rinse thoroughly, and dry with a blower or in warm air. For the Wirehaired coat, bathe the dog at least a week before a show, and several days beforehand for the Smooth, to allow enough time for the coat's natural oils to be replenished.

- Check the Dachshund's nails. Nails should be regularly trimmed for both show and pet dogs, and this must be done with great care since the quick (the nerves and blood supply) cannot be seen.

- The ears can be wiped with cotton batting, and the teeth should be kept clean by regular brushing.

- Add sparkle to the dog's coat by lightly spraying (or applying with your hand) some coat-finish lanolin. Of course, if you are showing your dog, no substances can be added to the coat.

DALMATIAN

COAT: The coat is short, hard, dense and glossy in appearance.

MAINTENANCE: The Dalmatian's coat benefits from regular grooming, as plenty of hair comes out during molting periods. I once had a car that previously belonged to the owner of a Dalmatian. I had it two years and never did get rid of all the hairs stuck in the rear carpets (and it wasn't from lack of trying)!

PROCEDURE

Equipment needed: Hound glove, bristle brush.

Breed tip: When the Dalmatian is being bathed, rub the go vigorously to remove dead and molting hairs, which like to stick everywhere.

- Bathe the Dalmatian in a suitable natural shampoo.

- Rinse thoroughly, ensuring all the suds are removed.

- Rub vigorously with a rubber brush or hound glove while the dog is in the bath, to remove dead or molting hairs.

- Towel-dry the coat.

- Check the dog's nails, ears and teeth.

- Brush with a hound glove or natural bristle brush, and go over the coat one final time with a chamois cloth.

DOBERMAN PINSCHER

COAT: The coat is smooth, short, harsh, thick and close-lying. The color is definite black, brown, blue or fawn, with rust red markings.

MAINTENANCE: Benefits from regular grooming with a sisal brush and hound glove.

PROCEDURE

Equipment needed: Hound glove, bristle brush, fine-toothed comb, chamois cloth.

Breed tip: A final rub-down with a chamois cloth will produce a polished finish.

- Brush daily with a rubber mitten to remove dead hairs.

- Bathe in a suitable natural shampoo only a couple of times a year, unless it falls or rolls in something obnoxious. Wipe over with a damp cloth (no soap) once a week or as necessary.

- Vigorously rub the dog with a hound glove while it is damp.

- For that extra sparkle, apply baby oil or

coconut oil (though this should not be used for the show ring).

- Towel-dry any excess water from the coat.

- Check nails, ears and teeth once a week.

FOXHOUND (AMERICAN AND ENGLISH)

COAT: Short, dense and waterproof.

MAINTENANCE: This coat is easy to maintain even for the show ring.

PROCEDURE

Equipment needed: Hound glove, fine-toothed comb.

Breed tip: Demandingly energetic, so be warned!

- Brush through the coat with a hound glove on a regular basis.

- If bathing for the show ring, use a natural-ingredient shampoo, and, if required, replace the natural oils with a suitable light, oily conditioner.

- Towel-dry and finish in warm air.

- Check the dog's nails, ears and teeth regularly.

- Brush with a cloth/glove to enhance the coat.

- For the show ring, a mink-oil spray and a rubdown with a chamois enhances the coat color and gives a good shine to the coat.

FRENCH BULLDOG

COAT: The coat is fine, smooth, lustrous, short and close.

The colors available include brindle, pied and fawn.

MAINTENANCE: Brush the French Bulldog's coat regularly using a bristle brush and a hound glove.

Particular attention must be paid to its "bat" ears, facial wrinkles and the base of its tail. These areas must be kept thoroughly clean.

PROCEDURE

Equipment needed: Bristle brush, hound glove, fine-toothed comb.

Breed tip: Smoothing the coat with a silk cloth gives a professional touch.

- Brush through the entire coat with a hound glove.

- Bathe in a suitable natural shampoo, and rinse.

- Cage-dry or blow-dry after using absorbent towels.

- Check the dog's nails, ears and teeth on a regular basis.

- Lightly spray or rub in lanolin conditioner for that added sparkle.

- Finally, go over the entire coat with a silk cloth.

GERMAN SHORTHAIRED POINTER

COAT: The German Shorthaired Pointer's coat is short and thick. It is somewhat longer on the underside of the tail and the back edges of the haunches, and softer, thinner and shorter on the ears and head. Some pet dogs have a longer coat, but this is not desirable in the show ring.

MAINTENANCE: Maintenance is easy with regular brushing with a bristle brush or a hound glove.

PROCEDURE

Equipment needed: Bristle brush, hound glove.

Breed tip: Using the hound glove while the dog's coat is still wet will remove excess shedding hair.

- Brush through the entire coat with a bristle brush or hound glove to remove dead hairs and dust.

- Bathe the dog in a purifying shampoo, followed by a suitable mask or conditioner to enhance the coat's sheen, and rinse thoroughly.

- Vigorously use a hound glove while the coat is still wet to remove excess molting hair.

- Dry with absorbent towels, and finish in a cage or with a blower.

- Check the dog's nails, ears and teeth.

- Go over the coat one last time with a cloth or a bristle brush.

GREAT DANE

COAT: The coat is short, dense and sleek-looking, never inclined to roughness. The colors include the following:
- Brindle: a striped coat. The ground-color from the lightest buff to the deepest orange, the stripes are always black.
- Fawn: various shades from lightest buff to deepest orange, dark shading on head and ears acceptable
- Blue: varying in shade from light gray to

deep slate. The nose may be blue.
- Black: obviously, all black.
- Harlequin: a pure white underground, with (preferably) all black or all blue patches, having the appearance of being torn.

MAINTENANCE: Easy and clean by habit and the short coat is easy to maintain.

PROCEDURE

Equipment needed: Hound glove, bristle brush, fine-toothed comb.

Breed tip: Unless your bath is at ground level or you can walk the dog in along a ramp, you will need help to lift it in.

- Brush the dog with a bristle brush or a hound glove.

- Bathe in a suitable shampoo, making sure the coat is rinsed thoroughly.

- Towel-dry and finish in warm air.

- Check the nails, ears and teeth.

HAMILTONSTÖVARE

COAT: The Hamiltonstövare is double-coated. The undercoat is short, close and soft, and is especially thick during winter. The upper coat is strongly weather-resistant and lies close to the body.

This dog is richly colored in black, tan and white.

MAINTENANCE: This is an easy breed to maintain.

PROCEDURE

Equipment needed: Hound glove, bristle brush, fine-toothed comb.

Breed tip: Use the hound glove in a vigorous round action to remove dead or molting hairs.

- Brush through the coat with a bristle brush or a hound glove.

- Bathe the dog in a natural, mild shampoo when necessary.

- Rinse thoroughly.

- Remove excess moisture from the coat with an absorbent towel.

- Finish the drying process by putting the dog in warm air or a cage-dryer, or use a blower.

- Check the dog's nails, ears and teeth regularly.

IBIZAN HOUND

Smooth-coated (left) and rough-coated (right) Ibizan Hounds.

COAT: Whether smooth or rough, the coat is always hard, close and dense. It is longer under the tail and at the back of the legs.

The Ibizan Hound color is white, chestnut or lion solid color, or any combination of these.

MAINTENANCE: The coat is easy to maintain, requiring only a weekly brush.

PROCEDURE

Equipment needed: You will need a good-quality hound glove and a bristle brush.

Breed tip: To give the coat a nice sheen, give a final polish with a glove or a velvet cloth after brushing.

- Brush on a regular basis with a bristle brush and a hound glove.

- The dog should need a bath only for the show ring – in which case, use a natural-ingredient shampoo.

- Towel-dry the coat, and finish in warm air.

- Check the dog's nails, ears and teeth.

ITALIAN GREYHOUND

COAT: The hair is short, fine and glossy. The color is black, blue, cream, fawn, red or white, or these colors broken with white.

MAINTENANCE: The coat is easily taken care of by regular, daily attention with a velvet pad or a piece of silk.

PROCEDURE

Equipment needed: Hound glove, velvet glove or pad.

Breed tip: Looks wonderful when groomed daily with a velvet pad.

- Bathe the dog in a good-quality protein shampoo.

- Use a purifying shampoo and mask on occasions, or a conditioner to enhance the gleam of the coat.

- Cage- or blow-dry.

- Check the dog's nails, ears and teeth.

- Go over the entire coat with a velvet pad or a piece of silk.

LABRADOR RETRIEVER

COAT: This gentleman of a dog has a distinctive coat, which is short, dense and without wave or featherings. It has a hard feel to the touch and a weather-resistant undercoat.

The Labrador colors are wholly black, yellow or liver/chocolate. The yellow color ranges from light cream to red fox. Small white spots on the chest are permissible.

MAINTENANCE: This breed is easy to look after with regular brushing and loves a good bath.

PROCEDURE

Equipment needed: Bristle brush, medium-toothed comb.

Breed tip: Generally, a twice-yearly bath should be sufficient.

- Work through the entire coat with a bristle brush.

- Bathe the Lab in a suitable natural shampoo, such as tea tree and lavender.

- Rinse thoroughly, taking care to remove all the soap.

- Soak up the excess moisture with towels.

- Finish drying the dog in warm air or a cage-dryer, or with a hair-dryer.

- Check the Labrador Retriever's nails, ears and teeth.

- Finally, for pet dogs, lightly spray the coat with an enhancing conditioner for that extra finish. Remember that this is not permissible in show dogs.

LANCASHIRE HEELER

COAT: The coat is short, and consists of a fine undercoat covered by a short, thick, hard, flat topcoat. The topcoat is slightly longer on the neck. The undercoat should not show through the topcoat nor allow any longer hair at the mane to stand off. The mane may be noticeable in the winter.

MAINTENANCE: The coat is easy to maintain, requiring little more than a chamois cloth and a quick brush.

Equipment needed: Bristle brush, medium-toothed comb.

Breed tip: Polish with a cloth for the show ring to enhance the natural gleam of the coat.

- Brush the entire coat with a bristle brush.

- Comb through with a medium- to fine-toothed comb to remove dead hairs.

- Bathe the dog in a natural-ingredient shampoo, such as tea tree and lavender oil.

- Towel-dry and finish with warm air, cage or gentle blower.

- Check the nails, ears and teeth.

- Brush over with a bristle brush and chamois cloth to finish.

MANCHESTER TERRIER

COAT: It has a short, close, smooth, glossy coat of firm texture. The color is jet black and rich mahogany tan.

MAINTENANCE: Easy.

PROCEDURE

Equipment needed: Hound glove and a bristle brush.

Breed tip: The Manchester Terrier's smooth, glossy coat will benefit from a polish with a cloth.

- Brush through the coat with a hound glove or bristle brush.

- Bathe in a natural shampoo to enhance the coat gleam.

- Rinse well.

- Towel-dry and finish by leaving the dog in warm air or a cage-dryer, or gently blow-dry.

- Check the nails, ears and teeth.

- Brush over and use a cloth or a velvet pad to enhance the quality of the finish.

MANCHESTER TERRIER (TOY)

COAT: Known as the English Toy Terrier in the U.K., this breed has a short, glossy coat and is well balanced, elegant and compact, sleek and cleanly built.

The coat is thick and glossy, with a density of short hair required.

MAINTENANCE: Regular brushing with a hound glove and bristle brush will keep the coat in tip-top condition.

PROCEDURE

Equipment needed: Hound glove, bristle brush, fine-toothed comb.

Breed tip: Use the hound glove while the Manchester Toy Terrier is still wet. This will help to remove excess dead hair.

- Brush through the entire coat with a hound glove.

- Bathe the dog in a natural shampoo.

- Rinse thoroughly, ensuring you have removed all the suds.

- When the dog is molting, a hound glove can be used in the bath to remove any excess dead hair.

- Use conditioner, if required, to enhance the shine.

- Towel-dry, and finish in warm air, a cage or with a light blow.

- Don't forget to check the dog's nails, ears and teeth.

- Finally, brush over the coat once again with a bristle brush, a hound glove or with velvet cloths.

MASTIFF

COAT: The Mastiff's coat is short and close-lying, but not too fine over the shoulders, the neck and the back. The color is apricot-fawn, silver-fawn, fawn or dark-fawn brindle. Muzzle, ears and nose are black.

MAINTENANCE: This breed needs regular brushing with a bristle brush and a hound glove to keep the coat in good condition. It also benefits from a good bath – if you can get the dog in it!

PROCEDURE

Equipment needed: Hound glove and a bristle brush.

Breed tip: The Mastiff is renowned for its slobber, and you will need to pay this frequent attention.

- Thoroughly brush the coat to remove dead and molting hairs.

- Bathe the dog in a suitable, good-quality protein shampoo.

- While the coat is wet, groom the Mastiff with a hound glove to encourage the removal of dead hairs.

- Rinse thoroughly.

- Use a coat-nourishing conditioner, and rinse well.

- Dry thoroughly with superabsorbent toweling.

- Remember to check the dog's nails, ears and teeth.

- Give a final brush with a hound glove or bristle brush.

MINIATURE PINSCHER

COAT: The Min Pin coat is smooth, hard and short, as well as straight and lustrous, and is close to the body.

Color: there are various colors, including solid clear red of various shades, black, chocolate and blue, with sharply defined tan markings on the cheeks, lips, lower jaw, throat, twin spots above the eyes and chest, lower half of the forelegs and vent region, and also on the lower portions of the hocks and feet. All Miniature Pinscher colors have pencil marks on their toes – with the exception of the red.

MAINTENANCE: Easy to maintain. Regular brushing, using a sisal brush or a bristle brush, as well as a hound glove, will help to keep the Min Pin in tiptop condition.

PROCEDURE

Equipment needed: Hound glove, bristle brush, chamois cloth.

Breed tip: Brushing several times a week will keep the coat and skin in good condition. A velvet pad will bring out the coat beautifully.

- Brush through the entire coat with a pure bristle brush.

- Bathe the dog in a natural ingredient shampoo, making sure you rinse thoroughly.

- Towel-dry, and then finish in a warm-air cage or with a light blower.

- Check the dog's nails, ears and teeth.

- Finish with a light brush of the coat with a bristle brush, or use a pad or cloth for a silky effect.

NEAPOLITAN MASTIFF

COAT: Short, dense, hard texture, with a good sheen and no fringe.
  Colors: black, blue, all shades of gray, brown (from fawn to red). Brindling on either of the latter colors. A small star on the chest and white toes are permitted.

MAINTENANCE: Easy to care for with regular weekly brushing. The folds and wrinkles must be kept clean and dry or sores may develop.

PROCEDURE

Equipment needed: Hound glove, bristle brush, fine-toothed comb.

Breed tip: Dribbles a lot of saliva, so have a large towel on hand to mop it up.

- Brush over the coat to remove dead hairs.

- Get help to lift the dog into the bath or walk it up a bath ramp.

- Bathe in a mild-ingredient, natural shampoo.

- Rinse thoroughly.

- Dry in a cage-dryer or in warm air (i.e., a warm room or outside on a warm, sunny day).

- Lightly spray the coat with conditioner to enhance the gleam.

- Check the dog's teeth, brushing them if necessary.

- Check wrinkles and folds of the to ensure they are free from moisture, or they could develop eczema or sores.

- The Neapolitan Mastiff's eyes should be bathed as often as possible.

- The ears should be cleaned inside weekly or as part of the grooming routine so as to avoid recurring problems.

- Clean under the dog's chin regularly, as food collects in this area very quickly.

PHAROAH HOUND

COAT: A striking feature of the breed is its shiny, glossy coat. Hair ranges from fine and close to slightly harsh, with no feathering. The coat is tan or rich tan in color. White is allowed on the chest (the "star") and the toes, and a slim white blaze down the center line of the face is also permissible. A white tip to the tail is highly desirable.

MAINTENANCE: Easy.

PROCEDURE

Equipment needed: Bristle hound glove, rubber grooming mitt and chamois cloth.

Breed tip: Dry the dog quickly after a bath, as it really dislikes the cold.

- Brush through the entire coat with a bristle hound glove.

- Bathe in a natural ingredient shampoo with conditioner, removing dead hair with the rubber mitt.

- Rinse thoroughly, ensuring all soap is removed.

- Remove excess moisture with towels, and then leave to dry naturally – preferably in front of a warm fire.

- Check the nails. The Pharaohs' nails grow at a remarkable rate, so they need checking on a weekly basis.

- Gently clean the ears with cotton batting. Do not insert cotton swabs into the ear canal, as these can damage the Pharoah's sensitive ears.

- Next, check the teeth.

- Finally, go over the coat with a chamois cloth to provide that extra show shine.

POINTER

COAT: The smooth, hard coat should have a definite sheen, and is fine and short. It should be evenly distributed over the body and perfectly straight.

MAINTENANCE: Easy with regular brushing with a bristle brush or hound glove.

PROCEDURE

Equipment needed: Bristle brush, hound glove.

Breed tip: Using the hound glove while the coat is still wet will remove excess shedding hair.

- Brush through the entire coat with a bristle brush or hound glove to remove dead hairs and dust.

- Bathe the Pointer in a natural, purifying shampoo and mask/conditioner to enhance the coat's sheen.

- Vigorously use a hound glove while the coat is still wet to remove excess molting hair.

- Remove excess moisture with absorbent towels.

- Finish the drying process in a cage or with a blower.

- Check the dog's nails, ears and teeth.

- Go over the coat one last time with a cloth or a bristle brush.

PUG

COAT: The coat is fine, smooth, soft, short and glossy, neither harsh nor woolly. The colors are fawn or black. Fawn Pugs have a clear contrast of black masks, ears and facial wrinkles. The nails should be black.

MAINTENANCE: Easy to maintain, as it only needs regular brushing. The Pug's overnose wrinkle and ears should be checked daily and kept spotlessly clean. If a sore should develop, a vet should be consulted. Special care should be taken with the breed's eyes. They should be kept clear, and a vet should treat any damage to the eye immediately. The older Pug's eyes are particularly vulnerable, and occasionally require eye drops.

PROCEDURE

Equipment needed: A suitable brush or a grooming glove. A selection of combs is useful.

Breed tip: Watch for any sores in the facial folds.

- Brush the coat daily.

- Bathe in a suitable natural-ingredient shampoo and rinse thoroughly.

- Make sure that the Pug is completely dried.

- Check the dog's nails, ears and teeth.

- Check that any wrinkles on the face are clean and dry, wiping with cotton batting if necessary.

RHODESIAN RIDGEBACK

COAT: The Rhodesian Ridgeback's coat is short, dense, sleek and glossy, never woolly nor silky. The color is light-wheaten to red-wheaten.

MAINTENANCE: The Rhodesian Ridgeback only requires regular brushing with a bristle brush or a hound glove.

PROCEDURE

Equipment needed: Bristle brush or hound glove.

Breed tip: A hound glove or cloth will produce a sleek appearance at the end of the grooming session.

- Brush over the body with a bristle brush or hound glove.

- This breed of dog requires bathing very rarely. When bathing is necessary, use a suitable natural, mild shampoo.

- Ensure that all evidence of the shampoo is rinsed well from the coat.

- Towel-dry the coat and finish with warm air, a cage-dryer or a blower.

- Check the dog's nails, ears and teeth.

ROTTWEILER

COAT: The Rottweiler has a shiny double coat, which consists of a topcoat and an undercoat.

The topcoat is of medium length, coarse and flat. The undercoat is essential on the neck and thighs but should not show through the topcoat. The hair is also permitted to be a little longer on the back of forelegs and the breeching.

The color is black with clearly defined markings of rich tan to mahogany – a spot over each eye, on the cheeks, as a strip around each side of the muzzle (but not on the bridge of the nose), on the throat, two triangles on either side of breastbone, on the forelegs from the carpus to the toes, on the inside of the rear legs from the hock to the toes (but not completely eliminating black from the back of the legs), and on the undertail.

MAINTENANCE: The Rottweiler is easy to maintain, although regular brushing will be required at least three days a week to keep the coat at its best.

PROCEDURE

Equipment needed: Bristle brush, hound glove, fine-toothed comb.

Breed tip: If the dog is being shown, bathe it a couple of days before the show to allow the coat to settle, as the coat should not be soft.

- Brush with a hound glove or a bristle brush, or both, against the lie of the coat, (i.e., the wrong way) in order to remove loose and dead hair. Then brush back the correct way to induce polish. Finish with a comb to encourage

the coat to lie flat and to remove surface hair.

- Bathe the dog with a pH-balanced natural shampoo and use purifying shampoo and a mask a couple of times a year. Or use a shampoo especially for black- or wirecoated breeds. Alternatively, walk the dog in the rain then finish off with a dry, rough towel. This works wonders!

- Make sure you rinse thoroughly.

- Use a hound glove when the dog is in the bath to help remove loose, molting hairs.

- Towel- or cage-dry.

- Check the Rottie's nails and keep them short.

- Check the dog's ears and teeth.

- Go over the coat with a velvet pad or a silk cloth after using a spray conditioner very lightly, if required. If your dog is to be shown, conditioner should not be allowed to remain in the coat.

SLOUGHI

MAINTENANCE: Requires only regular brushing to keep clean and healthy.

PROCEDURE

Equipment needed: Hound glove, sisal brush or bristle brush, and a fine-toothed comb.

Breed tip: A hound glove is a must to remove loose hair.

• Brush with a sisal brush or a hound glove.

• Bathe the dog in a natural shampoo, and rinse.

• Dry the coat with towels and finish in warm air or a cage-dryer, or with a light blower.

• Check the dog's nails, ears and teeth.

• Go over the coat with a hound glove or a cloth for a final polish.

COAT: The coat is tough and fine. Colors include sable or fawn in all shades with or without a black mask. Also permissible is a coat that is dark, white, brindle, black with tan points, or a brindle pattern on a fawn background on the head, feet and sometimes the chest.

STAFFORDSHIRE BULL TERRIER

COAT: The coat is smooth, short, close and gleaming. It comes in a variety of colors: red, fawn, black or blue, and white. In addition, any of these colors may come with white. There is also a brindle variety, and brindle and white, which gives plenty of choice.

MAINTENANCE: The Staffordshire Bull Terrier requires no trimming, but brushing on a regular basis with a hound glove or a pure bristle brush will keep its jacket in perfect order.

PROCEDURE

Equipment needed: Hound glove, bristle brush, fine-toothed comb.

Breed tip: Most Staffords like water and enjoy a good bath – which is helpful for removing short hairs too.

- Brush through the entire coat with a hound glove.

- Bathe in a natural shampoo.

- Make sure you rinse thoroughly.

- While the dog is molting, use a hound glove when you are bathing it, and scrub thoroughly around the coat to remove any dead hairs.

- Rinse again.

- Air-, cage- or blow-dry.

- Remember to check the Stafford's nails, ears and teeth.

SWEDISH VALLHUND

COAT: The coat is harsh, close-fitting, of medium length, with a tight topcoat and an abundant, soft, woolly undercoat. The color is steel-gray, grayish yellow and reddish brown, with darker guard hairs on the back, neck and sides of the body. Saddle markings should be present. The muzzle, throat, chest, belly, feet and hocks are usually cream in color. White can sometimes occur under the throat or around the collar (one-third white is permissible).

MAINTENANCE: Easy. The breed sheds its coat twice a year – the undercoat molts first, hence the need for a rake (below).

PROCEDURE

Equipment needed: A rake-type comb (which ensures the groomer can get down to the bottom layer of the coat), hound glove, fine-toothed comb.

Breed tip: A chamois cloth is a useful addition to its grooming bag.

- Brush through the coat with a rake-type

comb and a hound glove.

- Bathe in a natural tea tree shampoo, or similar.

- Towel-dry and finish in a cage or with a blower. Allow a few days for the coat to settle if the dog is about to be shown.

- Check the nails, ears and teeth.

- Finally, go over the coat with a bristle brush and a chamois cloth.

VIZSLA

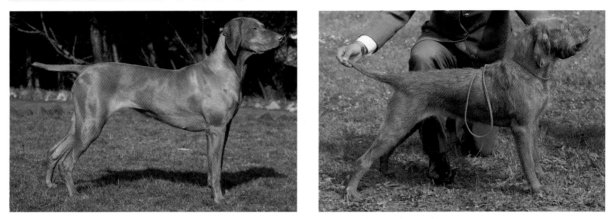

The Vizsla comes in two coat varieties: smooth (left) and wirehaired (right).

COAT: Russet-gold in color; small white marks on the chest and feet are acceptable, though undesirable. The coat is short, dense, smooth and shiny, feeling greasy to the touch.

MAINTENANCE: Requires only a regular brush with a bristle brush and a hound glove.

PROCEDURE

Equipment needed: Rubber mitt, hound glove, fine-toothed comb.

Breed tip: Use a bristle brush from a young age to encourage a healthy coat and skin.

- Brush over the coat with the bristle brush.

- Bathe only when necessary, as it removes the natural oils and often encourages dandruff. Use a natural shampoo, and rinse well.

- Spray a little stay-in (nonrinse) oil-based conditioner over the entire dog.

- A quick rub-over with a towel is all that is necessary to dry the coat.

- Brush through the coat with a hound glove.

- Check the dog's nails, ears and teeth.

WEIMARANER

COAT: The Weimaraner's coat is short, smooth and sleek.

MAINTENANCE: Maintenance is very easy – just give a quick brush through with a hound glove to remove any dead, loose hairs.

PROCEDURE

Equipment: Hound glove.

Breed tip: Bathe only as necessary – the hound glove usually keeps the coat clean.

• Brush through the coat with a hound glove.

• If necessary, bathe in a natural-ingredient shampoo, and rinse thoroughly.

• Towel-dry well and finish drying in a cage or in warm air.

• Don't forget to check the dog's nails, ears and teeth.

• Finally, go over the coat with a chamois cloth to give a gleam to the coat.

LONGHAIRED WEIMARANER

This type has a coat that is around 1 to 2 inches (2.5 to 5 cm) long, which is longer on the neck, chest and belly. There is feathering on the tail and the back of the limbs, which will need extra attention when brushing to ensure all tangles are removed.

Pay particular attention to the trousers and tail, which collect debris on walks. The feet should also be checked, particularly for grass seeds.

Brushing at least three times a week is recommended, using a bristle brush and comb on the feathering.

WELSH CORGI (CARDIGAN AND PEMBROKE)

The Welsh Corgi: Pembroke (left) and Cardigan (right)

COAT: Coats do not vary to a great degree, being short to medium on the Cardigan and slightly longer on the Pembroke. The coat is truly dense in its undercoat and it would be difficult to imagine this breed feeling the cold to any great degree.

MAINTENANCE: A practical breed that is easy to live with and maintain.

PROCEDURE

Equipment needed: Slicker brush, bristle brush, medium-toothed comb.

Breed tip: Low to the ground, the Corgi stomach can collect mud, seeds and bits of twigs while outside, so give a thorough brush after every walk.

- Brush thoroughly with a slicker or curry brush.

- Bathe the Corgi in a protein shampoo, using white-enhancing shampoo on the white parts. (However, if you are using a natural tea tree and lavender shampoo, it seems to bring white coats up beautifully and white-enhancers are not always necessary.) Remember, coat-altering products are not allowed on show dogs.

- Use a conditioner to nourish (but not soften) the coat.

- Towel well, then use a blower in the direction of the hair growth.

- Check the dog's nails, ears and teeth.

- Brush the coat with a bristle brush to finish.

WHIPPET

COAT: The coat is fine, short and close in texture, easy to keep clean and looks great after a bath. The color is any mixture.

MAINTENANCE: Easy to keep and maintain.

PROCEDURE

Equipment needed: Hound glove or rubber grooming glove.

Breed tip: A thorough rub with the hound glove when wet will remove excess hairs.

- Bathe in a suitable shampoo, using a hound glove to help remove molting and dead hair.

- Use a purifying shampoo and conditioner a few times a year to encourage healthy skin and to add luster.

- Towel-dry. Finish in a cage or with a blower.

- Check the Whippet's nails, ears and teeth.

- Lightly spray the coat with a conditioner to enhance the finish, if required.

14 *STRIPPED BREEDS*

COAT CARE

There are various ways of stripping a dog. Some breeds are hand-stripped, some are stripped with a knife; others are rolled, thinned with thinning shears, or scissored, clipped, or both.

CLIPPING PETS

Using clippers on some types of coats ruins the natural growth of the hair, and the dog may become very woolly. For the pet dog, this may not matter, and it certainly saves time for the groomer and is less expensive for the owner.

Hand-stripping a large dog may take several hours, but to clip the same amount of hair from the dog would take about five to ten minutes! Therefore, clipping might be the better option in some cases.

The groomer and the dog's owner must decide what is the best for all concerned in advance. Among the issues to consider are the stress factor, the time available, the grooming expenses involved and whether or not the dog is to be shown.

For the professional groomer, it is essential to know if a dog of any breed is likely to be shown in the conformation ring before putting clippers anywhere near it. Certainly, most pet owners have absolutely no intention of showing their dogs, and they don't care two hoots for the intricate details of finger and thumb plucking, or knife-stripping, and so on – they just want their dogs to look as smart as possible and to smell lovely.

SHOW DOGS

Those wishing to show their dogs at top level will certainly learn the skill of presenting each breed to its own breed standard, and this includes understanding that many of the different breeds of terrier have slightly different shapes – such as eyebrows, beard, whiskers, and so on. Lots of people call Scotties black Westies! But you will soon discover that they have completely differently shaped heads.

TERRIERS

Once upon a time, terriers were trimmed once a year or every six months. Nowadays, it is much more respected to keep all terriers looking smart at all times and they are trimmed regularly every six to eight weeks, and even more frequently when they are being shown.

Attention should be paid to the coat on a weekly – and sometimes even daily – basis, for the best-looking guys always get the prizes.

IGNORE AT YOUR PERIL!

As with all terrier breeds (and, in fact, every breed of dog), read the breed standard to be sure that any trimming does not fall into the category of disobeying your national kennel club rules where show dogs are concerned.

WEST HIGHLAND WHITE TERRIER

Featured is the West Highland White Terrier Kenex Cartan Lass, owned by Ann Gardner.

COAT: The Westie's double coat needs ongoing attention to keep it smart and clean. The outercoat consists of 2 inches (5 cm) of harsh hair, which is curl-free. The undercoat, which resembles fur, is short, soft and close.

MAINTENANCE: Westies are stripped by hand or knife, thinned or clipped, depending on their coat and if they are to be exhibited.

This is a constant visitor to the grooming salon, with mats and tangles underneath. For most pet owners, and for the comfort of the dog, it is better to trim this hair short. Westies are not shaved close. An Oster No. 4 or No. 5 is short enough, unless the owner requires a shorter trim. When stripped, the hair is roughly 2 inches (5 cm) long, with fringing underneath and blended in on the legs. The face is never clipped, but is rounded into a chrysanthemum shape with scissors.

PROCEDURE

Equipment needed: Stripping knife, clippers, slicker brush, wide-toothed comb.

Breed tip: Brushing and combing must be done on a regular basis to prevent mats from forming, as the Westie is a sensitive breed that hates being tugged at to remove tangles.

- Brush the entire coat **1** removing tangles with an anti-tangle spray, if necessary.

- Trim the neck from 2 in (5 cm) behind the ears, **2** downwards over the shoulder, incorporating the chest **3 4** along the body to the tail, down the sides to a level line from the elbow to the pelvis, leaving a skirt. **5 6**

- Trim the tail **7** This hair is shortened by

using the stripping knife, hand-plucking, thinning scissors or merely, for the pet dog whose owner requests it, clipped with a No. 4 or 5 Oster, or a No. 40 blade with a $\frac{1}{2}$ inch (1.25 cm) universal comb attachment for a hand-stripped appearance.

• Trim the hair from under the tail and around the anal area  always holding the dog's genitals for safety when scissors and clippers are close to delicate parts. Clip or scissor these parts, going in the direction of the growth of the hair.

• Strip or lightly clip the upper side of the tail, or blend to the required length with scissors.

• Bathe in white-enhancing shampoo, and apply a conditioner where necessary.

• Blow the coat dry, while using a pin brush or slicker on long hair.

• Check the Westie's nails ears and teeth.

• Trim off any hair lifted from the bathing.

• Blend the skirt into the body with the stripping knife or thinning shears to ensure a smooth, balanced appearance with no "stepped" effect. See.

• Comb through the hair on the head and allow the dog to shake.

• To deal with the ears, strip the stray hairs with a knife or with thinning scissors, and neaten the edges with scissors where excess hair has grown. Always hold the ear leather and clip to the fingers for safety.

• From the back of the neck, scissor the head round in a forward action to the chin hair to form a chrysanthemum appearance.

• Indent the stop (the area between the eyes) with thinning scissors to remove enough hair to reveal the eyes.

• Pet dogs usually have their legs scissored to about 4 inches (10 cm) in a downward blend, and the skirt shortened at the bottom. Some Westies have their underneath clipped with a No. 10 blade through from the chest to the stomach, incorporating the genital area. This should not be obvious when the dog is standing up, as the skirt falls over the clipped area.

• Some people have their Westies clipped all over, apart from the head, with a No. 4 or a No. 5 and they can look very smart when clipped. However, it is sad to see this lovely breed shaved to the skin, as it sometimes is, and it is not necessary. Even when matted, the coat can be attended to; if clipping is absolutely necessary to save the dog from experiencing too much trauma, then a coarse blade can be used.

• The finished dog.

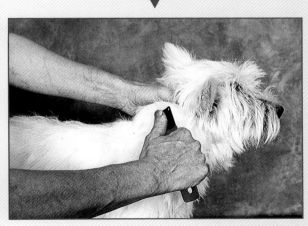

3

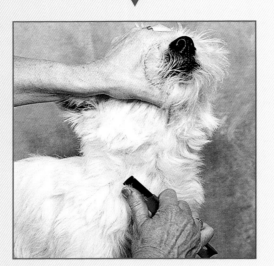

4

5

6

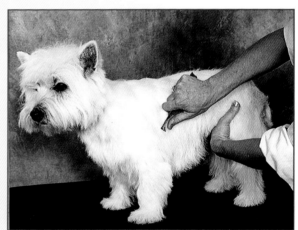

7

8

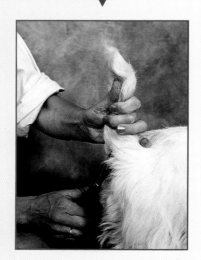

9

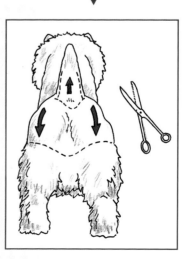

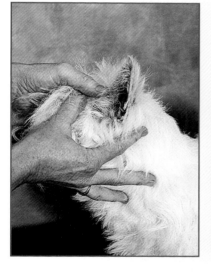
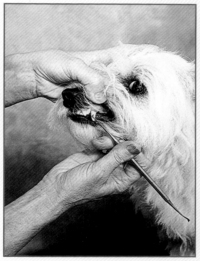

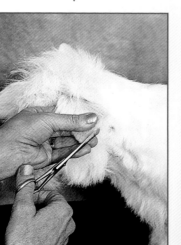

AIREDALE TERRIER

COAT: It has a double coat that is waterproof. It is hard, dense and wiry. It should not be so long as to appear ragged (it is very smart), and should lie straight and close, covering the body and legs. The outercoat is hard, wiry and stiff, and the undercoat is shorter and softer.

MAINTENANCE: A daily brush keeps this dog looking smart, but it needs professional stripping about three or four times a year. Being a breed that loves nothing more than to participate in family games and to go for long walks, the coat will need regular attention.

It is always a joy for any groomer to achieve perfection on this breed. Many groomers clip the coat rather than strip it and, professionally done, Airedales still look very smart whichever procedure is undertaken. Care should be taken with regards to the coat when showing, as hand-stripping only is acceptable.

Pet dogs are usually clipped, as are those that are retired from the show ring, as this is less time-consuming and stressful for the dog (especially older dogs). With regular clipping, the undercoat tends to take over and the coat becomes softer and loses color, which is not a problem to the pet dog, but will not be tolerated in the show ring.

PROCEDURE

Equipment needed: Terrier pin-pad brush, wide-toothed comb and narrow-toothed comb, clippers or stripping tools, scissors (rounded ones for the ears and around the face, and pointed ones for the rest of the body).

Breed tip: It is hard work to keep this charming breed stripped. Most pets and retired show dogs are clipped.

- Brush the entire coat with the terrier pin-pad brush.

- Trim closely and evenly from the back of the head and down into the back.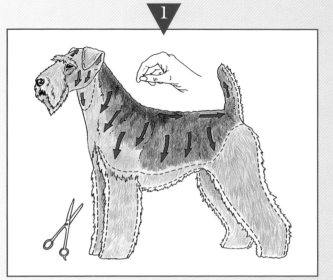

- Trim the level of the back, but not as closely as the neck area.

- The front parts of the neck and brisket are trimmed very closely, with just a shade more hair left on, as you work down to where the front legs join the body.

- The shoulders are trimmed evenly and closely.

- The front legs should be merely trimmed to straightness. This can be done carefully with scissors, taking off only the hair that stands out. Trim from the rear line. Take out a few hairs from the front and outside the front legs where they join the shoulder to give a straight line from the top of the shoulder to the feet, and from the brisket to the tips of the toes.

- Shape the ribs to follow the body conformation, working hair evenly from a closely trimmed back to a fairly heavy coat on the underpart of the ribs and chest. On the underpart of the chest, only remove those hairs necessary to prevent shagginess. Trim under the line of the chest to follow the bodyline.

- Take the hair in the loin area closer than the chest, but do not make it too fine. The underline is trimmed closely to emphasize the tuck-up.

- Do not take all the hair off the belly, but only those hairs that are snarled or shaggy.

- For the hindleg areas, trim to achieve a fine back to a fairly heavy-coated thigh.

- From the middle of the thigh to the hock, trim only those hairs that are shaggy.

- The back line of the hock should be trimmed straight. Superfluous hairs should be trimmed from the edges of the feet and between the toes. Shape to create a round outline.

- Trim the insides of the back legs to a clean finish, taking care to give a straight, even line to the hindlegs (from the rear view).

- Trim the tail closely to the tip, toward the head. Trim very fine in the rear, where it joins the stern. 1 3

- Trim the stern very closely where it joins the tail, working it heavier toward the hindlegs. 3

- Trim the skull very closely. Trim the eyebrows evenly and closely at the outside corner of the eye, with plenty of length over the inside corner. 4

- Trim the cheeks closely from the outside corner of the eye to the corner of the mouth. 4

- Trim very slightly from the inside corner of the eye, downward to the corner of the mouth, to achieve the characteristic breed facial expression. 4

- Trim the hairs on top of the muzzle from slightly between the eyebrows to the nose to give a straight line from the top of the skull. 4

- Leave the chin whiskers, but brush them forwards. Clean under the jaw from the corner of the mouth to the back of the neck. 4

- Clean off the ears closely inside and out, giving particular attention to the edges of the ears, which should have a clean finish. 4

- Remember to check the Airedale's nails, ears and teeth.

- Avoid bathing unless absolutely necessary – regular brushing should keep the coat clean. If a bath cannot be avoided, wet the coat thoroughly, apply a mild shampoo and rinse thoroughly. Brush the coat through with a hound glove to remove loose hairs, and towel off excess moisture. Leave to dry naturally in a warm room.

- Pet dogs are often clipped rather than stripped and trimmed.

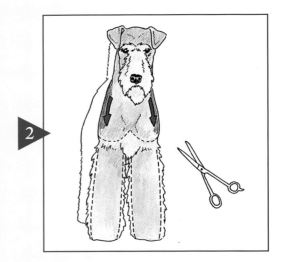

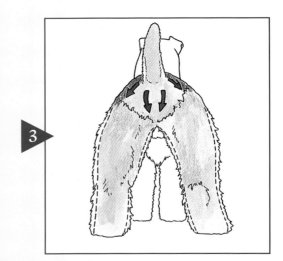

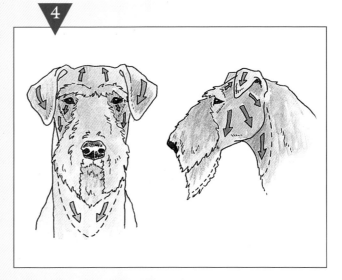

BORDER TERRIER

COAT: The coat is harsh and dense, with a close undercoat and thick skin.

MAINTENANCE: The coat is not clipped, but will require stripping out by hand twice a year. This will give the dog a new lease on life, as well as removing uncomfortable and itchy layers of dead coat. When the hairs start to form a natural parting and fall into clumps, the dog is ready to be stripped.

Some grooming salons do not hand-strip, but it is a pity to ruin this wonderful little dog's coat by running the clippers over it. Stripping takes time; the groomer must discuss this with the owner and charge accordingly.

PROCEDURE

Equipment needed: Stripping knife, fine-toothed comb, slicker or pin brush, scissors.

Breed tip: The coat could be rolled (page 48) on a regular basis to keep the dog looking smart throughout the year.

- Comb the dog thoroughly with a fine-toothed comb.

- Starting behind the shoulders, and working down the entire body, finger and thumb hand-stripping is the correct practice ▼1 . However, should a knife be used, one with a serrated edge is preferable. The coat is easier to strip when it is rubbed up the wrong way. Be sure to pull the coat in the direction of the hair growth. It should come out easily if it is ready to strip.

- Part the hair underneath the tail to remove the hair on either side. Trim with scissors around the anal area.

- Take the long hair from the skull and inside the ear. ▼2

1

2

- Trim the hair of the foot upward, removing the long hair on the back of the pastern with a stripping knife.

- If absolutely necessary (e.g., the dog has rolled in something nasty), then bathe it. Show dogs are rarely, if ever, bathed, as it can soften the required harsh coat. Use a protein shampoo, and rinse thoroughly.

- Dry in a cage or with a dryer on a low blow setting.

- Most dogs, however, only require daily brushing to keep the coat clean and in good condition.

- Finally, remember to check the dog's nails, ears and teeth.

BRUSSELS GRIFFON (GRIFFON BRUXELLOIS)

COAT: There are two types of Brussels Griffon – the Rough and the Smooth. This breed comes in three colors (red, black, and black and tan).

MAINTENANCE: The Smooth coat is comparatively easy, only necessitating brushing with a natural bristle brush, and using a pair of curved scissors to remove hair from between the toes and to remove the curl that forms at the end of the tail.

A very fine comb is useful when the Smooth is molting to speed up hair removal. The tail can be also trimmed underneath and around the anus area for tidiness.

The Rough coat requires more detailed stripping.

PROCEDURE

Equipment needed: Bristle brush, small slicker, medium-toothed comb, fine-toothed comb, thinning scissors and tweezers.

Breed tip: This is a rugged little dog that should look natural and not overly trimmed. Some Griffons lack undercoat, so will look a little bare for a few weeks after being stripped.

- Work though the coat with a bristle brush, and comb through with a medium-toothed comb. Lift a few hairs on the back between your finger and thumb and gently pull. If the hair comes out easily, the coat is ready to strip.

- Commence stripping the topcoat at the withers or base of the neck between the shoulder blades, and continue stripping down the back and side of the tail. Always strip with the growth of the hair toward you. ▼

- Remove the long hairs from the dog's thighs, taking care to retain a balanced outline. ▼

192

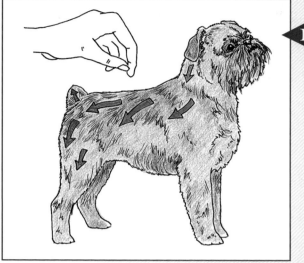

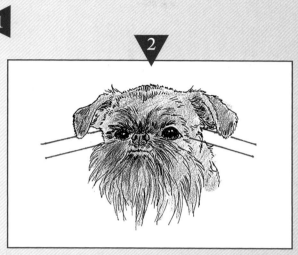

• Remove the thick hair growing on the back of the hindlegs below the hock. Also remove the longest hairs from the front of the legs and feet. Overstripping here can make the feet look long as opposed to the desired cat-like appearance. **1**

• Strip the shoulders around to the chest, removing long hairs from the leg. **1**

• Strip the long hair on the outside of each shoulder, down to the elbow to present a straight front. **1**

• The chest is now stripped at the front to the lowest point.

• Scissors or clippers (Oster No. 10) can be used under the stomach and around the sensitive genital area.

• Look over the complete picture of the dog as it stands on the table and remove stray hair that detracts from a smart, balanced look.

• The head: start behind the eyes, being careful to strip only a few strands of hair at a time. Work back to each ear and over the top of the head **2**. Leave some longer hairs over the eyes to form eyebrows. Strip the back of the ears, down to the chest. Continue down the side of the neck toward the jawbone, to give a distinct beard and blend in to the chest.

• Comb the beard forward to enable you to pluck the ear and below the beard to the throat to give a clean neckline, and to accentuate the head. Remove long hairs from the inside of the ear. The edge of the ear can be closely trimmed with scissors to give a neat finish.

• The stop (the point between the eyes, just above the nose) is a tender part and may need tweezers to remove a small amount of hair.

• Hairs from the corner of the eye should be removed with tweezers or curved scissors to prevent them sticking into the eye or accumulating debris.

• The hair of the beard that adjoins the ears can be removed in a direct line from the corner of each eye. **2**

• Tidy around the anus with scissors or thinning scissors to give a neat finish.

- Trim the hair from under the feet and between the toes.

- Bathe the Griffon in a natural mild shampoo, and rinse well.

- Towel-dry thoroughly. Cage- or lightly blow-dry.

- Check the dog's nails, ears and teeth.

- Note: For the pet, a complete strip twice a year is fine with a little tidying in between.

- The show strip is ideally done in stages – side of body and legs first, then back, then head, as they grow in different stages.

- The pet dog can be trimmed lightly with a coarse blade if required, rather than hand-stripped.

CAIRN TERRIER

COAT: The Cairn has a weather-resistant double coat. The outercoat is profuse, harsh, but not coarse; the undercoat is short, soft and close.

The color is cream, wheaten, red, gray or nearly black. Brindling in all these colors is acceptable.

MAINTENANCE: The Cairn is usually hand- or knife-stripped; pet dogs are sometimes clipped to give a cleaner, smarter appearance, but it ruins the coat, as the undercoat and topcoat are then the same length and the coat becomes quite soft.

PROCEDURE

Equipment needed: Clipping/stripping materials, scissors, stiff bristle brush, fine- and coarse-toothed combs.

Breed tip: The Cairn Terrier is not shaved short.

- Brush the coat through to remove dead hair and tangles. Often pet Cairns are never brushed by their owners, so they can respond negatively until they are used to being handled and brushed.

- With neglected coats, use a spray conditioner and lightly brush it in before grooming commences.

- Remove hair from under the feet and around the anal area with scissors.

- Where stripped (or clipped with a coarse No. 7 blade), go through the coat with the growth of the hair from the neck downwards. ▼

- Strip the untidy hairs from the back of the ears at the tip to define.

- Bathe with a mild shampoo for its natural and

therapeutic action, and use a conditioner where required.

- Dry with a blow-dryer, after toweling. The Cairn, like the Westie, really enjoys a good rub with a towel after a bath.

- Check the dog's nails, ears and teeth.

- If required, the underneath can be clipped with a No. 10 blade to remove all unnecessary hair that will trail in the mud, etc. This should be done so that it is impossible to see unless the dog rolls over on his back, and should only be done on pet dogs.

- Show Cairns should never be clipped. In fact, except for around the feet and at the end of the male dog's sheath, a blade should not go near them. Some exhibitors use thinning scissors but this usually shows as a harsh line on the coat. The Cairn, unlike the trimmed terriers, should give the impression of not having been trimmed, and this takes time and skill to achieve. Newcomers to the show ring

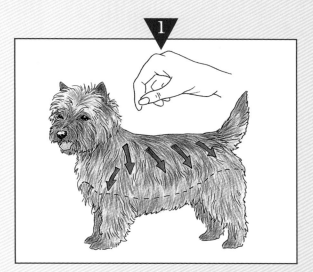

should seek help from an experienced exhibitor to learn how to prepare Cairns.

- Using thinning scissors, tidy the head to give an indentation between the eyes, and leaving a well-furnished round shape to the outline of the head, but in proportion to the body.

- Trim the tail upwards to balance with the stripping or clipping of the body coat.

- Check the dog's nails, ears and teeth.

DANDIE DINMONT TERRIER

COAT: The coat is a very important feature of this breed. The Dandie coat should be a mixture of two-thirds hard (not wiry) and one-third linty (not silky) hair.

The coat should be 2 inches (5 cm) long. The topknot should be soft and silky, and very pale.

MAINTENANCE: When grooming the Dandie Dinmont, only dead hair should be removed. The dogs should be hand-stripped – clipping (even in pet dogs) ruins the coat, although it is sometimes done in older dogs for ease.

PROCEDURE

Equipment needed: Pin brush or slicker, medium-toothed comb, stripping knife.

Breed tip: A small amount of baby oil mixed with the chosen conditioner helps to give extra nourishment to the Dandie Dinmont's coat.

- Brush with a pin brush or a slicker, spraying untangle or dematter on dry or felted areas to remove mats without breaking too much hair. The mat-breaker will thin excessively soft hair that has bunched. Be sure all mats are removed before bathing.

- If bathing is unavoidable, bathe the Dandie in a protein shampoo and rinse thoroughly.

- Apply coat-protecting conditioner if necessary (for pet dogs only – not show dogs, as this could lead to disqualification).

- Towel-dry and finish with a blower, brushing continuously with a pin brush, away from the heat.

- Do not bathe just prior to a show, as this will tend to soften the coat texture, which must be crisp to the touch.

- Check the dog's nails, ears and teeth.

- Comb through the coat.

- About eight weeks before a show, remove most of the old hair from the topcoat only. The Dandie's coat is at its best when about 1 1/2 to 2 inches (4 to 5 cm) long. Do not interfere with the undercoat. The neck and shoulders should be trimmed carefully between the second and third weeks prior to a show.

- About two weeks before a show, trim the ears, leaving the hair at the top of the ears to be combed to join the topknot. This will give an effect of added width to the head. Leave a good inch of hair tapering to

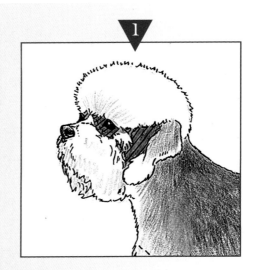

the tips of the ears where the "tassel" hangs down. **1**

- Remove all the hair from the underside of the ear, which will allow the ear to hang down very close to the cheek.

- Clear all the long hair from the nose to the stop, taking care to make it close. Remove the hair in the crevice or dip between the eyes to accentuate the stop, but do not remove the hair too far toward the forehead. **1 2**

- Trim under the eyes, removing all superfluous hair. This will enhance their beauty and largeness. Care must be taken not to overdo this trimming, and to give time for the "spectacles" to refurnish or the expression of the dog will be marred. **1 2**

- The forelegs should be cleared of most of the long hair at the front and inner sides only, leaving a slight "feathering" toward the back of the legs. **2**

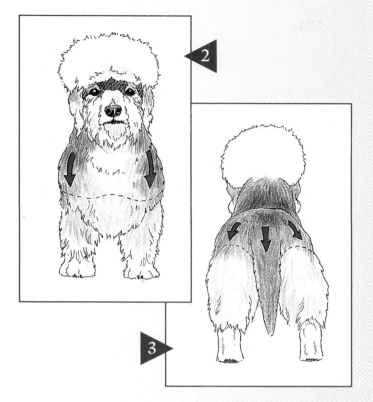

stripping knife, but preferably with finger and thumb, taking pains to taper it naturally. Remove all hair that is wispy and superfluous to the natural feathering.

- Tidy the feet to look round and neat. Cut the nails, should this be necessary, being sure not to damage the quick.

- Trim the underbody with a stripping knife or finger and thumb from the end of the ribs to the hindlegs in order to show a carefully graduated and natural cut-up of loin and shapely waist.

- The topknot is the Dandie's crowning glory, and deserves special care and attention. The topknot should be trimmed to give a rounded effect. All wispy, untidy hair should be foreshortened with the finger and thumb only a day or so before the show, and many enthusiasts will whiten it for added effect with a little chalk and powder – but be sure to remove all chalk before entering the ring or you will lose the silvery sheen. Comb the hair upwards from the neck, and get it to stand softly all over the head, but clear of the eyes.

- The hindlegs should be cleared of all the long hair from the hocks to the ground. Tidy the hair, which ranges from the base of the tail right down to the hocks.

- The tail should be thick at the base, tapering to a point. All hair beyond the bone of the tail should be carefully and lightly taken off with a

FOX TERRIER (WIRE AND SMOOTH)

The two varieties of Fox Terrier: the Smooth (left) and the Wire (right)

COAT: There are two varieties of Fox Terrier – Smooth and Wire. The Smooth coat does not require so much attention, but will benefit from a bath and a good brushing with a hound glove to remove dead hairs.

The Wire variety has a dense, wiry texture of about 3/4 inches (2 cm) on the shoulder to 1 1/2 inches (4 cm) on the withers, back, ribs and quarters, with an undercoat of short, softer hair. The hair on the back and quarters is harsher than that on the sides. Hair on the jaws is crisp and of sufficient length to impart the appearance of strength to the foreface. The leg hair is dense and crisp. The eyes are well defined by careful trimming.

MAINTENANCE: This classy little dog really looks his best when nicely trimmed.

The Smooth molts, but regular brushing keeps loose hairs to a minimum. The Wire does not molt and the coat of a pet Wire dog should be stripped or clipped about three to four times a year, and then brushed a couple of times a week with a pin brush to keep the coat free of mats and tangles. The coat of a show Wire requires more regular attention and fine trimming.

Although it is quicker to clip a pet Wire, and they will still look very smart, clipping will make the distinctive rich colors in the coat quite a lot paler and will make the coat lose its typical wiry texture.

PROCEDURE

Equipment needed: The Smooth requires a hound glove and thinning scissors; the Wire requires a pin brush, combination comb (narrow one end, wide one end), ordinary scissors for cutting between the pads, thinning scissors, stripping knife.

Breed tip: The following details a basic outline of grooming a Fox Terrier; however, the best advice if you want to show a dog is to consult with experienced breeders who can guide you on the finer points of grooming – achieving an expert trim comes only with experience.

WIRE FOX TERRIER

- Brush the Fox Terrier's coat with a pin brush and follow by combing through.

- Hand- or knife-strip the neck and body to the required length, from the point of the neck down to the elbow and along the body with the growth of the coat, arching slightly over the hips to give shape. Where pets are concerned, this part is frequently clipped with a No. 5 or No. 7 blade. ▼1

- Clip the stomach and the inside of the groin. ▼1

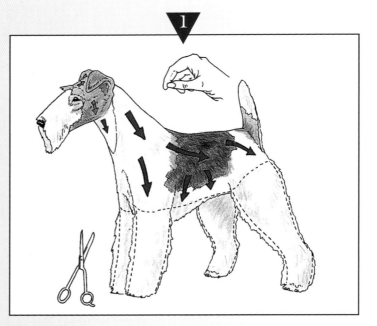

• Hand- or knife-strip (or clip) the head from the brows to the base of the skull, down both sides of the ears. ▼2

• Trim from the outer corner of the eye, down the cheek and under the neck to taper to a V at the throat. ▼2

• If hand-stripping, ears should be hand-stripped or plucked using finger and thumb, including the edges. If you are clipping the ears, you should use the scissors on the edges to neaten them. ▼2

• Strip or clip the top of the tail and scissor underneath, cleaning the hair from the anal area. ▼1

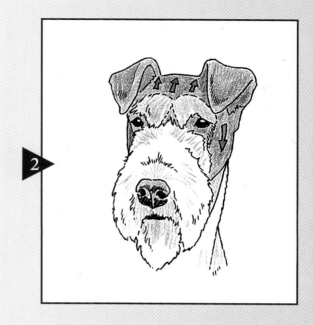

• Bathe the dog in a plain, mild shampoo, and rinse thoroughly. Bathing can soften the coat, so bathe only when necessary.

• Towel-dry in the direction of the coat. Brush the coat to keep the coat flat and use a handheld hair-dryer to dry, or air-dry. Avoid using a cage-dryer, as the coat will "lift," and most Fox Terriers will hate being in a cage dryer.

• Check the dog's nails, ears and teeth.

• Go over the trimmed parts to remove any lifted hair. Use a knife or thinning shears, or clippers where applicable.

• Comb through.

• Comb the eyebrows forward and pull the hair, using your fingers, into a V in the center. Use the scissors to tidy the ends.

• Comb down once again, pulling the eyebrows to a triangle. Scissor the ends to get a neat finish.

• Trim out the hair from between the pads and around the toes to give a round, compact appearance. When scissoring the feet, put the dog's foot on the table, as you will get a better finish.

• Comb forward and trim the beard.

• Pull some of the longer hair on the front legs using your fingers to get a tubular shape, leaving the hairs still fairly dense, and then scissor the ends to get a neat finish. Pulling some of the hair on the legs helps to keep the white a bright color and stops the legs becoming too soft in texture.

• Trim the bottom of the chest fringe and under the chest, following the contours of the body.

• Pull some of the longer hair, using your fingers. When standing behind the dog, the back legs should appear straight from the top of the leg to the feet. The top and middle part of the back legs over the thighs should therefore have short, neat hair with slightly longer hair around the lower part of the leg and the hock area. Use the scissors to tidy up the ends of the hair.

SMOOTH FOX TERRIER

- Brush through the entire coat with a hound glove.

- If preparing for a show, tidy the hair with thinning scissors and clippers to sharpen the outline and to clean around the side of the cheeks. ▼

- For bathing, see instructions for the Wire Fox Terrier.

- As above, check the dog's ears, teeth, nails and pads.

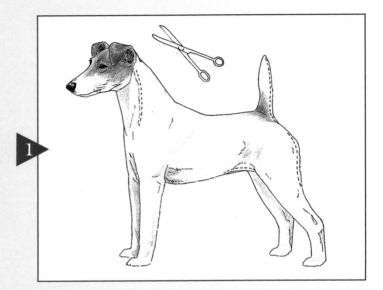

IRISH TERRIER

COAT: The coat is a distinctive red, harsh and wiry, and has a broken appearance. It should be free from softness or silkiness, and the length should not hide the outline of the body, particularly the hindquarters. The hair should be straight and flat, with no shagginess, and should be free of lock or curl. At the base of the stiff hair is a growth of finer and softer hair: the undercoat. The hair on the foreface is crisp. The leg hair is dense.

MAINTENANCE: Regular brushing is required to keep this breed looking smart, and the coat clean and healthy. Use a slicker brush, terrier palm pad and a stripping stone, and brush with the lie of the coat.

PROCEDURE

Equipment needed: Slicker brush, terrier palm pad, stripping stone, medium-toothed comb, stripping knife, clippers and scissors where applicable.

Breed tip: Done on a 12-week basis, the thorough strip described below will keep the breed looking every bit as distinguished as it should. Show dogs are given more regular attention.

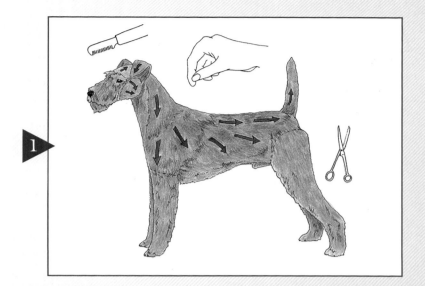

- Brush with a slicker brush.

- Comb with a medium-toothed comb.

- Using your finger and thumb or an all-in-one stripping knife, strip from the corner of the eye to the edge of the mouth down, incorporating the cheeks. ▼1

- Shorten the hair on the ears by stripping. The stripping stone can be used on the ears as well as the body, etc. – rubbed across the coat, it tidies up loose hairs. ▼1

- The muzzle hair is left to form the correct, grand expression, but should not be so full or long as to upset the balance of the head.

- Strip down the neck and along the body, being careful to blend the hair to give a smooth appearance. It should be shorter at the back of the hindlegs. ▼1

- Hand or knife-strip those hairs that are easy to see as being longer. Make sure you only take a few hairs at a time, as described in the plucking procedure. Always pluck with the grain of the growth. ▼1

- Pet dogs are sometimes clipped with a coarse blade, but consult with the owner first. This routine is far quicker and less costly, but the coat never looks the same as when regular attention is paid to stripping and general grooming.

- Pay particular attention to the armpits, and around the genital and umbilical areas, as the undercoat can felt. Comb regularly to prevent matting.

- Strip the tail in the direction of the hair growth from the base to the tip. ▼1

- The legs have slightly more furnishing than the body, but the hair should still remain short and smart. This can be achieved by stripping or scissoring. ▼1

- Bathe the dog in a natural shampoo and rinse well.

- Dry with a blower or air- or cage-dry after combing through.

- Tidy any loose hairs when the dog is dry.

- Check the dog's nails, ears and teeth.

- Scissor all hair from underneath the pads and check between the toes.

- Many breeders are happy to help with any grooming problems.

LAKELAND TERRIER

COAT: A trimmed breed, this dog has a coat that is dense, harsh and weather-resistant, with a good undercoat.

MAINTENANCE: It requires regular brushing and grooming, as well as a complete professional strip twice a year.

For the show ring, the coat will probably be worked on twice a week to keep it in tiptop show condition and to ensure it is never out of coat. Using scissors and clippers alters the color and texture of the hair – only hand- or knife-stripping maintains the vibrant coat color and slightly wavy, harsh coat. The show dog should be hand- or knife-stripped everywhere, except for between the pads of the feet, under the stomach and where the dog may be particularly tender.

Pet owners often ask for this breed to be clipped and bring them to the salon at least every 10 to 12 weeks. Either way, this dog benefits from daily brushing.

PROCEDURE

Equipment needed: Slicker brush, medium-toothed comb, stripping knife, thinning scissors, scissors, clippers where applicable.

Breed tip: Should look smart at all times with the correct grooming techniques.

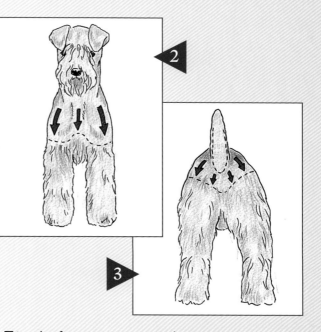

- Brush through the entire coat with a slicker brush, removing dead hair and tangles.

- Follow this by combing with a medium-toothed comb.

- Strip, thin or clip (with a No. 10 Oster) the head. Work from the eyebrows to the top of the skull, down the ears and from the outer corner of the eye, down the cheek to the corner of the mouth, then backwards down the throat to the neck. **1**

- Strip, thin or clip (with a No. 7 Oster) from the skull down the neck, over the shoulder to where the legs join the body at the front. **1 2**

- Trim the chest to leave a fringe at the brisket, downwards with growth of coat to the rear, just above the hip. **2**

- Blend the hair into the legs evenly. **1**

- Trim the tail with the hair growth, and scissor underneath and around the anal area, or clip lightly. **3**

- Clip under the tummy and inside the groin with a No. 10 Oster. **1**

- Trim the hair away from between the toes and under the foot.

- Bathe the dog in a suitable shampoo and use conditioner to complement the wiry coat.

- Blow the coat dry, following the direction of the hair growth.

- Check the Lakeland's nails, ears and teeth.

- Tidy the trimmed parts where they have lifted with the bathing.

- Comb through the hair on the front legs with a slicker brush.

- Trim the foot to give a round, compact appearance.

- Lift the foot so the hair on the front leg falls naturally. Then, scissor into a cylindrical shape.

- Trim the furnishing under the chest. Work with the contours of the body, and scissor up toward the loin.

- Trim the hindlegs to blend into the body at the hip joint. **3**

- Comb the eyebrows forward. Next, trim the hair (in the direction of the hair growth). The fall is full between and over the eyes, and from the eyebrows down, blending in with the face hair. **1**

- Comb the beard forward to trim away any untidy hair, and to give a neat appearance.

- Note: all furnishings (e.g., face, legs, under the chest) are better trimmed by hand, not scissors. Using your thumb and forefinger, tease the hair out in the direction of growth. This maintains strong hair which is less likely to mat and tangle.

NORFOLK TERRIER

COAT: Described as shaggy, the Norfolk Terrier coat is hard and wiry. It is straight and lies close to the body, as well as being weatherproof. The hair is longer and rougher on the neck and shoulders, while the hair on the head and ears is short and smooth, except for slight whiskers and eyebrows. The ears need to be picked to keep the hair on them short.

MAINTENANCE: This dog is hand-stripped. Overtrimming is undesirable, but regular brushing on a daily basis is essential.

PROCEDURE

Equipment needed: Stripping knife, medium-toothed comb, pin brush or slicker brush.

Breed tip: Establish whether the owner likes the natural or smart look before starting.

• Brush and comb through.

• Strip the body by hand or knife, to remove any straggly hairs and to neaten its appearance to a natural-looking finish. ▼ **1**

• Bathe the dog in a mild shampoo and thoroughly rinse.

• Air-, cage- or gently blow-dry.

• Comb with a medium-toothed comb.

• Check the dog's nails, ears and teeth.

• Check between the toes for excess hair and remove with scissors.

• Both the pet and show dog will need the genital/anal area kept clean and hair-free for hygiene. The pet dog should also be scissored down the legs to neaten its appearance, as well as having the head tidied of straggly bits.

• The show dog needs constant attention to the coat, with finger-, thumb- and knife-stripping. The coat is required to be brushed frequently enough to keep it in good order, and will not be bathed as often as the pet dog.

• See also pages 205–206.

NORWICH TERRIER

Photo: Edwin.

COAT: The coat is wiry, straight and lies close to the body, with a thick undercoat. It is longer and rougher on the neck, forming a ruff to frame the face. The hair on the head is short and smooth, except for slight whiskers and eyebrows. The color is red, wheaten, black and tan, or grizzle. White marks or patches on the chest are undesirable but permissible.

MAINTENANCE: Excessive trimming to leave a sculptured look, as in some terrier breeds, is undesirable. Trimming of a different kind is required for show dogs – e.g., rolling the coat to keep a new coat growing amongst the older coat is done in most cases. Pet owners usually prefer all the old coat removed to help prevent molting hair on clothes and furniture.

PROCEDURE

Equipment needed: Pin brush/slicker brush, medium-toothed comb, stripping knife, straight-bladed scissors, thinning scissors.

Breed tip: Brush on a regular basis to keep the coat free from burrs and debris.

- Brush and comb through the coat, using a slicker or pin brush, and a medium-toothed comb.

- Strip cut any loose hair with your finger and thumb or a stripping knife **1**. Then work backwards from the stop to the point of the neck, and from the outside corner of the eye to where the corner of the ear joins the top of the skull. Strip straggly hairs from the ears.

- When all dead hair is removed from the body, blend into the underskirt **1**. If this is more than 2 inches (5 cm) long, shorten with thinning scissors to give a smart appearance.

- Strip out hair from the front of the tail. Using thinning scissors, trim down the back of the tail and around the anus to leave a neat appearance.

- Using straight-blade scissors, cut the hair a round the outside of the feet and, underneath

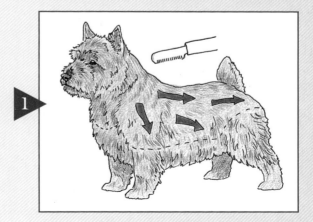

the feet, excessive hair growing over the pads. Remove straggly hairs from the legs.

• Bathe the dog in a good-quality, natural-ingredient shampoo.

• Air-, cage- or blow-dry the coat.

• Brush and comb through.

• Check the dog's nails, ears and teeth.

• Norfolk and Norwich Terriers are often clipped because the owners want them shortcoated. This is a shame, as they are lovely when carefully trimmed. Where the owner insists, a coarse blade is sufficient to maintain a natural look and smart appearance.

PARSON RUSSELL TERRIER

◄ *Smooth*

◄ *Broken – similar to the Smooth, but with more profuse hair around the neck and shoulders.*

▲
Rough – with the longest top coat of the three varieties.

COAT: The coat is naturally harsh, close and dense – whether Rough, Smooth or Broken – and has an undercoat. The belly and undersides are coated.

MAINTENANCE: In most cases, provided that the dog is well cared for, little maintenance is required. Once dry, dirt can be easily removed from the coat by brushing. Bathing is not recommended unless really necessary, as it can affect the coat's texture and waterproofing. This is particularly important if you show your Russell. When show Russells are stripped, it is always done by hand. They are never clipped.

Pet owners may wish their Russells to visit a grooming parlor from time to time, although it is not strictly necessary. Normally, this will be to strip the Rough variety, or to provide a bath if a pet Russell has become a little enthusiastic in the mud when out on a walk or at play. Grooming Russells normally involves little more than some stripping or clipping in order to maintain the smoothness of the coat – although coat quality in Russells is dependent on little more than good diet and overall health.

PROCEDURE

Equipment needed: Comb, bristle brush.

Breed tip: A hound glove is great at removing excess hair when the dog is shedding.

- Brush through the coat and use a fine comb to remove dead hairs.

- Strip with a serrated-edged, deep-toothed knife.

- Trim around the feet.

- Only bathe your Russell if absolutely necessary. If this is the case, make sure you use a suitable canine shampoo. At the time of molt, a hound glove can be used to remove excess hairs.

- Check the nails, ears and teeth.

SCHNAUZER (MINIATURE, STANDARD AND GIANT)

COAT: The Miniature (pictured left and ▼1), Standard (▼4) and Giant (▼5) are classed as separate breeds, but their coat care and grooming requirements are the same.

The topcoat is harsh and wiry, just short enough for smartness on the body. It is slightly shorter on the neck and shoulders, but blends smoothly into the body coat. It is clean at the throat, skull, ears and under the tail. The hair on the legs is harsh. The breeds have a good undercoat.

The color is pepper and salt, black, and black and silver.

MAINTENANCE: Seen frequently in the grooming parlor. Grooming entails using many grooming skills – from hand-stripping and scissoring, clipping and blending, to rolling. The coat requires regular brushing with a slicker and combing with a medium-toothed comb, particularly on the legs and whiskers. The coat is stripped completely when it blows twice a year.

PROCEDURE

Equipment needed: Trimming scissors, two slicker brushes (one small, soft one for the face, and a harder one for the rest of the coat) and a terrier pad for the main jacket.

Breed tip: Pay attention to stripping/rolling the coat on a more regular basis to keep it looking smart all year round. Show dogs are frequently rolled every week to keep them in a full coat. Rolling consists of continually removing longer dead hairs by finger and thumb so that new coat growth is continuous. The undercoat can be kept in check by removing with a blunt stripping knife.

- Starting with the head, strip the top of the skull, the neck and the body down over the shoulder to where the front legs join the body. **1**

- Work along the back and down the back legs, to blend the coat in at a line running from the groin to the hock. **1**

- Follow the underline through to the rump and down to just above the indentation of the hock and the tail. **1**

- Trim the tail by hand- or knife-stripping (working with the direction of the hair growth). Some pet dogs are clipped. The underside of the tail is trimmed short. **2**

- Clip the ears downwards with a No. 10 Oster, or use thinning scissors to shorten the hair. Tidy the edges with scissors. **1**

- Then clip the cheeks and under the throat and down the front of the chest. **3**

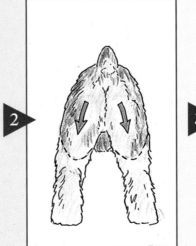

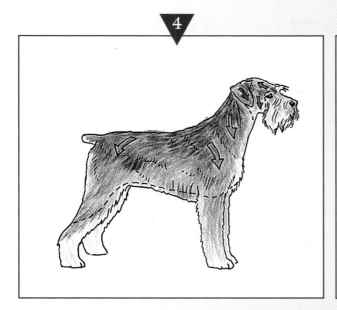

- The belly can be clipped to incorporate the insides of the groin. However, leave part of the rib cage to be tapered up with scissors to make a short fringe. This will enhance the contours of the body.

- Brush the coat out using a fine spray of conditioner if dry, or where tangles are to be removed.

- Comb through the coat once more.

- Bathe in a natural-ingredient shampoo.

- Towel-dry and finish in a cage or with a blower.

- Trim with scissors under the body upwards, working with the contours of the body.

- Tidy the trimmed parts to remove stray hairs.

- Comb the eyebrows and beard forward, and scissor diagonally from the bridge of the nose to the outer corner of the eye, then scissor a small inverted V-shape between the eyes to make a distinct eyebrow and to show the stop.

- Using scissors, trim between the eyebrows into a diamond shape.

- Scissor the edges of the ears to a rectangular shape. The head should give the impression of a "house brick."

- The hair on the chest, between the legs, should now be scissored to look flat and smooth.

- Scissor the front legs to achieve a neat appearance, with the elbows close to the body, taking more hair from the outer elbow to give the appearance that the forelegs are close together, and are not sticking out.

- Scissor the feet to give them a round, catlike appearance.

- Trim the back legs, blending the longer hair into the shorter body coat.

- Pet dogs are very often clipped instead of being stripped, as this is far quicker and, therefore, cheaper. They can look extremely smart and chic when this is undertaken with consideration.

SCOTTISH TERRIER

COAT: The Scottie's coat is close-lying. It has a double coat, which consists of a short, dense undercoat and a harsh, dense and wiry outercoat that is weather-resistant.

MAINTENANCE: Requires regular brushing at least three times a week, especially the long hair of the skirt and the beard, and so on.

PROCEDURE

Equipment needed: Slicker brush, wide-toothed comb, stripping knife, clippers, scissors.

Breed tip: The Scottish Terrier presents

more work than at first appears, so give yourself more time than you initially think you'll need.

- Brush with a slicker to remove tangles and dead hair.

- Clip with a No. 10 from the eyebrows to the back of the skull to the base of the ears, down the cheek, in a line from the outer corner of the eye to the outer edge of the mouth. ▼1

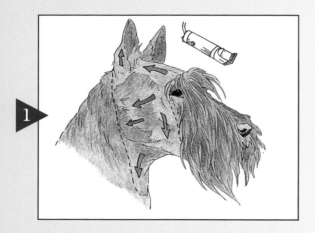

- Clip a narrow strip between the eyes to within 1 1/2 inches (4 cm) of the nose.

- Use scissors to shape the ears, leaving tufts inside at the base.

- Hand- or knife-strip, thin or clip from the head, down the neck, to leave a skirt from just above the elbow. Show dogs should not be clipped. Always remember to work in the direction of the coat growth. If stripping, remove only dead hair with a blunt stripping knife. ▼2

- Continue trimming down the back, taking in the sides of the body to a line level from just above the elbow to the bottom of the pelvis. ▼2

- Trim the upper part of tail by stripping or clipping it to tidy. ▼2

- Clip carefully under the tail and around the anal area with an Oster No. 10. When using clippers, do make sure first that the dog is not going to be shown.

- Clip the abdomen area. (Check with the owner first.)

- Clip down the front of the dog, below the throat to the breastbone, and blend in to the sides. ▼2

- Bathe the dog in a suitable shampoo, conditioning where necessary.

- Blow-dry the coat with the growth of the hair, brushing the long hair with a pin brush or slicker.

- Check the dog's nails, ears and teeth.

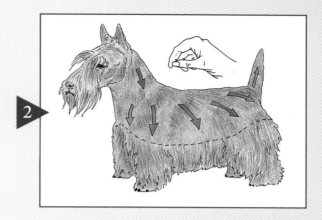

- Blend the skirt into the body all around. ▼2

- Trim around the feet to neaten their appearance.

- Cut the hair short between the pads and the toes.

- Comb the eyebrows and beard forward.

SEALYHAM TERRIER

COAT: The coat is long, hard and wiry with a weather-resistant undercoat.

MAINTENANCE: The dog's low carriage and long skirt attracts dirt, and grooming is required on a regular basis to keep the white or white-and-lemon coat smart.

PROCEDURE

Equipment needed: Slicker brush, wide-toothed comb, stripping knife, clippers.

Breed tip: Regular expert trimming is a must.

- Brush the coat with a slicker to remove debris and tangles.

- Comb with a wide-toothed comb.

- Strip or use thinning scissors on the head if it is not being clipped (show dogs should be stripped). Start from above the center of the eyebrow, as shown in the diagram, so the eyebrows will fall over the inner part of the eye, forwards toward the nose. Work backwards toward the back skull or the point at the top of the neck. Next, trim down from the inner corner of the eye to the edge of the mouth, and backwards to the throat. ▼1

- Then trim again from the center to the outer corners of the eye, down the cheek to the outer edge of the mouth and back to the throat **2**. For both pet and show dogs, clip from the sternum up to the line of the mouth and as far as the inner edge of the ear. **1** **2**

- Trim both sides of the ears downwards, and trim the edges with scissors. Pets can be clipped with a No. 10. **1** **2**

- For the pet dog, clip from the groin to the navel, and the insides of the thighs. Clip the anal area in a triangle shape for show dogs. Use a No. 7 Oster. **3**

- For show dogs, strip or thin from the head, down the neck and over the shoulder, taking in the brisket to the elbow. Pet dogs can be clipped with a No. 5.

- Continue stripping with a knife or finger and thumb, along and down the sides of the back to leave a skirt to be blended in with the line from the elbow to the pelvis.

- Trim the dog's tail by stripping or clipping from the base to the tip (obviously, do not clip a show dog, however).

- Comb the coat to remove loose hairs.

- Bathe the pet dog in white-enhancing shampoo, and apply conditioner where necessary. An ordinary dog shampoo should be used for show dogs – no substance can be used to enhance the coat.

- Blow the coat dry using medium heat, brushing the long hair in the direction of the hair growth with a pin brush or slicker.

- Check the dog's nails, ears and teeth. Hair inside the ear canal needs removing with forceps.

- Go over any lifted hair to neaten appearance.

- Blend the skirt and legs into the body with thinning shears, going with the hair growth at all times. **2**

- Scissor around the feet to give a catlike appearance. Remove hair from in between the pads. This is done for both show and pet dogs.

- Comb the fringe of the face downwards and scissor it level.

- Comb the eyebrows and beard forwards, and scissor with the hair growth to trim any stray or straggly hairs. The fringe falling from the eyes is solid and is not cut between the eyes.

WELSH TERRIER

COAT: The black-and-tan coat is wiry, tight, close and abundant. The top or guard coat is rough and wiry, and the undercoat is fairly soft. A single coat is undesirable.

MAINTENANCE: Starting at about 5 months of age, the jacket is hand- or knife-stripped every three months. Clipping will destroy the joyous color, though this procedure may be sought by pet owners requiring a cheaper grooming bill and for older dogs and those unable to sustain long hours of grooming.

PROCEDURE

Equipment needed: Two stripping knives (coarse and fine), scissors, thinning scissors, terrier pad, and a coarse- and fine-toothed comb.

Breed tip: This dog should look tailored and smart, yet natural.

- Using a terrier pad or pin-pad brush, work through the entire coat to remove tangles and any debris that may remain from the dog's exciting walks and investigations.

- Comb the jacket with a fine, metal comb. Use a coarser comb for whiskers and longer hair.

- Strip (with a fine knife) the head, neck, front and shoulder. Working from the middle of the eye to retain the eyebrows, strip backwards to the point of the neck, and down from the inner corner of the eye to the edge of the mouth, backwards to the throat. ▼1

- The eyebrows should preferably be trimmed with finger and thumb. They are left over the eyes but are not scissored off to a sharp edge like Schnauzer brows. The eyebrows create the mean look desired. Hair is not removed under the eye. The face should not look scooped out or trumpetlike. ▼1

- Closely trim the ears with a stripper or thinning scissors. Neaten the edges with scissors. ▼1

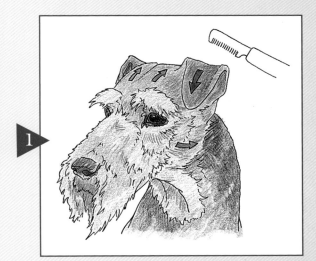

- Hand-strip down the neck and over the shoulder to the elbow point, leaving a fringe of hair at the lower chest and along underneath the rib cage, which is trimmed with scissors to accentuate the outline.

- A coarser knife is used to strip the body down to the base of the tail and over the dog's hip joints.

- Strip the tail with the growth of the hair, leaving the hair moderately long on the black side of the tail, and short on the tan side. The tail should not be left looking "whippy."

- Strip the legs to blend in or use thinning scissors or shears to carefully shape with the contours. This dog should look tailored and smart, yet natural.

- The Welsh Terrier is not frequently bathed. However, pet owners may like to bathe the dog when it becomes necessary, using a mild, natural shampoo to enhance the texture, then cage-, air- or gently blow-dry.

- Tidy loose hairs and shorten the beard to face forward, and tidy the eyebrows with thinning shears. (The eyebrows are not left long, as in the Schnauzer.)

- Check the Welsh Terrier's nails, ears and teeth, being careful to remove hair from the inside of the ear, using ear powder first to loosen the hair.

- Scissor the hair between the foot pads.

- With the pet dog, it is a good idea to clip a 2-inch (5 cm) line from the genitals to the chest to keep this area clean and hygienic. The genitals are also clipped short for the same reason. The best blade is an Oster No. 10, as this will not shave so close as to make the skin sore, but will be short enough to keep the whole area clean.

- Note: the use of chalk aids stripping. A good pointer is to mark the area requiring stripping with a chalk outline. If a trimming tool is used for stripping, it should be a blunt, dull, serrated-edged tool so as not to cut the throat. As with all terrier breeds, read the breed standard, and contact an expert in the breed or the breed club to be sure any trimming does not breach kennel club rules.

15 *THICK, DENSE-COATED BREEDS*

THICK, DENSE-COATED BREEDS FEATURED IN THIS SECTION:

CHOW CHOW
- Akita (Japanese)
- Alaskan Malamute
- Anatolian Shepherd Dog
- Canaan Dog
- Collie (Rough)
- Estrela Mountain Dog
- Finnish Lapphund
- Finnish Spitz
- German Shepherd Dog
- German Spitz
- Great Pyrenees
- Greenland Dog
- Hovawart
- Japanese Spitz
- Keeshond
- Kuvasz (Hungarian)
- Leonberger
- Maremma Sheepdog
- Newfoundland
- Norwegian Buhund
- Norwegian Elkhound
- Norwegian Lundehund
- Pomeranian
- Samoyed
- Schipperke
- Shiba Inu (Japanese)
- Siberian Husky
- St. Bernard
- Swedish Lapphund
- Tibetan Mastiff

COAT CARE

These dogs are truly handsome, mostly with wedge-shaped heads and beautiful eyes. They are designed to cope with nature, sometimes in extremes of cold weather. Mostly, they are well domesticated, as with the Keeshond and Norwegian Elkhound who are lovely to live with, but it is as well to remember they are usually very active dogs at heart and will not be content to lie on the sofa all day while their owners go out to work. Plus, their coats take considerable looking after.

When these dogs molt, they mean it. Fluffy hair will come out in handfuls. In a few days, a good molt can completely cover the living room carpet. Unfortunately, because these dogs are kept in a warm climate, they seemed to moult continuously, so vacuuming is a must on a daily basis. I know several owners of these breeds that have varnished wood floors rather than carpets for ease of cleaning.

A professional bath and groom will remove most of the offending hair in a few hours and save the owner considerable work. The quick removal of the molting coat may not be popular with the show exhibitor where most breeds require an abundance of coat. For pet owners, however, it is usually more practical to remove excess coat, especially when their dogs take up residence on the sofa for the evening to watch television with the family.

QUICK DRY

With all these breeds, the groomer will save considerable time drying the dog if the power blaster dryer is used to force water from the coat following the bath. The power blower can also be used to blow a considerable amount of dead hair from the coat, even before the bath. However, dogs need to get used to the high velocity of this blower, and some will not tolerate it at any cost.

DISLODGING THE COAT

With these breeds, it is sometimes as well to comb the hair initially, taking first a wide-toothed comb to dislodge the most offending hairs, and then a medium-toothed comb. Brushing can then be done to enhance the finish.

In some cases, the following procedure will budge most hairs:

- Brush thoroughly with the slicker or pin brush, first using the brush in an upwards stroke.
- Clean the hair out of the brush regularly.
- Then brush the coat in a downward stroke.
- Comb through to remove any loose hairs.

PROFESSIONAL GROOMING

These breeds are not clipped, stripped or thinned, but there is plenty of grooming to be undertaken, and more and more frequently they are coming into the salon to be professionally presented, whether as pet or show dogs.

These breeds are usually nice to work on, provided they have been accustomed to being brushed from an early age. However, they are mainly good-natured dogs that soon respond to a kind, firm hand and really enjoy all the attention they are given. All pet owners should be made aware that brushing and combing puppies is essential to their well-being and good health. Responsible breeders will remind them of this.

CHOW CHOW

Featured is the Chow Chow Brosscroft Madonna Bear, owned by Pippa Clare.

COAT: The Chow has an abundant coat, which is thick and stands off from the body. The Smooth Chow has a woolly undercoat with a short topcoat of plush texture, abundant, dense, straight and upstanding. The Rough Chow has a coat that is profuse, abundant, dense, straight and standoff. The outercoat is rather coarse, with a soft woolly undercoat. It is especially thick around the neck, forming a mane or ruff. It also has good culottes or breeching on his back thighs.

The color is whole black, red, blue, fawn, cream or white. The coat is frequently shaded, but not in patches or parti-color. The underpart of the tail and the back of the thighs are often of a lighter shade.

MAINTENANCE: This dog looks gorgeous when properly presented, but requires very regular brushing and combing, which few pet owners feel able to take on. However, if done frequently from a very young age, it becomes a pleasure for both Chow and owner.

PROCEDURE

Equipment needed: Wide-toothed comb, slicker brush, pin brush, trimming scissors.

Breed tip: Chow Chows are prone to matting around the ears, so be careful to remove any tangles.

- Brush the entire coat with a slicker , getting right down to the skin to remove dust and prevent any buildup of dead hairs or felting in any area where the coat is regularly compressed. Hold the coat down with one hand and brush upwards with the other. Start with gentle surface brushing and work through the depth of the whole coat, brushing the coat toward the head. Be thorough when brushing the breeching and always comb through in an upwards direction.

- Put the dog in the bath and wet the coat thoroughly, right down to the skin.

- Bathe with a suitable shampoo, being vigilant to remove all lather when rinsing. Then apply a coat-protecting conditioner.

- Rub the dog with an absorbent towel to remove the majority of the moisture.

- Blow the coat dry while brushing with a pin or slicker brush. Alternatively, use a power blower to remove excess water from the coat.

- Comb through with a wide-toothed comb.

- Check the dog's nails and trim if necessary.

- Ears should be checked for any dirt, soreness, or odor.

- Teeth should also be cleaned and checked.

- Hair from underneath the feet should be removed to prevent mud from sticking to the fur and causing sores.

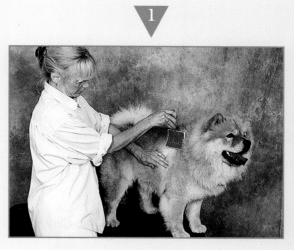

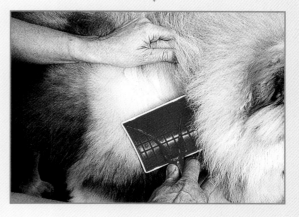

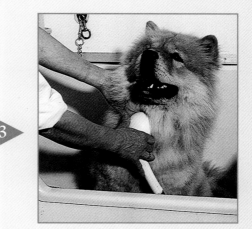

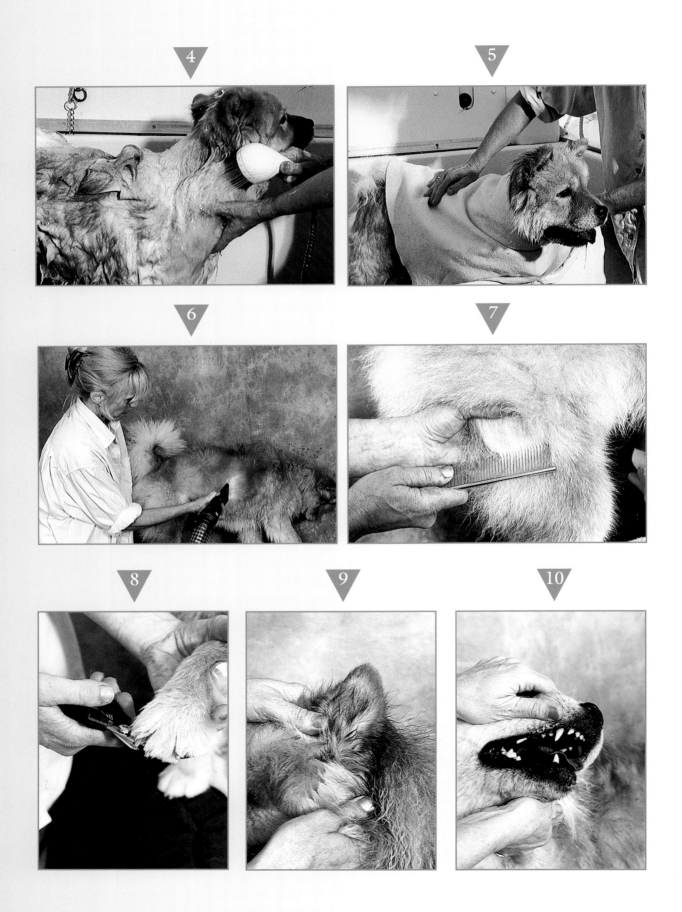

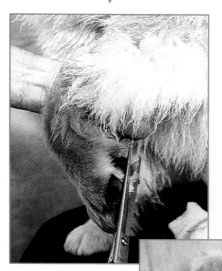

- Trim the feet to help produce the round, catlike appearance required. Please note: the Chow is not trimmed for show purposes.

- The finished dog.

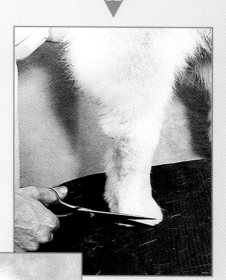

AKITA (JAPANESE)

COAT: The Akita is double-coated. The outer coarse coat is straight and stands off the body. The undercoat is soft and dense, and the coat on the tail is profuse.

The coat can be any color. Markings are well defined, with or without a mask or blaze.

MAINTENANCE: Regular weekly brushing will keep the coat healthy. The undercoat, as well as the outercoat, normally sheds twice a year.

PROCEDURE

Equipment needed: Slicker or pin brush, wide-toothed comb.

Breed tip: Use a bristle brush on a young pup to introduce it to grooming and handling.

- Brush the entire coat with a pin brush or slicker brush.

- The undercoat is not stripped out, but is untangled and groomed with a metal comb.

- Bathe the dog in a good-quality, pH-balanced or natural shampoo.

- Blow- or air-dry after soaking up any excess water with towels.

- Check the dog's nails, ears and teeth.

- Show people tend to tidy the feet if required by trimming the excess hair between the pads, enhancing their tight appearance. You should be very careful if you choose to do this.

ALASKAN MALAMUTE

COAT: The Alaskan Malamute's coat is thick in the coarse outer guardcoat; the undercoat is dense, oily and woolly. The coarse guardcoat stands out, with thick fur around the neck. The coat is of medium length, increasing around the shoulders and the neck, down the back, over the croup and in the breeching and plume.

MAINTENANCE: Regular brushing is essential from puppyhood.

PROCEDURE

Equipment needed: Slicker or pin brush, wide-toothed comb, rake.

Breed tip: Brush against the lie of the coat on a regular basis.

- This coat often benefits from a protein coat conditioner to aid grooming and to help protect the hair from breaking.

- Brush with a slicker to remove dead hair.

- Comb with a molting comb to remove any loose undercoat.

- Bathe the dog in a good-quality shampoo. Many breeders recommend a pH-alkaline shampoo when bathing is undertaken. It is not a breed that is frequently bathed, but Alaskans do look stunning after such ablution. Certainly, a warm bath helps to lift the coat during shedding.

- Dry with a power dryer to blow out any excess water after toweling to speed up drying time.

- Finish with a blower, brushing the coat with a pin brush, being careful not to dry out the coat. Or allow the coat to dry in warm air.

- Remember to check the dog's nails, ears and teeth.

- With pet dogs, you might want to neaten the hair on the back of the pastern with small scissors or thinners, but show dogs should be left natural.

OVER THE MOON

Jannat Al-Haddad's kennel of Highmoon was top of the league in Alaskan Malamutes for many years until she recently started to cut down on her showing activities. Having bought her first pup in 1960, Jannat has been a devotee of the breed for more than 40 years. She judges in many countries around the world and has twice judged the breed at Crufts. She was Honorary Secretary of the Alaskan Malamute Club for 25 years and now writes the breed notes for a dog paper.

DAILY MAINTENANCE

Grooming the Alaskan Malamute, Jannat says, is surprisingly easy, despite its dense, heavy coat. This coat should never be long and this means it doesn't normally mat. And, like many of the Spitz breeds, the Malamute's coat doesn't smell. A daily brush against the lie of the coat is basically all that is needed and bathing isn't required on a regular basis. Brushing the coat against the lie helps for the offstanding requirement of the breed standard.

MORE AT MOLTING

At the time of molting, more attention will be required. There is a difference between males and bitches at this time. Males tend to have one molt heavier than the other, whereas the bitches have two roughly equal molts. This molting has been described as being like a mattress coming unstuffed and also as resembling an exploding thistle; Jannat says that both comparisons are valid.

Raking or combing at this time is required every day or every other day to remove the dense, oily, woolly undercoat as quickly as possible to allow the new coat to come through. It is particularly important to get the dead hair out of the feathering and the tail to prevent matting. A pin or slicker brush is used, as is a medium- to fine-toothed comb, and simple hand-plucking is also effective.

When the dog is being shown, it is better to bathe it at least two days before a show to allow the coat to regain its desired texture and oiliness. Chalk is sometimes used to harshen the coat but all traces must be removed before the dog enters the ring.

The Alaskan Malamute molts profusely – something prospective owners should be prepared for.

ANATOLIAN SHEPHERD

MAINTENANCE: This is a breed that is comparatively easy to look after. However, it looks stunning after a bath and professional groom.

PROCEDURE

Equipment needed: Bristle brush, medium-toothed comb.

Breed tip: An occasional bath will help to remove loose hair from the Anatolian's thick, dense coat.

- Brush through the entire coat with a bristle brush.

- Bathe the dog with a protein pH-balanced shampoo.

- Rinse thoroughly, taking care to ensure all soap has been removed.

- Remove any excess water from the coat while the dog is still in the bath. Follow this by drying the dog in a cage-dryer or by blow-drying. To avoid skin problems, it is important to ensure that the undercoat is not left damp after bathing.

- Check the dog's nails. The adult dog weighs about 130 pounds (60 kg) and so regular exercise on hard surfaces is normally sufficient to keep the claws naturally short. Hind dewclaws may be present and these will need regular trimming to prevent problems such as overgrowth or snagging.

- Next, check the dog's teeth and ears. Regular cleaning with antiseptic wipes will avoid irritation caused by the waxy deposit that can build up in warm, damp conditions.

COAT: It has a relatively short, dense coat with a thick undercoat. It is flat, close-lying and neither fluffy nor wavy. The coat is slightly longer and thicker at the neck, shoulder and tail, with no feathering on the ears or legs. This double coat is designed to protect the working dog against the extremes of temperature it faces on the bleak high plateau of central Turkey. The coarse outer coat naturally sheds water and mud while the dense, soft undercoat, which is slightly less thick in summer, provides insulation against the cold and sun.

All Anatolians, whether kept as working, pet or show dogs, undergo a complete molt twice a year, a process that takes two to three weeks. The outer hair is loosened and replaced gradually over this period, but the woolly undercoat is shed quite spectacularly, and can be gently plucked away in great handfuls or carefully raked out, taking care not to scratch the skin.

CANAAN DOG

COAT: The coat is described as having a dense outercoat, harsh and straight, of short to medium length. The undercoat is close and profuse according to the season.

Color: solid-colored sand to red-brown, white or black, or spotted white with any of the aforementioned colors. Both patterns can be with or without a mask. If the dog is masked, it must be symmetrical. A black mask is permitted on all colors, and white markings are also acceptable.

MAINTENANCE: Regular brushing will keep this dog looking good.

PROCEDURE

Equipment needed: Bristle brush or slicker brush, medium-toothed comb. When the dog is molting, a grooming rake should be used, as it gets through the thick undercoat more easily than a comb or bristle brush.

Breed tip: The coat is thicker than you would imagine, so make sure it is well dried after bathing.

- Brush thoroughly with a bristle brush.

- Comb through with a medium-toothed comb to remove dead hairs.

- Bathe the dog in a natural-ingredient shampoo, and rinse well.

- Towel the excess water from the coat, then warm air- or cage-dry.

- Check the dog's nails, ears and teeth.

COLLIE (ROUGH)

COAT: The coat fits the outline of the dog's body and is very dense. The outercoat is straight and harsh to the touch. The undercoat is soft, furry and very close, almost hiding the skin. The mane and frill (neck hair) are very abundant, and the mask and face are smooth. The ears are smooth at the tips, but carry more hair toward their base. The front legs are well feathered, and the

hindlegs are profusely feathered above the hocks (smooth below the hock joint). The hair on the tail is very profuse.

MAINTENANCE: Either as a pet or a show dog, regular weekly grooming will maintain the glamorous coat and featherings. It is only during a molt/shed that extra, daily grooming or a bath is required.

PROCEDURE

Equipment needed: A pure bristle brush, wide-toothed comb, scissors (thinning and blunt-nosed), water spray or spritzer, towels. A pin brush is required only during a molt.

Breed tip: Due to the nature of the double coat (the long outer hair and the thick undercoat), only a pure bristle brush should be used. The use of a pin brush on a regular basis will remove all the undercoat and spoil the elegant outline of the Collie. A coat conditioner may be added to the water spray (for pet dogs), but regular bathing is not required, as this will soften the coat and cause tangles and matted hair to collect.

- Due to the texture of the coat (which should be harsh), never groom the dog without using a fine water spray, otherwise the hair could be broken.

- Remove your dog's collar and stand your collie. Lightly spray all over with a fine water spray containing only water (for show dogs to comply with regulations), but with a coat conditioner for all other dogs.

- Towel off the coat. This will remove most surface dust and dirt. The majority of Collies will only require the feet and legs to be bathed. This can be done by standing the dog's front feet and then its back feet in a bowl of water and bathing them (see below).

- Starting at the back, while the coat is still damp, brush against the lie of the coat, lifting it in layers. Continue through, covering the front mane and frills, not forgetting the tail. By the time you have finished, a collie with the correct textured coat will be dry.

- Use a wide-toothed comb to tidy up the leg featherings and behind the ears.

- Gently comb the fine hair that grows around the ears and, if preparing for the show ring, use your thinning scissors to remove excess hair. The long, fine hair, which can grow around the back of the head, can also be removed by using finger and thumb and plucking the hair out.

- Using blunt-nosed scissors, trim around the line of the foot and remove the long hair which grows between the toes. Comb out the feathering on the hindlegs. In pet collies, this may be trimmed using scissors, cutting a line parallel to the bone. In show dogs, this is usually trimmed using thinning scissors, which gives a softer, more natural look.

- At this stage, check the length of the Collie's nails, not forgetting the dewclaws, which can be found on the front legs, just above the foot. Trim the nails with specialized nail clippers.

- During the coat molt, daily grooming will be required for all Collies. The use of a pin brush is quite acceptable at this time, as the object of this exercise is to remove all the dead undercoat to allow new hair growth. The undercoat can easily mat up at this time, especially under the elbows, around the ears, and around the hindlegs. If mats do occur, use your blunt-nosed scissors to cut into the mat, away from the skin, and loosen off the mat. A comb-through will remove most mats. A well-cared-for Collie will not mat up if regular grooming takes place.

- In the unlikely event that an allover bath is required, use a medicated or conditioning shampoo (if your Collie has rolled in something unpleasant, a medicated shampoo is preferable). Remember, though, that constant bathing will soften the coat.

- Wash the dog all over. Make sure that the water reaches the skin – the thick, woolly undercoat protects the skin and it may take some time to soak through. Protect the ears with cotton batting to stop water from entering. Shampoo and rinse thoroughly with plenty of warm water. Remove your dog from the bath and allow your Collie to shake itself dry.

- Towel down and gently brush with a bristle brush. Hand-held dryers or power blasters will hasten drying, but constant use, especially of the blaster, will speed up coat loss!

- If you are bathing to remove dead coat, using a pin brush will quicken coat loss, especially if used two to three days after a bath.

- The addition of any coloring (blue whiteners, etc.) is not permitted for shows, but may be used at home to enhance the white.

- Finally, don't forget to remove the cotton batting from the ears and to check the condition of the ears, eyes and teeth.

ESTRELA MOUNTAIN DOG

COAT: There are two types – long and short. The outercoat on the long variety is thick and moderately harsh, resembling goat hair. It lies close over the body, and is flat or slightly wavy, never curly. The undercoat is very dense and normally lighter in color. The hair is short and smooth on the head, and abundant around the neck and chest, forming a ruff. The short coat variety is thick, moderately harsh and straight, with a shorter undercoat.

MAINTENANCE: Needs regular brushing.

PROCEDURE

Equipment needed: Pin, slicker or bristle brush, a medium-toothed comb and a good rake.

Breed tip: Do not overlook the grooming needs of the short-coated variety, which requires as much regular attention as the long coats.

- Brush with a pin, slicker or bristle brush.

- Comb through to remove dead hairs.

- If bathing is undertaken, use a natural-based shampoo and be careful to rinse thoroughly.

- Dry with absorbent towels.

- A good rake should be used to remove the shedding coat when the dog molts.

- Check the dog's nails, ears and teeth.

- Check for clogged hair under the pads and remove with scissors.

FINNISH LAPPHUND

COAT: The coat is profuse. The outercoat is long and coarse, the undercoat soft and thick. The coat is shorter on the head and the front parts of the legs.

The coat comes in all colors, but the main color must dominate.

MAINTENANCE: The Finnish Lapphund needs regular brushing, especially when kept mostly in the house as a family pet. However, an outdoor type of family will suit it better.

PROCEDURE

Equipment needed: Slicker brush, wide-toothed comb.

Breed tip: Some Finnish Lapphunds seem to have a deep-seated fear of water, perhaps relating to the fact that a wet dog could quickly become a dead dog in the freezing

Finnish conditions its ancestors endured.

To prevent this from becoming a problem, be organized when grooming this breed. Before you begin, make sure you have everything on hand that you will need, to minimize the length of time during which your Lapphund is wet. If you don't, the dog will roll and shake itself excessively following bathing.

- Comb through the entire coat with a wide-toothed comb, removing any excessive and molting coat.

- Brush the entire coat with a slicker, brushing upwards and then downwards to remove dead hair.

- Bathe the dog in a good-quality, natural-ingredient shampoo, such as tea tree and lavender.

- No conditioner should be used on the Finnish Lapphund's coat – just rinse the coat well, taking care to remove all the soap. The coat should be clean, healthy and have a matte finish.

- After rinsing, towel the coat well and finish with a normal blower. Make sure the dryer blows the hair and not the skin, or it will be very uncomfortable for your Finnish Lapphund.

- Remember to check the dog's nails, ears and teeth.

- Check underneath the feet for clogged hair, and remove only the minimum of hair with scissors. Otherwise, the dog should be left natural – never trimmed elsewhere on the body.

FINNISH SPITZ

COAT: The coat on the head and on the front of its straight legs is short and close. On the body and the back of the legs it is longish, semi-erect, and is stiffer on the neck and back. The outercoat on the shoulders is considerably longer and coarser. The hair is longer and denser on the back of the thighs and on the tail. The undercoat is short, soft and dense. The color is reddish brown or red gold, preferably bright.

MAINTENANCE: No trimming is necessary, but brushing is a must.

PROCEDURE

Equipment needed: Slicker brush, wide- or medium-toothed comb.

Breed tip: As with all Spitz breeds, brush against the lie of the coat.

- Brush the coat, and then comb through with a wide-toothed comb.

- Bathe only when necessary. Use a natural shampoo and rinse well.

- Check the dog's nails, ears and teeth.

- Run over the coat with velvet or a silk pad.

GERMAN SHEPHERD DOG

COAT: The German Shepherd Dog has a thick, double coat. Some have long coats.

MAINTENANCE: The German Shepherd's coat is relatively easy to maintain and looks positively sparkling after a bath. Regular brushing will keep it in great condition.

PROCEDURE

Equipment needed: Curry or slicker brush, medium-toothed comb.

Breed tip: The dog can lose so much hair that it is best to groom it outside (in fair weather) or in a noncarpeted room.

- Brush the body hair thoroughly with a curry brush or slicker to remove dead hair.

- Bathe the dog in a pH-alkaline balanced shampoo or with a purifying shampoo and mask.

- Blow the coat with a blaster to remove excess water.

- Finish the drying process with a blower, or air- or cage-dry.

- Check the dog's nails, ears and teeth.

- Brush the coat with a sisal brush and, if necessary, lightly spray with coat conditioner.

GERMAN SPITZ

COAT: Its coat is double and consists of a soft, woolly undercoat and a long harsh-textured, perfectly straight topcoat covering the whole of the body.

The hair is very abundant around the neck and forequarters with a frill of profuse off-standing straight hair extending over the shoulders.

In some countries, there are color restrictions – contact your national kennel club or breed association for details of the breed standard.

MAINTENANCE: Grooming should be regular and thorough, but the coat is easy to maintain.

PROCEDURE

Equipment needed: Slicker brush, medium- or wide-toothed comb.

Breed tip: The German Spitz is not a trimmed breed, although some breeders do tend to tidy the hair on the hock and around the feet.

- Brush through the entire coat with a slicker brush or pin brush, removing mats and dead coat.

- Bathe the dog in a suitable good-quality shampoo.

- Rinse thoroughly, ensuring that all soap has been removed.

- Apply a conditioner and again rinse thoroughly.

- Blow the coat dry, brushing with a pin brush.

- Don't forget to check the dog's nails, ears and teeth.

GREAT PYRENEES (PYRENEAN MOUNTAIN DOG)

COAT: The coat consists of a profuse undercoat of very fine hair and an outercoat of longer, coarser-textured hair that is weather-resistant. The coat is thick, straight or slightly wavy, but it is never curly or fuzzy.

The Great Pyrenees color is mainly white with patches of badger, wolf gray or pale yellow.

MAINTENANCE: This breed needs thorough grooming at least once a week. In addition, the Great Pyrenees should always be groomed thoroughly before bathing.

PROCEDURE

Equipment needed: Pin brush, wide-toothed comb and a fine-toothed comb (the finer-toothed version is for knots around the ears).

Breed tip: A huge breed, the Great Pyrenees puppy must get used to grooming from a young age; persuading a reluctant adult to be bathed is not an easy feat.

- Brush through the entire coat with a pin brush. Be extra vigilant at getting underneath the body and in the breeches, as you must ensure you remove dead hairs that will otherwise cause clogging.

- After brushing, comb with a wide-toothed comb.

- Bathe the dog in a white-enhancing shampoo (but use an ordinary shampoo before a show, as most kennel club rules state that no substance is allowed to be used that will alter the coat).

- Rinse thoroughly.

- If possible, allow the dog to shake a good deal of the water from its coat.

- Towel-dry with a superabsorbent towel.

- After removing the excess moisture with a towel, use a domestic hair-dryer to dry the rest of the coat. While you are drying the coat, smooth down the hair with the brush so the topcoat lies close and flat to the undercoat.

- Complete the drying process with warm air or with a blower.

- Do not forget to check the dog's nails, ears and teeth.

- Finally, brush over the coat once again, using a spray conditioner if required.

GREENLAND DOG

COAT: Thick, double coat, consisting of an impenetrable undercoat and protruding outercoat of coarser hair.

MAINTENANCE: Brushing is all that is required for this breed, together with an occasional bath.

PROCEDURE

Equipment needed: Bristle brush, wire brush, medium-toothed and wide-toothed combs.

Breed tip: Never underestimate the Greenland Dog's size and weight – you may need to enlist help for bathtimes.

• Brush through with a bristle brush.

• Next, comb to remove dead hairs.

• Bathe when required in a natural-ingredient shampoo, and rinse well.

• Towel-dry and then finish in warm air or a cage.

• Check the dog's nails, ears and teeth.

• For show dogs, towel off, use a blaster to remove all excess water and any remaining loose coat, then blow-dry to finish.

HOVAWART

COAT: The coat is long in appearance, but is short on the face and front legs, and is not as long on the rib cage and the thighs. It has a fine, light undercoat, which is straight or slightly waved. The color is black/gold, black or blond.

MAINTENANCE: Relatively easy to look after, only requiring regular brushing and the occasional bath. Trimming is done only on the feet.

PROCEDURE

Equipment needed: Curry brush or slicker brush, wide-toothed comb.

Breed tip: For the show ring, bathe the Hovawart well in advance, leaving enough time for the coat to settle.

- Brush through the entire coat with a curry brush or slicker.

- Comb with a wide-toothed comb.

- Bathe the dog in a natural-ingredient shampoo.

- Rinse thoroughly, ensuring that all the shampoo has been removed.

- The coat can be blow-dried after using a light conditioner to enhance the coat and to prevent dryness.

- Check the dog's nails, ears and teeth.

- Check underneath the feet for excess hair and remove with scissors.

- The feet can be trimmed round with scissors to enhance their oval, well-arched appearance.

JAPANESE SPITZ

COAT: It has a profuse standoff outercoat and a thick, short, dense undercoat, which is soft in texture. The mane on the neck and shoulders reaches down to the brisket. The tail is profusely covered with long hair and is curled over the back. The hair on the face is shorter, as it is on the ears, on the front of the forelegs, the hindlegs and below the hock.

MAINTENANCE: Regular brushing is essential.

PROCEDURE

Equipment needed: Pin brush or slicker, wide-toothed comb.

Breed tip: Should the dog get muddy and dirty, do not try to brush or wash him clean. Wait for the mud to dry, brush, and the mud will fall off the hair, leaving it white and clean.

- Brush the coat thoroughly with a pin brush or slicker. Brushing against the lie of the coat keeps it clean and dust-free.

- Comb with a wide-toothed comb.

- Bathe in a white-enhancing shampoo and apply a suitable white conditioner for that extra sparkle. (Prior to a show, no coat-enhancing substances should be used, of course.)

- Blow-dry while brushing the coat with a pin brush.

- Remember to check the dog's nails, ears and teeth.

- Use thinners to tidy any straggly hair from the hocks.

- Trim hairs under and around the feet to give them a catlike appearance.

- Check under the feet for excess hair and trim with scissors to prevent clogging.

KEESHOND

COAT: The coat is a harsh, standoff and straight one. It has a dense ruff and is well feathered on the forelegs. The trousers are profuse. The Keeshond is not feathered below the hocks. It has a soft, thick, light-colored undercoat.

MAINTENANCE: Less arduous than it appears. Brush regularly with a pin brush or slicker and comb out dead hairs.

PROCEDURE

Equipment needed: Bristle or nylon brush (with the bristles well spaced – not close), and a wide, long-toothed comb.

Breed tip: Easier to keep groomed than its coat would have you believe.

- Brush the coat in layers, right down to the skin. Do this by first brushing toward the tail and then finish by brushing toward the head.

- Comb the feathering and hocks.

- Trim around the feet to give them a catlike appearance, and check under the feet and remove excess hair between the pads.

- Check the dog's nails, ears and teeth.

- Tidy the hocks with scissors.

- Use a comb only when the dog is molting, to remove loose undercoat.

- Bathing is seldom necessary as the coat is not oily. If the coat gets muddy, let it dry and then it can be brushed out easily. Bathing softens the coat, which is not desirable in the show ring and makes it less easy to keep.

- If a bath is unavoidable (e.g., if the dog has a skin infection), use a shampoo recommended by your vet, and rinse thoroughly.

- Blow-dry, brushing the hair away from the heat and not blowing the skin.

- For showing, the feet, stomach and sometimes the trousers are bathed with a harsh-coat shampoo. A pin brush can be used on the ruff, trousers and tail plume at the very last minute before going into the show ring (used more, it will remove too much undercoat).

KUVASZ (HUNGARIAN)

COAT: The Kuvasz coat is pure white. It has a slight wave and is double-coated, with a medium-coarse topcoat and a fine, woolly undercoat.

MAINTENANCE: Regular brushing is required, and perhaps a bath.

PROCEDURE

Equipment needed: Slicker brush, wide-toothed comb.

Breed tip: Be prepared for profuse shedding in warm weather.

• Brush the entire coat with a slicker to remove dead hairs.

• Follow by combing with a wide-toothed comb.

• Bathe the dog in a tea tree and lavender or protein-balanced shampoo.

• Rinse well, leaving no trace of shampoo suds in the thick coat.

• Towel-dry, then blow-dry with warm air or use a cage-dryer or a blower.

• Don't forget to check the dog's nails, ears and teeth.

LEONBERGER

COAT: The coat is medium-soft to hard, fairly long and lies close to the body, despite a good undercoat.
   Slightly wavy, but never curled, the coat is very evident on the mane, throat and chest, and the color is light yellow, golden to red-brown.

MAINTENANCE: The Leonberger's coat requires regular brushing to keep it in good condition.

PROCEDURE

Equipment needed: Slicker brush, metal comb.

Breed tip: It is very important to get the Leonberger puppy used to regular grooming, before it grows!

• Brush through the coat with a slicker brush.

• Comb with a metal comb.

• Bathe only as necessary. Use a good-quality proprietary shampoo. Rinse thoroughly.

• Remove excess water with absorbent towels or blast out with a power blower.

• Finish the drying process by using warm air or a blower.

• Brush through the coat with a slicker.

• Check the dog's nails, ears and teeth.

MAREMMA SHEEPDOG

COAT: The dog's coat fits its outline and is long, plentiful and rather harsh. It has a slight waviness but curliness is not permitted. The coat forms a thick ruff on the neck. A thick, close undercoat is present, especially in winter.

The color is usually all white.

MAINTENANCE: Requires regular brushing. The coat sheds once or twice a year.

PROCEDURE

Equipment needed: Bristle brush/slicker, medium-toothed comb.

Breed tip: A white-enhancing shampoo is a useful addition to the grooming collection (though, given show regulations, it should not be used on show dogs).

• Brush the entire coat with a bristle brush.

• Use a comb to remove excess undercoat.

• Bathe the Maremma in a white-enhancing shampoo (only for pet dogs – show dogs

should not have their coat altered) and rinse well to ensure all suds are removed.

• Remove excess water from the coat with a superabsorbent towel, or use a power blower.

• Finish the dog in warm air or a cage, or with a blower.

• Check the dog's ears and nails, and clean and trim where necessary.

• Finally, brush its teeth.

NEWFOUNDLAND

COAT: Double, flat, dense, coarse and oily.

MAINTENANCE: This water-resistant coat is extremely time-consuming.

PROCEDURE

Equipment needed: Slicker brush, wide-toothed comb.

Breed tip: Early socialization and an introduction to grooming is essential.

- Brush through the coat from root to tip with a slicker brush to remove dead hairs.

- Comb with a wide-toothed comb.

- Bathe in a protein pH-balanced shampoo, and rinse thoroughly.

- Blow excess water from the coat with a power blower or let the dog shake outside if the air is warm enough. Then power-dry.

- Newfies have hair that grows under and over the ear, which should be trimmed (to let air circulate and to prevent infection, and so that the ear looks neat and tidy). The excess hair around the ear flap should be trimmed, following the natural curve of the ear. Then the long hair over the flap can be slightly trimmed, using thinning scissors – only take a little hair off at a time, so there is less chance of making a terrible mistake. This will create more of a natural appearance. Thinning scissors can be used on other parts if needed.

- Check the dog's nails, ears and teeth.

- Check between the pads for matted, excess hair and remove.

- Trim the anal area, if necessary.

- Spray with a coat-protecting conditioner – obviously, show dogs cannot have anything applied to the coat.

- Extra grooming is required during molting.

NORWEGIAN BUHUND

COAT: The Buhund's coat is harsh but smooth, and the undercoat is soft and woolly.

MAINTENANCE: A breed that is easy to keep clean.

PROCEDURE

Equipment needed: Bristle brush, medium-toothed comb.

Breed tip: In common with other Spitz breeds, the Norwegian Buhund enjoys a good chat with other dogs – something to bear in mind if you run a salon. If you have a Buhund booked in, avoid having other known "barkers" scheduled for that morning or afternoon, or you could end up with a headache!

- Brush through the entire coat with a bristle brush.

- Comb to remove dead hairs.

- Bathe the dog in a natural shampoo, and rinse well.

- Towel-dry and finish with warm air or a blower, or cage-dry.

- Remember to check the dog's nails, ears and teeth.

NORWEGIAN ELKHOUND

COAT: This most attractive hound has a close, abundant and weather-resistant coat, with a soft, woolly undercoat that will molt profusely. The coat is short and smooth on the head and front legs, and longest on the neck, back of the thighs and the tail.

The color is gray or various shades with black tips to the outer coat. It is lighter on the chest, stomach, legs, underside of the tail, buttocks and in a harness mark (a darker patch across the body). The ears and foreface are dark, with a dark line from the eye to the ear being desirable. The undercoat is pure pale gray.

MAINTENANCE: The coat is not trimmed, but will benefit from a bath at molting time to help rid it of all the dead hairs.

A bitch sheds twice a year, just prior to a season; males will shed around once a year. They do not necessarily shed in the summer, as the thick undercoat insulates against heat as well as cold. Requires regular brushing.

PROCEDURE

Equipment needed: Slicker brush, wide-toothed comb.

Breed tip: Keep the Elkhound groomed regularly unless you want a heap of hair on the carpet!

- Thoroughly brush the coat with a slicker and remove dead hairs with a medium-toothed comb.

- Bathe as necessary, using a good-quality shampoo.

- Rinse thoroughly, making sure all the soap has been removed.

- These dogs usually shake off the excess water, and the coat can then be dried with a towel.

- In the United States, the dogs are often bathed prior to a show, and the coat is dried by blasting out the excess water (where the dog will tolerate the high-velocity blower). Otherwise, use superabsorbent paper towels.

American owners also generally blow-dry the coat, while brushing with a pin brush or slicker. However, this is not done in Europe and the U.K.

- Brush and comb through the coat with a light spray of stay-in-the-coat conditioner.

- Do not forget that show dogs are not permitted to have any coat-altering substances used on their coats.

- Do not forget to check the Elkhound's nails, ears and teeth. Clean the ears and teeth as necessary, and trim the nails if they have grown too long.

NORWEGIAN LUNDEHUND

COAT: It has a dense, rough outercoat with a soft undercoat. The coat is short on the head and front legs, and is longer on the neck and thighs.

The color is reddish brown to fallow, preferably with black tips on the hairs. Black or gray are also acceptable. All colors with white markings or white with dark markings.

MAINTENANCE: Fairly easy to maintain with regular brushing.

PROCEDURE

Equipment needed: Bristle brush, medium-toothed comb.

Breed tip: A quick once-over with a sisal brush or cloth after grooming will give the coat a marvelous gleam.

- Brush the coat thoroughly with a bristle brush.

- Comb out the dead hair.

- Bathe the dog, if required, with a natural-ingredient shampoo, and rinse well.

- Use an absorbent towel to take away excess moisture from the coat and finish the drying process with warm air.

- Check the dog's nails, ears and teeth.

POMERANIAN

COAT: The coat is made up of an undercoat and an outercoat. The former is soft and fluffy; the latter is long, straight and harsh, and covers the whole of the body.

The coat is very abundant around the neck and the fore part of the shoulders and chest, forming a frill that extends over the shoulder. The forequarters are well feathered, and the thighs and hindlegs are well feathered to the hocks.

MAINTENANCE: It needs regular attention to keep it clean and attractive. Thorough brushing, checking nails, cleaning ears and teeth, and trimming should be done once a week.

Males cast their coats once a year and bitches twice a year (usually after a season), ending up looking quite sorry for themselves. Do not worry, it will grow back, sometimes better than ever.

PROCEDURE

Equipment needed: Slicker/pin brush, medium-toothed metal comb, scissors, cotton buds.

Breed tip: Brush against the lie of the coat to give the Pomeranian its round pompom appearance.

- Brush the coat with the slicker/pin brush. Work from the top of the head, layering the hair as you go and making sure you reach skin level.

- Next, work through the coat with the comb. If you encounter any tangles, try to tease them out gently using finger and thumb or a comb. If you need to use scissors, cut down

the length of the knot – not across – to ensure minimal coat loss.

- A bath should only be considered when the dog is out of coat – when in coat, use a dry shampoo. For a wet bath, use a suitable pH-alkaline-balanced shampoo, rinsing carefully.

- Blow-dry the hair. Work from the head, layering the hair as you go. Brush as you dry.

- Check the dog's nails and clean its ears and teeth.

- Trim the hair with thinning shears or scissors from the hocks in order to give a smooth finish.

- Trim the hair from under the feet where necessary, tidying around the feet to give them a catlike appearance.

- The hair around the anus should also be trimmed for hygiene reasons.

SAMOYED

COAT: The body coat is thick and close, with a soft and short undercoat. It has harsh (but not wiry) hairs growing through it, forming a water-resistant outercoat, that stands away straight and is free from curl.

MAINTENANCE: This thick, luxuriant coat requires much attention, but the dog looks magnificent when well turned out.

Samoyeds shed their coats periodically and will require extra grooming during this time.

PROCEDURE

Equipment needed: Pin brush, wide-toothed comb.

Breed tip: This dog is worth all the attention that its coat requires.

- Brush through the coat with a pin brush to remove dead hairs.

- Comb with a medium- or wide-toothed comb.

- Bathe in a superwhite enhancing shampoo to help remove stains or discoloring, applying a nourishing white conditioner. Remember that for the show ring no substances must be used on the coat.

- Blast excess water from the coat and blow-dry.

- Check the Samoyed's nails, ears and teeth.

SCHIPPERKE

COAT: It has a typically crisp, dense coat, which is abundant. It is smooth on the head, ears and legs, and lies close on the back and side.

The Schipperke's coat is erect and thick around the neck, forming a mane, ruff and frill, and there are good culottes on the back of the thighs.

MAINTENANCE: The Schipperke is easy to maintain.

PROCEDURE

Equipment needed: Pin brush or slicker, wide- or medium-toothed comb.

Breed tip: The tight-fitting coat makes this an easy dog to keep clean.

- Brush with a pin brush or slicker, removing dead hairs.

- Bathe in a suitable pH-balanced shampoo.

- Rinse thoroughly.

- Apply a quality conditioner to add that extra sparkle to the Schipperke's dark coat.

- Blow the coat dry, following the hair growth.

- Check the dog's nails, ears and teeth.

SHIBA INU (JAPANESE)

COAT: The coat is thick. It has a hard, straight outercoat, with a soft, dense undercoat. The hair on the tail is slightly longer.

The Shiba Inu color is red, black, black and tan, or brindle. White with red or gray tinge.

MAINTENANCE: Easy to maintain, with only regular brushing required to keep the dog looking smart and clean.

PROCEDURE

Equipment needed: Slicker brush, wide-toothed comb.

Breed tip: Don't neglect to gently brush the tail, which has slightly longer hair than on the rest of the body.

- Brush through the entire coat with a slicker brush. Brush in the opposite way to how you would normally groom – i.e., brush toward the head. Along the top of the back, however, brush toward the tail.

- Next, comb the coat with a wide-toothed comb to remove dead hairs.

- Bathe the dog in a natural shampoo, and rinse thoroughly.

- If necessary, condition the coat with a light cream to suit the coat texture, and rinse out thoroughly.

- Remove excess water from the coat with an absorbent towel and finish by drying with warm air, in a cage or with a light blower.

- Check the nails, ears and teeth.

SIBERIAN HUSKY

COAT: The Siberian has a double coat, which is medium in length, giving the dog a well-furred appearance. The undercoat is soft and dense. Guard hairs of the outercoat are straight and smooth-lying, never harsh, rough or shaggy.

MAINTENANCE: It is easy to groom with regular weekly brushing with a bristle brush. Comb out dead and molting hairs with a medium-toothed comb.

If you have any difficulty with the coat or require more specialist supervision, contact your breed club for advice.

PROCEDURE

Equipment needed: Bristle brush, medium-toothed comb.

Breed tip: A heavy molter, the Siberian will need regular grooming to collect loose hair and to minimize that which accumulates on your carpet or furniture.

- Brush with a slicker brush if the dog is molting, or use a bristle brush. Then comb through with a medium-toothed comb. The undercoat will fall out during molting.

- Bathe the dog in a suitable, quality pH-balanced shampoo and apply a conditioner.

- Blow-dry the coat.

- Check the dog's nails, ears and teeth.

- Trim the feet to look oval and compact, if required.

ST. BERNARD

The St. Bernard coat comes in shorthaired (left) and longhaired (right) varieties.

COAT: There are two coat types. Longhaired dogs have a dense, flat coat that is rather fuller around the neck and the thighs, and the tail is well feathered. Shorthaired have a close, houndlike coat, with slight feathering on the thighs and tail.

MAINTENANCE: This is a dog with a fair acreage of coat to be groomed.

PROCEDURE

Equipment needed: Slicker brush, medium- or wide-toothed comb.

Breed tip: The St. Bernard generally loves being bathed and brushed, but don't take any chances – get it used to being groomed from a young age. Because of its size, a helper may be required.

- Brush the dog with a slicker to remove dead hairs.

- Comb with a medium- or wide-toothed comb.

- Bathe the dog in a suitable shampoo, using white-enhancing shampoo on white parts to give a finish of splendor. Do not use any shampoo that will affect the coat if you intend to show your dog.

- A purifying shampoo and mask can be used three times a year, if required, for that extra-special finish – but is not for frequent use.

- Blast the excess water from the coat with a power dryer or use superabsorbent towels.

- Then blow-dry.

- Don't forget to check the St. Bernard's nails, ears and teeth.

- Remove untidy hairs on the hocks with thinning shears.

- Additional trimming of the hair on the feet is sometimes required on the longhaired variety.

- The ears need plucking and the underline should be tidied with scissors.

- With the show dog, consideration must be given to the condition of the coat when bathing, as too much undercoat may be pulled out, leaving the dog looking short of coat.

SWEDISH LAPPHUND

COAT: The coat is weather-resistant, with the hair standing straight out from the body. It is short on the head and front legs, and longer on the brisket, thigh and tail. There is a ruff around the neck. The undercoat is dense and finely curled.

The color is bear-brown, black, brown and a combination of black and brown. A white mark on the chest, white feet and a white tip on the tail are acceptable.

MAINTENANCE: Relatively easy to maintain with regular brushing.

PROCEDURE

Equipment needed: Slicker brush and a wide-toothed comb.

Breed tip: A bristle brush can be used on the softer puppy coat.

- Brush the entire dog with a slicker.

- Comb with a wide-toothed comb.

- Bathe the dog in a natural shampoo, and rinse well.

- Dry with a blower, brushing the hair away from the direction of the heat with a pin brush.

- Check the dog's nails, ears and teeth.

- Check under the pads for excess hair and remove with scissors, if necessary.

- Brush the coat once more, adding a fine sheen spray to enhance the coat.

TIBETAN MASTIFF

COAT: The males carry more coat than the females. It is fairly long, thick and woolly, with a heavy undercoat in cold weather. The hair is fine but straight, and never silky, curly or wavy. There is a heavy undercoat, giving a manelike appearance. The tail is bushy and densely coated.

Color: rich black, gold, black and tan, brown, various shades of gray, and blue tan.

MAINTENANCE: Low maintenance – just needs a weekly brush. The breed molts only once a year on average (in the spring).

PROCEDURE

Equipment needed: Slicker brush, wide-toothed comb.

Breed tip: It is essential to get the puppy used to grooming to prevent problems later.

- Brush through the entire coat with a slicker brush.

- Comb with a wide-toothed comb.

- If it is necessary to bathe the dog, use a natural-ingredient shampoo.

- Rinse thoroughly, making sure that all suds have been removed.

- Blast water from the coat or use super-absorbent towels, and leave the dog to dry naturally.

- Check the dog's nails, ears and teeth.

16 *CLIPPED AND TRIMMED BREEDS*

The Poodle belongs in this category, but because of the intensive work involved and the number of different trims it is being dealt with in Chapter 17.

COAT CARE

Pet dogs often have their hair cut, as do retired show dogs. Sometimes, owners of such dogs can no longer maintain the coat and, rather than let the dog become a neglected mess, the coat is trimmed back to a manageable length.

This task is usually undertaken with the aid of a coarse clipper blade, such as a No. 5 Oster, or a pair of scissors. Clipping, obviously, is far quicker and many groomers resort to using clippers through sheer need. Time is of the essence and hand-stripping takes hours. Clipping keeps the dog extremely smart at a much-reduced cost. Breeds like the Bichon Frise, Löwchen, Portuguese Water Dog, Poodle and Cocker Spaniel can look beautiful when clipped down, provided this is carefully and expertly executed.

REGULAR CARE

On-growing coats like the Poodle's are wool-like, and they need brushing and combing, if not daily, then certainly three or four times a week, especially when the dog is young and at coat-changing adolescent time.

Very young puppies rarely mat, as the hair is thinner, but they should still be brushed and combed to accustom them to the practice. From the age of 8 weeks or even less, the Poodle will have its feet, face and the base of its tail clipped. Poodles can also be bathed very regularly. Show dogs are always bathed once or twice a week when shows come thick and fast. This does not harm the coat at all – in fact, it encourages growth – but a good-quality shampoo should be used, together with the complementary conditioner. Brushing and combing must be thorough.

When combing the coat, the hair needs to be combed from the skin downwards, so separating the hair is essential. Otherwise, stubborn mats will form close to the skin, which could harbor parasites and cause scurf. This happens particularly with adolescent dogs.

ADOLESCENT COAT CHANGES

From about the age of 7 months, the coat begins to change and the old coat must be removed or it will clog into a mass. When the full adult coat has arrived, and this could take months, the hair will be harsher and easier to groom in most cases. Only some dogs will retain an awful cotton coat that is difficult at the best of times; it is nearly impossible when it is not brushed and is left unclipped or between trims.

AMERICAN COCKER SPANIEL

Featured is the American Cocker Spaniel Davcan Bombastic from Calmolly, owned by Mr. and Mrs. P.R. and M.E. Jones.

COAT: Its most characteristic attribute is its coat, which is short on the head and slightly longer on the body. The hair is profuse on the legs and abdomen. However, this should not be so excessive as to impair its function as a sporting dog. The coat is silky, flat or slightly wavy.

MAINTENANCE: Very few pet owners can maintain this breed in all its splendor, as dedication to the coat is essential. We see many dogs of this breed with a "short back and sides" because they have become matted solid.

PROCEDURE

Equipment needed: Mat-breaker (if necessary), pin brush or slicker.

Breed tip: The nurtured coat is not brushed out while dirty, as this removes too much hair.

- Brush out the entire coat using an untangle product or a dematter, and mat-breaker where necessary 1. However, if the coat is so severely felted or clogged that brushing will cause the dog severe pain or undue stress, then the only solution may be to remove the coat and ensure the dog is then groomed on a regular basis to prevent this happening again.

- With pet dogs, it is a good idea to clip under the arms, under the elbows, along the stomach and inside the thigh with an Oster No. 10 blade, even when the dog is coated. Carefully done, this is not seen when the dog is standing. One would not do this to a show dog.

- Clip the dog's face with an Oster No. 15 blade from the top of the eye to the back of the skull. 2 3

- Clip above the ears, including about one-third downwards to accentuate the ear. 3 4

- Clip down the cheeks to produce a clean appearance, tightening the skin where necessary to ensure a smooth finish and so as not to catch loose skin.

- Clip under the chin, down the neck to the chest in a V-shape to each side of the chest bone.

- The coat on the body is clipped, stripped, carded or thinned according to requirement (i.e., if it is a pet or show dog), but the shape is the same. Make a visual line between the chest bone and the bottom of the pelvis, and work from the neck down to this line. Leave a profuse skirt, which will almost reach to the ground in dogs whose coats are significantly groomed.

- Trim the tail upwards, away from the body.

- Clean off the hair from around the anus by clipping with an Oster No. 10, or by shortening the hair with scissors.

- Bathe the dog in a protein shampoo. ▽

- Rinse thoroughly and apply conditioner.

- Blow the hair dry, brushing with a pin brush or slicker. ▽

- Lightly spray with a coat-enhancer and brush through. ▽

- Check the dog's nails, ears and teeth.

- Trim the feet to a round shape and clip out the hair from under the pads. ▽

- Trim the bottom of the leg to give a bell-bottom appearance. ▽

- Blend in the clipped neck area to the shoulder, making the shoulder clean by shortening the hair to accentuate the outline. ▽

- Blend in the body skirt to a harmonious look without any appearance of a doorstep effect between the body and the skirt. Pay particular attention to the clipped area at the rear to ensure this is well blended. ▽

- Bring the hair on the ear fringe down. Hold it in your fingers and trim lightly across with curved scissors to enhance the look, rather than to shorten the hair to any degree.

- Strip the topknot where possible, depending on the coat texture and depending on whether the dog will be shown. Blend in with thinning scissors. Brush the hair first to one side. Then trim, using thinning scissors or by clipping with an Oster No. 10 with the growth of the hair. Then brush the hair to the other side and trim back. Then brush over the top to give a clean appearance.

- The hair at the edge of the skirt is leveled to appear neat. Remember, this dog should appear stunning.

- The finished dog. ▽

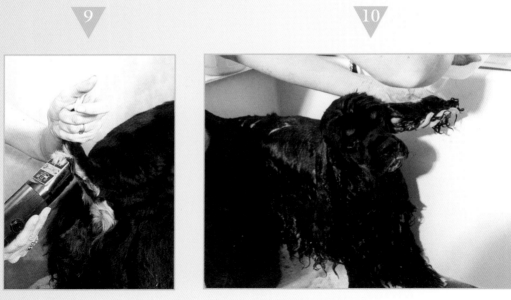

9

10

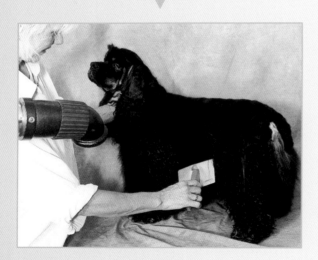

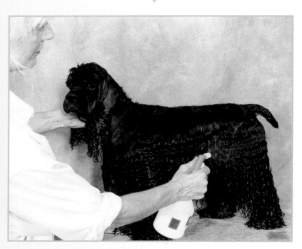

11

12

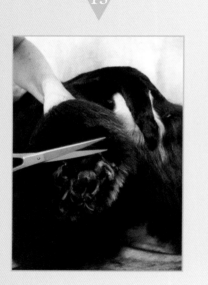

13

14

BEDLINGTON TERRIER

COAT: The coat is described as thick and "linty" and needs regular trimming, as it does not molt like most other breeds and is therefore a good breed for those allergic to dog hair, such as asthmatics. Standing well out from the skin, the hair is crisp and has a distinct tendency to twist, particularly on the head and face.

MAINTENANCE: The Bedlington should be trimmed on a regular four- to six-week basis to keep it smart and to prevent the dead hair from becoming tangled and matted. In addition, the dog should be thoroughly combed every two to three days, or its coat will quickly become matted.

PROCEDURE

Equipment needed: Slicker brush, wide- or medium-toothed comb, clippers, scissors.

Breed tip: Professional trimming is advisable unless the owner takes the trouble to learn the lengthy art of grooming. As a general rule, the coat trim and overall shape of the Bedlington should be a series of curves, with no harsh transitions between different lengths of coat.

- Brush through with a slicker brush and a comb.

- If the hair is dirty, it can be blown through with a power blower to remove grime and dirt, and to reduce matting. Note: A freshly washed coat will stand away from the skin, making the hair easier to trim.

- Depending on the predetermined length of hair to remain, use an Oster No. 10 or No. 15 against the grain of growth to clip the side of the face. Follow a line starting from the back corner of the eye to the front edge of the ear, and another from the back corner of the eye to the outer edge of the mouth. 1

- Clip the ears to leave a diamond-shaped tassel of hair. 1

- Clip the chin and underjaw down to the base of the throat, forming a V-shape to a point half way between the Adam's apple and the breastbone. Use a No. 10 or No. 15 Oster, as on the cheeks. 2

- Depending on the style of trim preferred, you will need to clip the hair on the back of the head slightly differently. For the traditional "U.K. trim," use a No. 5 Oster to trim the hair off the neck, starting from the back of the skull and moving down to the withers. For a more "U.S.-style" trim, also use a No. 5 Oster, but clip with the grain of the hair, starting from the base of the ear and progressing diagonally toward the center of the base of the neck, forming a V-shape of hair down the neck.

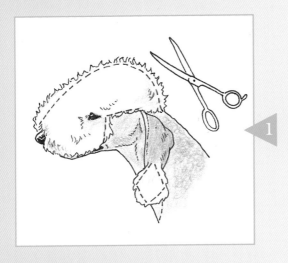

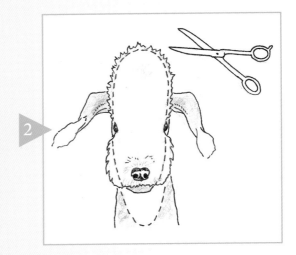

- Using a No. 5 blade, clip down the sides of the neck to the shoulders to blend the hair into the top of the front legs at the elbow. ▽

- Clip from the neck to the breastbone. With the show dog, this is shortened with scissors. Blend in the scissored and clipped edges. ▽

- With a No. 5, clip along the body and down the rib cage, leaving a fringe of hair under the chest and brisket. ▽

- Clip over the top of the back to the rear end, blending toward the top of the thigh. This can be done with scissors. ▽

- Using a No. 10 or No. 15 blade, clip beneath the belly from the navel to the groin and the inside of the thigh.

- Clip the tail. You can trim uniformly with a No. 10 or No. 15. Alternatively, for a more "U.S.-style" trim, leave a third of the hair at the base of tail and clip the remainder to the tip with a No. 10 or No. 15.

- Clip the anal area.

- Bathe the Bedlington with a canine shampoo recommended for harsh coats. If necessary, use a conditioner, but remember that a soft and fluffy coat is not desirable in this breed.

- Blow-dry the coat, using a pin or slicker brush to lift the coat away from the skin.

- Check the dog's nails, teeth and ears. It is important to pluck out the hair that grows deep into the ear canal, otherwise it can fall

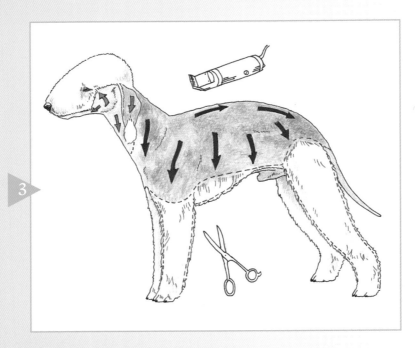

into the canal and cause a buildup of wax and possibly an infection.

- Clip over the clipped parts that have lifted in order to neaten them.

- Scissor the edges of the ears to neaten and comb down the tassels, scissoring them to form the required diamond shape.

- Scissor the head carefully to form a kind of Roman arch (the rise from the occiput to the nose). However, do not exaggerate this curve too much. Ideally, the profile should be wedge-shaped. Follow the line of the skull to form a smooth, unbroken, gentle curve. Blend the sides to taper, giving the side appearance of a long head, arching across the top between the ears to the tip of the nose.

- The hair on the tail is scissored to a tubular shape, blending into the body. However, take care not to leave too much hair at the base of the tail, as this can result in the tail looking as though it actually belongs to an Irish Water Spaniel!

- Scissor down the chest, down between the legs and then underneath the rib cage, scissoring down the front legs to form a tubular shape.

- Blend the rear legs with scissors to follow the natural contours.

- Clip or scissor between the toes and the pads, and then underneath the foot. Finish the feet with scissors to form a nice, neat appearance.

BICHON FRISE

COAT: It has a dense and soft coat with a tendency toward corkscrew curls.

MAINTENANCE: The Bichon needs a considerable amount of grooming to maintain its glamorous image. This breed was once presented with only its muzzle and feet tidied up, but now the whole coat is frequently seen scissored. It needs regular four- to six-week trimming and frequent baths to keep the coat in order and to give it the stunning appearance befitting the breed.

PROCEDURE

Equipment needed: Long-bladed scissors, short-bladed scissors, bristle brush, large slicker brush, small slicker brush and steel combs with wide-set teeth and close-set teeth.

Breed tip: The coat needs plenty of attention, but these delightful little dogs are worth every second of your hard work.

- Be vigilant about removing tangles before bathing, as, once wet, mats are virtually impossible to remove without cutting. On occasions, it has been necessary to put a filthy, dirty Bichon into the bath and put in spray conditioner (anti-tangle or dematter) while the dog is soaking wet, and brush out the mats with the mat-breaker. This is avoidable if the dog is well combed before bathing.

- Try to split the felts by parting small sections at a time with your fingertips, and by spraying in an untangle product or a dematter.

- Brush with a slicker and comb through with a wide-toothed comb.

- Bathe regularly, at least once a month, in an appropriate shampoo, being careful to use a good-quality conditioner. Sometimes, add a teaspoonful of baby oil or similar to the conditioner, to help prevent the coat from drying out.

- Rinse thoroughly. The Bichon may need two shampoos to get it clean.

- Not all groomers consider it necessary, but many choose to brush through the dog's wet coat hair with a slicker brush before beginning blow-drying.

- Blow-dry the hair after using absorbent towels to lightly swab up excess moisture. Professional groomers and showdog owners will use a high-velocity hair-dryer to first remove excess moisture (it does not dry the coat). Then, a dryer with variable heat/ strength settings will be used to dry the coat while brushing.

- Starting with the tail, dry only small sections at a time, brushing continuously with a slicker or bristle brush. Next, brush and dry the legs, followed by the body hair and then the head and ears. Make sure you comb the hair away from the body. If you are aiming for the show-quality "powderpuff" effect, it

is important to ensure that all the hair has been thoroughly groomed while drying, so the Bichon's natural curl is brushed out into a soft-textured, straighter puff.

- Comb through the coat before trimming, taking care to brush the hair up, away from the coat. The coat should be combed constantly while trimming.

- If you are scissoring for the first time without the aid of an experienced groomer, look carefully at the photograph on page 251. Try to copy the perfect rounded appearance.

- The ears are so well blended, it is hard to distinguish them. It may be necessary to use thinning scissors underneath the ears if aiming for a show-standard finish.

- Trim excess hair from under the feet.

- Trim the hair from under and around the anus, leaving the tail hair long.

- Scissor the rear legs, always keeping the scissors parallel to the body. When viewed from behind, the dog's legs should resemble a straight-sided, upside-down letter U.

- Next, trim the body hair. Begin with the sides and move down and underneath the body.

- Scissor the front legs to look straight when viewed from the front, but cylindrical (roller-shaped) from a distance. The feet are included in this line, hidden by the continuous line of leg hair.

- The hair on the topline – along the back from the shoulder to the tail – should be level, and closer than the hair on the neck. Scissor, following the line of the body, to give a round appearance, taking care to blend in well with the neck hair.

- If necessary, retrim the hindquarters and body hair to give a well-blended appearance.

- Excess hair should be removed from the inside of the dog's ear leathers, using your fingers or blunt tweezers and removing only a little at a time. Blend in the remaining hair with the Bichon's characteristic topknot.

- The hair over the eyes is combed forward and trimmed back to allow full view of the eyes. Keeping the scissor ends away from the dog's eyes, start by removing the hair on the inside corners of the eyes.

- Neaten over the bridge of the nose, combing the remainder downward.

- Comb the topknot and trim to a smooth, rounded appearance, also trimming any hair falling over the top of the eyes.

- The line across the chin, incorporating the beard, is fairly straight. The beard hair should be blended with the ear furnishings, and the neck blended with the topline (see below).

- Give a final comb through and check the dog's nails, ears and teeth.

BLACK RUSSIAN TERRIER

COAT: The whole body is covered with a thick, tough coat, with decorative hair well defined on the head and limbs. The mustache and beard are features, and give the muzzle a blunt, rectangular shape. The hair is rough and thick, with a fold (crinkle), which, when pulled straight, will make the hair appear longer. The body hair is shortened to about 2 to 4 inches (4 to 10 cm). The front and rear legs are well protected by slightly longer rough hair. The color is black, or black with an insignificant amount of gray hair.

MAINTENANCE: Trimming is obligatory in accordance with the approved style. Regular brushing is essential (at least three times a week). Bathing and caring for the coat, keeping it in the desired attractive style, is usually done by an expert.

PROCEDURE

Equipment needed: Slicker brush, wide-toothed comb, scissors or clippers.

Breed tip: As this dog molts slightly, it is essential that it receives regular grooming.

• Brush through the entire coat with a slicker brush, lifting the coat to brush the hair in sections to ensure this is done thoroughly.

• Comb with a wide-toothed comb.

• Bathe in a suitable, natural shampoo that will not remove too much of the natural oil from the coat.

• Dry the dog with superabsorbent towels. Brush or comb through, and then finish with a blower or in a cage.

• Starting with the head: trim the ears from the fold of the ears to the tip by clipping downwards (away from the head) with an Oster No. 10 blade (or equivalent) or scissors. Trim on the inside and outside. Tidy the edge with scissors, while holding the ear with your finger and thumb for safety.

- The hair is fairly short on the top of the head from behind the eye to the back of the skull, and this is done with scissors.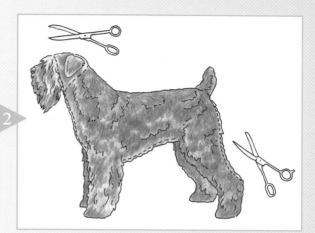

- Comb the beard forward and scissor downwards to give a deep-pointed look from the side view.

- The neck hair and body hair are shortened with scissors to about 2 to 4 inches (5 to 10 cm) and slightly tapered to the groin area. The underchest is fringed, and curves upwards towards the groin, giving the appearance of a deep chest.

- The front of the chest is accentuated in shape from the base of the neck to the front leg.

- The tail is fairly shortened with scissors and the undertail anal area is cut short.

- The front legs are scissored to tidy, and the hair on the foot is cut round to shape it into a neat finish. Unlike the Poodle (page 270), the legs are not "indented" to show the feet; with the Black Russian, the feet appear as a continuation of the leg.

- The back leg is trimmed to shape from the rump to the hock to accentuate angulations, and then from the hock to the foot.

- The front part of the back leg has more hair to accentuate the bend of the stifle, and then is trimmed down to the foot.

- The foot is cut in a round puff (i.e., a ball of hair) rather than a close cut.

- Trim under the foot to remove hair that might bunch and mat and cause the dog pain when it walks. Alternatively, clip this out with an Oster No. 15, ensuring that the top foot hair is left intact.

- Check the dog's nails, teeth and ears. Any hair inside the ears should be pulled out, as terriers should have an open ear canal.

- Note: the Black Russian Terrier needs trimming on a regular monthly basis (or for every show), much the same as the Kerry Blue (page 265).

BOUVIER DES FLANDRES

COAT: The coat is so abundant and thick that, when separated by hand, the skin is barely visible. Neither woolly nor curly, the hair should be about 2^1/$_2$ inches (6 cm), gradually becoming shorter on the legs. The undercoat is dense and close-grained. On the crown of the head, the hair is short and is close on the ears. The eyebrows do not veil the eyes. The eyebrows, beard and mustache are accentuated to give a formidable appearance, but the eyes should be seen.

MAINTENANCE: The breed has a rough, dry coat that should be easy to maintain. A visit to the salon every eight weeks will keep the coat in hand – it should not be allowed to get out of control.

PROCEDURE

Equipment needed: Slicker brush, wide-toothed comb, scissors, clippers.

Breed tip: Grooming with a bristle brush encourages growth of the undercoat in this breed.

- Brush the entire coat with a slicker brush. This hair is best groomed in sections. Lift the layer of hair and brush from the parting downward. Untangler or coat protector will aid brushing and help to remove mats and unwanted dead hair, without unduly softening the coat.

- Be systematic. Start on the left back leg and work through the front and head. Turn the dog and work through the right side from the back leg.

- Comb through. However, if the hair is too dirty, it will cause unnecessary discomfort to the dog.

- The crown, or top of the head from just above the eyebrow to the occiput, is clipped with an Oster No. 10 or scissored down to shorten the appearance. This can also be done with your finger and thumb or a coarse stripping knife. Clipping is more common and the breeder will usually put in the triangular shape required on the crown before the puppy leaves them. ▽I

- The ears are clipped short and the edges are tidied with scissors. Take care to hold the ear to prevent nipping the skin. ▽I

- Comb through and either leave natural or thin/strip the sides of the cheeks to enhance the appearance.

- Thinners are used to taper the throat and chest hair toward the shoulder, or the hair can be cut shorter with scissors. ▽I

- The hair on the body is shortened with scissors to a length of about 2 inches (5 cm), and the legs are blended in level with the body hair and shortened to enhance their shape. ▽I

- Bathe with a protein shampoo and apply conditioner. Use a dematting balsam conditioner and brush it through the coat to help aid grooming, if required. Use a spray conditioner otherwise.

- Use absorbent towels, or some of the excess water can be blown from the coat using a power dryer.

- Finish with a blow-dry, using a pin brush to lift the coat and remove any remaining dead hair.

- Comb through with a wide-toothed comb. The coat may need a few days to settle before the dog is shown in the ring.

- Check the dog's nails, ears and teeth.

- When using thinning scissors, keep the tool pointing downwards with the fall of the coat – never cut crossways. Scissor the hair to enhance the deep chest. The dog should not appear cylindrical, and has very little tuck-up.

- Remove the hair from around the anal area with scissors or a No. 5 clipper blade.

- Also remove the hair between the pads underneath the foot, using a closer blade or scissors.

- Trim the foot around the circumference to give an appearance of a cat's paw.

- With the pet dog, the entire body is frequently cut shorter with scissors or clippers than on the show dog. Some owners request that this breed is clipped all over, leaving just a shortened beard, as with the terrier trim. To do this, use a No. 5 Oster, going with the growth before the bath, and tidy with a blade or scissors after blow-drying.

BRITTANY

COAT: The coat is dense, fine, rather flat and slightly wavy. The color is orange/white, liver/white, black/white, tricolor, roan or any of these colors.

MAINTENANCE: Not difficult to manage.

PROCEDURE

Equipment needed: Bristle brush or pin brush, fine-toothed comb.

Breed tip: Stripping may be required, but should never be noticeable – the breed should look as natural as possible.

- Brush the entire coat with a bristle or pin brush, using a slicker on the long parts and on the feathering.

- Comb through, removing dead hair with a molting comb. Use thinning shears where any thick hair may need a cleaner appearance.

- Bathe the coat in a protein shampoo and condition with a conditioning enhancer.

- Towel-dry and then air-, cage- or lightly blow-dry, going with the growth of the coat to achieve a flat finish.

• Check the Brittany's nails, ears and teeth.

• Use a stripping knife to remove untidy hairs from the head. Thinners can be used on the hair below the ears to give a smoother appearance. ▽

• Continue stripping using the knife or thinners, down with the growth of the hair to smooth and taper the entire body coat. Some groomers may find carding useful to smooth hairs on the body. (Hold a No. 15 Oster blade or a blunt stripping knife in your hand and strip it through the coat, as detailed.) Removal of the coat should never be noticeable. ▽

• Then, thin the coat where feathering is too profuse. Spray the coat with an enhancer or a protein coat

conditioner, giving a final brush to add luster and sheen, and to give a more flattened appearance.

• Interestingly, in the U.K., clippers should not be used on the Brittany, but thinning scissors are very useful for tidying the ears, neck and excess feathering on the legs. ▽

CESKY TERRIER

COAT: The coat is silky in texture, slightly wavy and has a metallic sheen. The color is gray (of any shade), occasionally with tan markings on the cheeks, the underside of the muzzle, the lower parts of the legs and under the tail. Small white patches and a white collar or tail tip are permissible. Very, very rarely, a brown specimen is found.

MAINTENANCE: The coat requires daily grooming and regular trimming. The legs and belly are left unclipped to form a low skirt, while the hair on the foreface is grown into a beard and eyebrows. The hair on the body should be no more than ¹/₂ inch (1.5 cm) long.

PROCEDURE

Equipment needed: Slicker brush, wide-toothed comb, thinning and straight scissors, and clippers with No. 10 and No. 7F blades.

Breed tip: A slicker brush should never be used on a show dog's coat, which should be brushed with a bristle brush instead. Pet dogs should be trimmed approximately every eight weeks.

- Brush through the long hair with a slicker to remove tangles, paying attention to under the arm where mats may form.

- Bathe the dog using a combined shampoo/conditioner and make sure you rinse thoroughly.

- Blow-dry the coat, combing through the long hair with a wide-toothed comb.

- Clip the skull with an Oster No. 7F, from above the eyes moving back to the neck. Clip the ears against the growth of the hair, using a No. 10.

- Carefully trim the edges of the ears with scissors.

- Using a No. 7F and clipping against the growth of the hair, clip from 1 inch (2.5 cm) below the point of the elbow, over the shoulder and up the neck. Follow a horizontal line between the legs to the throat and up to a line from the edge of the mouth via the corner of the eye to the top edge of the ear.

- Clip the neck and body with a No. 7F, leaving a skirt.

- Using a No. 7F and clipping against the direction of hair growth, clip the hindquarters from just above the hock to the groin. Leave the feathering on the front of the hindlegs, as well as the hair from the hock to the foot.

- Clip the tail from base to the tip and around the anus area.

- Blend the different lengths of hair using thinning shears.

- Comb through with a wide-toothed comb.

- Trim under the feet and between the pads to prevent the hair from forming mats.

- Thin the beard and leg hair with thinning shears as necessary. Trim around the feet and the ends of the skirt. The finish should look natural, with no hard edges.

- Check the dog's nails, ears and teeth.

ENGLISH COCKER SPANIEL

COAT: The coat is flat, silky in texture, never wiry, wavy or curly. On some dogs, the coat is not too profuse, but many carry very heavy coats. The coat is well feathered on the forelegs, body and hindlegs above the hocks.

MAINTENANCE: This is a breed seen frequently in the grooming salon, and it should be trimmed every six to eight weeks. Ideally, Cockers will be hand-stripped as for the show ring. However, this is rarely the case – when the coat grows thick and the legs become matted, pet owners usually have their spaniels clipped short.

Thinning scissors can be used to thin and flatten the coat, and are used to take the tufty hair from the head in many cases where clippers are not used.

For the show dog, you should read the breed standard and adhere to any recommendations from experienced exhibitors on the correct procedure before putting a pair of clippers anywhere near the breed.

For the pet dog, you should consult with the owner for the most favorable method to suit all requirements, such as the time spent on daily brushing and combing, the kind of life the dog leads and the cost.

PROCEDURE

Equipment needed: Depends on whether it is a show dog or a pet. May include: slicker/pin brush, wide-toothed comb, thinning scissors, scissors, clippers and a stripping knife.

Breed tip: These dogs are best trimmed on a regular basis of not longer than eight weeks. Pet owners frequently have their spaniels clipped all over.

For show dogs, hand-trimming is recommended because it helps to maintain the coat quality. Roll the skin between the left thumb and index finger, gripping a few hairs at a time between the right thumb and index finger, and pull out the unwanted long hairs.

- Groom the entire coat with a slicker or pin brush.

- Comb through with a medium comb, removing tangles. Use a mat-breaker if necessary. Unfortunately, it is not always possible to remove matted hair by combing, in which case the dog may be hurt unless the mat is cut out. It is better to keep on top of things with regular grooming so that you are not faced with this problem very often.

- The pet dog is usually clipped underneath with an Oster No. 10 blade, incorporating under the elbows, the tummy, inside the thighs and under the tail, by at least one-width of the blade. No show dog would have this done (see below).

- The skirt line is not straight as in the American Cocker Spaniel; the lower line is

more of an inverted moon from the breastbone to the lowest point of the pelvis. For show dogs, if the coat is very heavy, the coat should be thinned down the line of the ribs. Comb the coat so that it lifts away from the skin, and remove the hair from underneath until the feathering falls naturally down from the ribs and does not billow out when the dog is moving.

• The top body coat is stripped, thinned or clipped . Remember, clipping is not desirable unless absolutely necessary as it will thicken the coat, making it almost fluffy in appearance and very curly. However, many pet owners ask for this breed to be clipped and they come to the salon every six weeks in order for the coat to be kept under control. Retired show dogs may also sport this type of cut.

• The head is thinned, plucked or clipped as required or desired; going away from the eye to the point of the skull and cleaned into the neck, incorporating the top of the ears to give flat, distinctive elegance of head. To create a neat finish, you will need to remove the excess hair – i.e., those that are longer and straggly. Show dogs will have this done by hand. Pet owners could use a clipper instead, although the coat will be left thicker and less smooth. It is also fairly common for the hair underneath the ears, where it meets the neck, to be thinned and trimmed, as this helps the ears to "breathe."

• Work down the cheekbone and muzzle, and down from under the chin to taper into the breastbone. (Only use clippers if essential.) Thinning scissors are generally used here on the show dog.

• Remove the long, straggly hairs from the front and sides of the forelegs. Many owners choose to taper the hair down the front of the leg up to and including the foot. When viewed from the front, you should not be able to see any feathering falling around the back of the leg; it should lie backwards naturally, from the elbow. Remove any excess hair. Feathering at the base of the leg should not touch the ground, so trim if necessary.

• For the hindlegs, show dogs should have the

feathering around their stifles shaped. Cutting to shape is not recommended, as plucking is relatively easy and looks more natural. The feathering should reach just to the knuckle, but it should be tapered, and not left looking like plus-fours! Shape down the hock to the pad. Do not trim the hocks too closely, as this makes for a spindly look.

- The tail should be thick at the root, tapering to a fine tip. Comb the feathering thoroughly and pluck out unwanted hair. The tail feathering should be as thick as the feathering on the legs – the aim is to achieve a balance throughout the whole coat. Plucking out the excess hair on the tail should create a neat, smooth finish on the top side of the tail and nicely but not overly thick feathering underneath. Trim the tail and cut neatly underneath it, shaping the feathering down to the top of the hock.

- Bathe the Cocker in a suitable shampoo and apply conditioner to help enhance the coat's appearance and to encourage it to lie flat.

- Blow the coat dry while brushing (with a pin brush) in the direction of the hair growth.

- Check the dog's nails, ears and teeth.

- Trim the clean hair from the hock down to the foot.

- Trim the toes to a round appearance, and take out any surplus hair from between the pads under the foot. Excess, untidy hair should be plucked out, but do not remove too much as this can look very ugly, and is not desirable in the show ring. Aim to achieve a neat and even, close-cut finish. In pet dogs, the hair between the toes is often extremely matted and dirty. This can lead to skin problems, so it is advisable for the pet owner to remove whatever hair has not been thoroughly cleaned by bathing.

- Comb through the feathering.

- When finished, the coat should look clean, and is stripped, thinned, carded or clipped with the hair growth, depending on the coat texture and whether the dog is a show specimen or a pet. This process can be helped by polishing the coat with a soft chamois cloth, which should leave it gleaming with good health and condition.

ENGLISH SPRINGER SPANIEL

COAT: The coat is close, straight and weather-resistant, never coarse. The feathering on the ears, forelegs, body and hindquarters is moderate. However, some ears seem to grow profusely and are better trimmed shorter to avoid matting and the collection of debris.

MAINTENANCE: Regular attention to the coat is necessary, which may include stripping, thinning and, sadly, even clipping – in the case of some pet dogs that have "runaway" coats. However, the natural look is desired and less trimming rather than more is usually sufficient to keep this breed looking good.

PROCEDURE

Equipment needed: Pin brush or slicker, metal comb.

Breed tip: Household rubber gloves or rubber thimbles will make the removal of dead, wispy hairs much easier – particularly on the top of the head and on the body coat.

- Brush the body and feathering with a pin brush or slicker, removing tangles with a metal comb.

- For a pet groom, trim (with thinning scissors) all the hair immediately under the ear. This will allow the air to pass freely into the ear and help prevent infection. Clean regularly with a proprietary ear cleaner.

- Carding is useful to thin the body hair where required. Use thinning shears where excess hair falls to give a tidy, clean – but not overtrimmed – look.

- Bathe the dog in a suitable shampoo.

- Lightly blow-dry the coat, going in the direction of the growth of the hair to dry it flat, or cage-dry after combing through the coat when wet.

- Check the dog's nails, ears and teeth.

- Check underneath the feet for the presence of debris and unwanted hair.

- Trim any excess hair from the back of the hocks to neaten, giving a clean look.

- Tidy the feet to a well-rounded, tight appearance.

- For a show trim, trim the hair underneath the ears so they lie flat.

- Using trimming scissors, trim the hair on the ears to about one-third of the way down, to achieve a smooth finish.

- Next, pluck out long hairs from the top of the dog's head.

- Trim the hair under the chin and on the brisket bone, again using thinning scissors. Thin the hair on the shoulders and blend the hair into the body. ▽

- Dead hair on the flanks and from the occiput and down the neck and back should be plucked out using finger and thumb. Scissors should not be used. ▽

- The hair around the tail should be trimmed to a neat appearance, and hair around the anus should be removed. Blend in to surrounding hair by using thinning scissors. ▽

- Trim the hair around each foot to neaten the shape, and cut any excess hair in between the toes and underneath the foot.

- Use thinning scissors to trim the hair and graduate back to the "stopper pad" to blend the hair in.

- Remove hair from the hocks, trimming to a close, smooth finish. Again, use thinning scissors.

FIELD SPANIEL

COAT: The coat is long, flat, glossy and silky in texture. It is never curly or wiry, but rather dense and weatherproof. Abundant feathering is seen on the chest, under the body and behind the legs, but the line is clean from the hock to the ground.

The color is black, liver or roan, or any of these with tan markings.

MAINTENANCE: Relatively easy to look after, the Field Spaniel needs regular brushing and combing, and stripping or thinning.

PROCEDURE

Equipment needed: Bristle brush, medium-toothed comb, thinning scissors, stripping knife, scissors.

Breed tip: The Field Spaniel coat should be as flat as possible.

- Brush with a bristle brush to remove dead hairs and tangles that may have formed in the feathering, under the arms and particularly around the ears.

- After brushing, thoroughly comb through with a medium-toothed comb.

- Using thinning shears or your finger and thumb, remove thick hair on the head to give a neat, clean appearance.

- Body hair is stripped or thinned where necessary to give a flat look.

- Bathe the dog in a suitable shampoo and conditioner to help enhance the gleam of the coat.

- Lightly blow-dry in the direction of the hair growth.

- Check the Field Spaniel's nails, ears and teeth.

- Comb through once more, and remove stray hairs with your finger and thumb. Alternatively, use thinning shears to produce a flat appearance.

- For pet dogs, lightly spray with a coat finish if extra shine is required. (Show dogs shouldn't have anything applied to the coat.)

KERRY BLUE TERRIER

COAT: The coat is quite a feature of this breed, being thick, soft and silky, and it does not shed. The coat, as well as being soft and silky, is plentiful and wavy. Puppies are born black and can take up to 18 months to clear to blue, of which there are many shades.

MAINTENANCE: It needs considerable trimming to keep it looking smart.

PROCEDURE

Equipment needed: Slicker brush, wide-toothed comb, scissors or clippers.

Breed tip: Preparing for the show ring, the Kerry Blue is washed and left to dry in warm air. The dog is then brushed, combed and scissored all over.

The pet Kerry is more often clipped, rather than scissored, to save time and money. A coarse blade should be used for this, with a finer one on the head.

- Brush the entire coat, including the beard, with a slicker.

- Comb through with a wide- or medium-toothed comb to remove all tangles.

- Bathe in a suitable shampoo for the blue coat, and then apply conditioner. Use a purifying shampoo and conditioning mask when required, up to three times a year.

- Dry in a cage or in warm air.

- Check the dog's nails, ears and teeth.

- The head is clipped. Using a No. 10 blade, clip the head – working away from the eye and leaving the eyebrows intact, clip or scissor back across the skull, leaving hair from the top eye level to form the shape of the face (see below). Make sure you work with the direction of the hair growth. ▽ ▽

- Next clip the ears, preferably using a slightly smaller blade. Going against the hair growth will produce shorter results. Neaten the edges with scissors. ▽ ▽

- Clip from the outer corner of the eye, backwards to the point of the neck. Trim down from this same marker to the edge of the mouth and under the chin to where you can feel a definite lump under the chin. Clip down the throat to taper at the base of the neck or the Adam's apple to a V-shape.

- Clip the body with the Oster No. 7/5/4, depending on the length required. Alternatively, scissor with the growth of the hair to the shoulders, down and back across the rib cage, down the back to the tail, and up the tail. Clip the body to leave a rise over the hip joint or the bone where the back leg begins ▽. All the leg hair is neatly blended into the shorter body hair.

- Clip under the tail upward, and then down the anal area. ▽

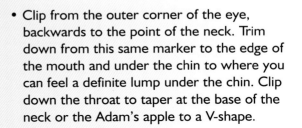

- Blend in the legs with scissors to complement the dog's angulations, giving shape.

- The front legs are blended in from the elbow down, to incorporate the feet.

- Scissor the hair out from underneath each foot.

- Trim the edge of the ears to neaten their appearance.

- Comb the Kerry Blue's eyebrows and beard forward. Next, trim the eyebrows and beard with the scissors pointing forward toward the nose. The hair between the eyes is shaped in a graduated fashion, so that face hair is prevented from falling sideways and impairing the dog's vision, particularly when on the move.

- Spray lightly with a coat gloss conditioner, if required.

- The hair on the head is taken shorter with clippers or scissors. With the show dog, the coat is scissored throughout as previously stated.

- Note: show dogs are clipped on the head as for pets, although many owners prefer scissoring, and it is always a good idea to check first with the breed standard recommendation.

LÖWCHEN

COAT: It has a fine, long, single coat, which comes in any color, marking or combination of both. The Löwchen cannot be bred for color – you get what you get!

MAINTENANCE: Its body is clipped from the last rib, down over the rear and down the back leg to the hock. It is clipped down the tail to leave one-third of the tail as plumage. It is also clipped from the elbow to just above the wrist.

The Löwchen requires regular brushing and grooming – this is a breed whose coat can mat within 20 minutes of bathing!

PROCEDURE

Equipment needed: Exhibitors tend to use a combination of clippers and a wide-toothed comb, although pet owners can manage the coat using a pin brush and a comb.

Breed tip: The soft coat will mat if not regularly brushed.

- Comb through with a wide-toothed comb or a pin brush.

- Bathe in a good-quality dog shampoo. Rinse well.

- Apply conditioning cream.

- Dry with a blower while gently brushing the hair with a pin brush or wide-toothed comb.

- If clipping your dog (most pet owners will not bother), use your chosen blade size. This is a matter of personal choice – some people use a No. 5 blade, while others use a No. 30 blade. Popular choices are No. 10 and No. 15 blades, which clip quite close to the body. Start just behind the last rib and incorporate the whole back leg down to the hock. ▼

- Clip the front leg with your chosen blade size. Clip from just below the elbow to a line that is level with the start of the hair left at the hock on the back leg. ▼

- Clip two-thirds of the tail with your blade from the base up, leaving a plumage on the end. ▼

- Comb all plumage.

- Check the dog's nails, ears and teeth.

PORTUGUESE WATER DOG

▲ *The "Retriever" trim*

COAT: The coat is described as profuse. There are two distinct types, born without undercoats: (a) Hair fairly long and loosely waved with a slight sheen; hair on head erect, ears well feathered; (b) Hair short, fairly harsh and dense, compact curls, lacking luster, head hair similar to body, hair on ears somewhat wavy.

MAINTENANCE: The hair doesn't molt, and needs brushing and combing frequently. These dogs are traditionally clipped on the face, hindquarters and on part of the tail, leaving a profuse plume at the end. The front end of the dog's coat is left to grow naturally.

PROCEDURE

Equipment needed: Slicker/pin brush, wide-toothed comb, clippers.

Breed tip: The pet dog can be clipped to about $1/2$ inch (1.25 cm) all over – this is called the "Retriever" trim (see page 268) and is used for showing in the U.S.

- Brush through the coat, removing tangles.

- Using an Oster No. 10 or 15 blade, clip the face from the corner of the eye to the corner of the ear in straight line.

- Clip down the muzzle from the eye.

- Clip the neck to the point of the throat.

- Clip the abdomen area.

- Clip the complete back leg from the last rib, including the back toes, with an Oster No. 10 or 15. Clip the tail two-thirds from the base to leave plumage on the remaining third.

- Clip the hair from between the pads underneath the feet.

- Bathe the dog in a suitable shampoo and apply a conditioner.

- Blow the hair dry using a pin brush, then comb with a wide-toothed comb.

- Remember to check the dog's nails, ears and teeth.

17 *THE POODLE*

CORDED POODLE

For details on coat care for the Corded Poodle, see page 75 (Chapter 10).

Featured: the Standard Poodle in "Lamb" trim is Tragapanz Chelsea Girl, owned by Carol Flatt.

COAT: The Poodle is the most intriguing of all breeds to trim – there are just so many styles into which its unique nonmolting coat can be artistically contoured.

MAINTENANCE: Poodle coats need constant attention. Pet owners invariably forget to brush their dogs, and they come into the grooming salon every six weeks or so with mats and tangles in their coats.

Once upon a time, the only considerate and kind way to deal with such felted mats was to get underneath the mat with a fine blade and clip it off.

With today's many preparations, conditioners and mat-breakers, the groomer has a wider choice and more capacity to sort out a neglected coat.

However, the prime consideration must be the welfare of the dog, and if the best solution is to clip off the coat, then this must be done. Given time, the coat will grow again.

POODLE EARS

Poodle ears have hair growing inside them. It is part of the grooming procedure to deal with this, and an experienced groomer should show a novice how to do this painlessly. You should lift the flap of the ear against the head, thereby protecting the inner ear. Hold the muzzle to keep the dog still, and then use forceps to tease out tiny bits of hair at a time. It is always a good idea to use some ear powder first, as this will help loosen the hair.

Where brown wax is evident, mites have probably invaded, so clean the ear with alcohol or ear cleaner and apply ear powder before and after removing as much of the offending mess as possible. Lemon juice and witch hazel ear-cleaning preparations are also available for this. This procedure may need to be repeated daily until the problem has cleared up.

SCISSOR WORK

There is a lot of scissor work to be done on a Poodle and only practice will allow the groomer to achieve a smooth, almost satin finish to the well-cared-for coat. Finishing is an art that some excel at more than others.

Different scissors give different finishes and the groomer must try several pairs of scissors in order to find the pair right for them. Most sales outlets are happy to help you choose the right type. Scissors vary in price. and to sustain the outstanding presentation that some groomers achieve it is imperative to buy high-quality equipment, such as clippers, scissors, shampoo and finishing sculpture conditioner. It really does make a difference and the investment is worthwhile.

Finishing is achieved by literally skimming over the coat with the scissors accurately placed to edge the coat. As the Poodle coat grows and moves constantly, and it has a natural tendency to curl despite straightening conditioners, this finish will not last, but still the dog will look expertly smart.

Good scissoring is an art. It is fascinating to watch groomers from different parts of the world scissoring in their own style to achieve perfection. If you visit grooming seminars, you will be able to see this interesting skill in action, and all the groomers' different styles. Some fluff the hair outwards and let it fall before commencing scissoring, while some comb it upwards. Some will say one way is the only correct way, but I have seen dogs turned out to sheer perfection both ways.

The same applies to how you hold a pair of scissors. Some use thumb and index, some thumb and middle finger, while others use thumb and fourth finger. I try all ways, and I don't see any difference! However, I do like scissors with a guard.

PROCEDURE

With all styles, the Poodle will need to have its feet, face and tail clipped. We will deal with this first. There are certain rules to observe:

- Apart from the feet, it is always safer to use clippers with the growth of coat to prevent rashing or grazing the skin.

- Where the face is concerned, always clip away from the eye.

- Unless you are experienced using clippers, it is quite likely that you will need time to get around all the delicate clipped parts of the Poodle, so use clipper lubricant frequently, every 10 minutes or less, and check the blade of the clipper for heat by putting it on your face. As soon as it feels more than a little warm, change the blade. Dogs have been burned with hot blades and it takes a long time for them to regain their confidence. My personal preference is for Aesculap blades.

FEET

Use blades that are meant for a closer finish on the dark colors only. Some people boast that they use a No. 40 blade on the feet and face, but the dogs invariably look as though they are grazed the next day, and I don't see why anyone wants to skin a Poodle. I have judged them in the show ring when their faces are livid red and even bleeding, and I consider this very wrong indeed. Feet can take a closer blade with less ill effect.

- Starting at the rear right foot (being sure the dog is standing square and is comfortable), hold the leg just beneath the hock joint, just above the foot. Take care that the foot is underneath the dog and not pulled out to the side. ▼

- Gently press open the toes with your fingers and clip the hair away from around the nails, flexing your wrist to turn the clipper to achieve this, and not twisting the dog's foot.

- Clip up each toe in turn, taking the hair from between the toes and being careful to avoid ramming the clipper into the web. Make sure you clip to the base of the toe and no higher, otherwise you will spoil the finished

appearance and give the Poodle what is known as a "chicken look."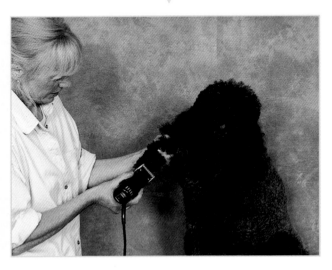

- Clip each foot in turn. Remember to change the blade if it gets too warm.

FACE

For the Poodle's face, we use an Oster No. 10 blade for most pet dogs and, for the thicker coat, a No. 15. The show dog is usually clipped closer with a No. 30, but this is not always advisable with a cream or white face. Always keep the blade as flat as possible without putting undue pressure on the skin.

- Hold the dog's muzzle in the right hand, folding the ear back over the head, and clip from the corner of the eye to the upper corner of the ear in a straight, neat line.

- Clip under the eye to the inner corner, then from between the eyes (at the stop) down to the tip of the nose.

- Clip from under the eye toward the muzzle to the nose. Repeat on other side of the face. 2 4

- From the base of the ear, clip down to the point of the throat – the Adam's apple. 3 4

- Clip the chin from the edge of the mouth to the nose, taking care to tighten the loose skin at all times. 4

- For the show Poodle, the neck is clipped into a U-shape, which involves shaving the hair down to an inch or two above the breast-bone, depending on the style of the mane, and the emphasis required to show off the length of the neck. 3 4

- Note: if you are unsure of the thickness of the facial hair, first clip the face with the coarser No. 10 blade – you can always take more off later, but if you start with, say, a No. 30 and it is too close for that individual dog, you could be in trouble, causing clipper rash, grazing or worse.

2

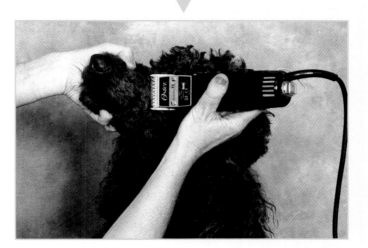

3

4

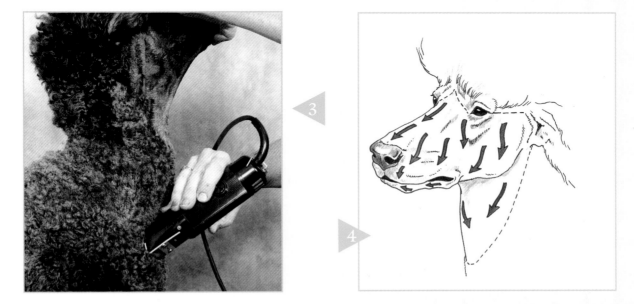

TAIL

Use a No. 15 Oster.

- Clip one-third of the (usually docked) tail from the base, leaving enough hair to create a pompom.

- Clip under the tail with a No. 10 blade, being careful not to use a clipper on the bulge of the anus.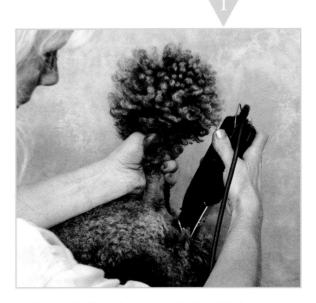

- The tail of an undocked Poodle can be clipped in the same way, but the amount of hair to leave can be confusing. It will depend on the trim: Lion, Sporting, or Lamb. How much hair has been left on the body? If it is a short backed Lamb, the unclipped hair on the tail generally looks better when trimmed with scissors into a large oval shape. Looking from any angle we should see about 1 inch (2.5 cm) of hair at the base and tip, blended to about double in the middle. A plume is the term often used to describe this finish. (See the photograph on page 284.)

- The show dog with a bad tail set – going too far towards the body – will have more hair left on the back of the tail and less on the front. This gives the illusion that the tail is better than it is. The idea is to make the finished effect look blended and balanced. Unfortunately many show dogs have an incorrect tail set. Where the tail curls right around, it can be made to look like a pompom with clever scissoring.

- Some people shave Poodle tails from end to end. I don't like this practice, as I prefer to see it looking more natural. If the dogs object to having their tails shaved in this way, it should not be done. Leaving even a short amount of tailored hair may be more comfortable for the dog. Or use a clipper with a coarser blade if the dog doesn't mind being clipped all the way along its tail.

BODY

LAMB TRIM

Use a No. 5 (summer) or a No. 4 (winter) Oster (for a longer finish).

- Clip from the base of the dog's head, just beneath the ears, down the top and underneath the neck, following the direction of hair growth. 1

- Lift the leg and clip under the arm and along the chest to the groin. 2 3 4

- Clip the neck to just above shoulder level, down the back to the tail, and just above the hip. Then clip along and downwards over the rib cage to the groin. 3 5

- Clip underneath the body – the stomach and

the groin – carefully taking hair from around the genitals. Always hold the delicate parts as you groom, to ensure safety. ▽3 ▽4

• Brush through the remaining hair, trousers, topknot and tail, removing all tangles with a slicker brush and a wide-toothed comb. Where necessary, to prevent causing the dog too much discomfort, use a mat-breaker. Anti-tangle conditioner can help too. ▽6

• Bathe the Poodle in a suitable natural, enhancing shampoo (such as tea tree and lavender), or a protein coat-strengthening formula with consideration to color and condition of the coat. ▽7

• Use a quality conditioner, such as sculpture finish, to aid scissoring.

• Blow the coat dry, brushing all the time in sections from the bottom of the leg upward with a pin brush or slicker. ▽8

• Check the dog's nails ▽9, ears ▽10 and teeth ▽11.

• Tidy all clipped areas where required by going over these parts with the same depth of blade as before.

• Hem the leg hair by neatening and blending the edge of the hair at the bottom of the leg, just above the toes. ▽12

• Scissor the legs, going with the contours of the body, or by using a silhouette line ▽3 ▽13. To do this contour edge, or to snip the hair, hold the scissors at a slight angle, pointing upward, and continue the line from bottom to top. Then take the next line and blend into the first line. Do not cut crossways (apart from when hemming across the toes). Trim with the scissors pointing downward or upward, at a slight angle but never crossways (apart from when hemming). Finally, skim across the hair to blend in any

stray hairs. Note: some groomers work (scissor) down from the body to the foot – it makes no difference if they get the correct neat finish.

• Holding the dog's muzzle, comb the head hair forward and scissor a topknot across the eye upward. ▽14

• Comb the hair to the left and trim across the top of the ears and the back of the neck, then repeat on the right side. ▽15

• Trim over the top, taking care to leave a nice topknot, but be sure that the dog can see clearly. ▽16

• For the tail, hold the pompom in one hand at the end of the dock (further up if the dock is short). Then cut straight across ▽17. Allow the hair to fall, and comb outwards. Hold up the tail at the tip and comb the hair outward, then scissor to a round appearance ▽18 or, in the case of a long tail, it may be more effective to trim into a brush, rather like that of a retriever.

• The finished dog. ▽19

▽1

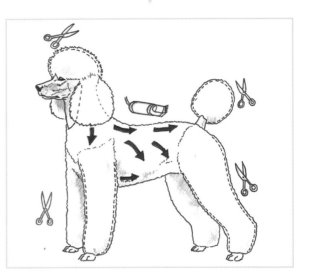

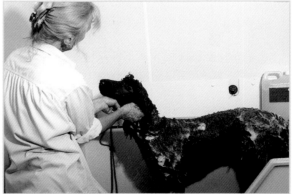

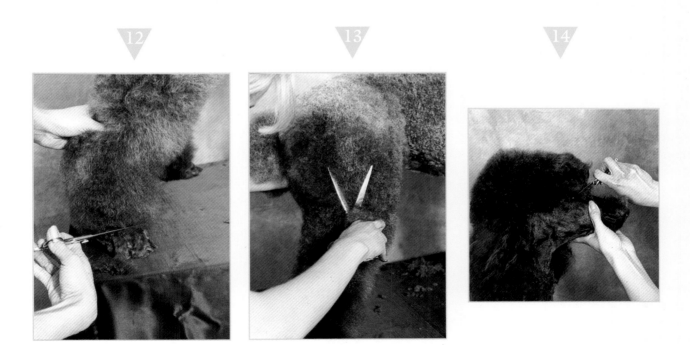

"SPORTING" OR "UTILITY" CLIP

Use a No. 5 Oster for the summer clip and a No. 4 for the winter clip. A thick coat can happily be taken down with the No. 10, going with the growth of the hair, in the summertime.

- Clip the neck from the base of the head, down over the shoulder, down the back to the tail, down and along the rib cage and under the chest, stomach and groin area.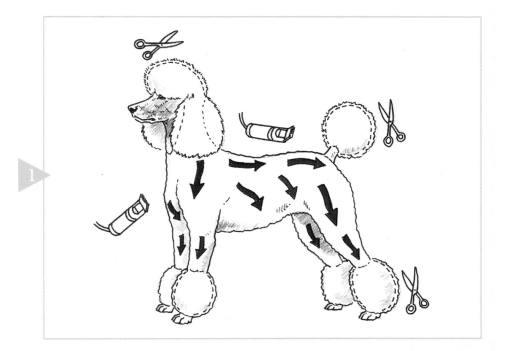

- Clip the back leg, inside and out, to an inch above the hock joint. Then, with an eyeline to balance, clip inside and out of the front leg to the same level. For the eyeline, just look at where the clip mark of the back leg ends and draw an imaginary line across to the front leg.

- Bathe and dry the Poodle, as for the "Lamb" clip (page 274).

- Check the nails, ears and teeth.

- Scissor the topknot as for the "Lamb" clip (page 274).

- Comb the long hair on the legs outward (bracelets) and scissor the bracelets into an oval shape.

- Trim the dog's tail as you would for the "Lamb" clip (page 274).

"DUTCH" CLIP

Use a No. 10 Oster.

- Clip the face, feet and tail, as with the instructions for the previous trims.

- Clip under the neck to the point of the breastbone, and then clip the rest of the neck to about 2 inches (5 cm) just above the withers.

- Taking a direct line, shave a blade's width between the shoulders, across the withers, and continue the line to the base of tail.

- Clip the abdomen from the groin to the navel and then downward, incorporating the insides of the thighs.

- Brush through the remaining unclipped hair with a slicker, and comb out any tangles.

- Bathe the dog in a suitable shampoo as for the "Lamb" clip (page 274).

- Blow-dry the coat, as described for the "Lamb" clip (see page 274).

- Check the dog's nails, ears and teeth.

- Go over the clipped part of the body to ensure a tidy finish.

- Scissor the topknot and tail as for the "Lamb" clip (page 274).

- Scissor the back legs to a neat finish, leaving a pronounced curve at the edge of the clipped parts, to give the impression that it is standing off.

- Scissor the front legs, leaving a pronounced curve to give the impression of the hair standing off the body. Scissor the front, leaving another pronounced curve that stands off from the body, rather than being blended into it.

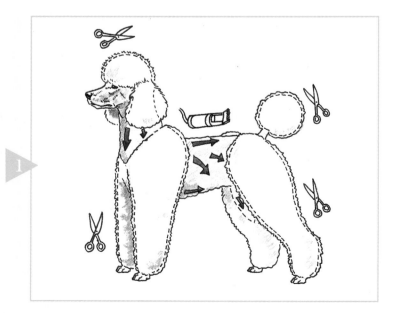

"FULL PUPPY" CLIP

A lot of time and effort goes into maintaining this style. It is mostly seen on puppies exhibited in the U.S. show ring, although there are some pet owners who adore their Poodles in this stunning trim and are happy to pay for the time and expertise the groomer takes in turning out an evenly scissored finish.

- Clip the face, feet and tail, as with the previous instruction.

- Thoroughly groom the coat with a slicker or pin brush, followed by a wide-toothed comb.

- Clip under the stomach/abdomen from the groin to the navel with a No. 10 blade.

- Bathe the dog in a suitable shampoo for the color and condition of the coat and apply a quality conditioner to aid scissor work.

- Blow-dry the hair away from the body, lifting with a pin brush to ensure it does not curl.

- Trim around the bottom of the legs to allow a peep at the toes.

- Snip off the very fine ends of hair to an even and dense-looking finish. As the coat grows in length, scissor slightly shorter at the base of the tail, blending the hair up toward the body to obtain an effective, pleasing, glamorous shape.

- Scissor the dog's tail as you would for the "Lamb" clip (see page 274).

"PUPPY LION" (OR "T-CLIP")

Strictly, the "Puppy Lion" and "T-clips" are different – the Scandinavian version of the "Puppy" clip accentuates the outlines slightly more.

In Britain, this trim is seen frequently in the show ring. In the U.S., show Poodles must be clipped into the traditional "Lion" at the age of 12 months.

• Clip the feet, face and tail, and groom and bathe the dog as for the "Puppy" clip (see page 281).

• Clip the abdomen area.

• Feel the body to ascertain the location of the last rib. For the uninitiated, it is a good idea to put a narrow bandage around the dog at just below this point to distinguish an even line and to be sure the balance is right. (Roughly one-third is trimmed shorter while two-thirds is left for the mane.)

• With the scissors held straight, cut upward along the edge of your line or bandage, from the near side, up one side, over the body and down the other side. This is more easily achieved when the dog is standing square with its rear end toward you. Remove your "guideline" bandage.

• In the "Puppy Lion"/"T-clip" (called "pajamas" by some) the back legs are trimmed with scissors as with the "Lamb" clip, but are left longer from the stifle down, and shaped over the hock with more accent on the rear angulations (to show, or to make the leg appear more angulated than it might be – clever trimming often scores more goals).

• Once you are well practiced with scissors, and if you have a good eye for the artwork involved, you can use a picture of your favorite dog and copy the up-to-the-minute trimming or the fashion of the current time.

• Flick the mane with the comb and allow the dog to shake and the hair to settle. Then, keeping the scissors level, scissor around, rather like skimming over the coat. The aim is to achieve a blend where the mane meets the shorter back hair to enhance the appearance of a well-defined neck.

• Work around the mane, shaping the incline from the brisket up toward the ear.

• Scissor the front legs to a tubular shape, accentuating where they join the mane at the elbow with a slight indent.

• Scissor the tail like the "Lamb" clip (page 274).

"TRADITIONAL LION" ("FULL PACK" OR "ENGLISH SADDLE")

• Clip the feet, face and tail.

• Groom, bathe, condition and blow the hair dry as for the "Puppy" clip (page 281).

• Part the coat behind the rib cage as in the "Puppy Lion" (page 282). It is always advisable to clip the mane in before the back end to make it easier to achieve a good balance. Again, a bandage can be used for forming lines. This is always a good idea as you can tie it around at the given points and move it up or down to achieve a balance before putting your scissors in. Once you've snipped, there is no turning back!

• Apply the bandage about 2 inches (5 cm) above the wrist, and look to see if this will allow you to scissor a nice oval bracelet. Cut above the bandage line, clip with a No. 10 up the front leg to remove the hair up to the joint of the elbow. Do not clip over the elbow. Trim the bracelet by combing the hair outward and allowing it to fall naturally. Then scissor the ends, tipping (scissoring) to form an oval shape.

• Scissor around the bottom of the mane to achieve a ball finish.

• Feel for the hock joint and apply the bandage about 1 inch (2.5 cm) above.

• Feel for the stifle joint, and apply a second bandage to define. Stand back and check that there is a good balance between the three defined points. Move the bandage slightly up or down until you feel happy that the dog looks right.

• With the scissors, cut a thin line above the bandage. These points can be carefully clipped, or defined with scissors.

• When starting on the other leg, do check that your lines correspond from behind (as seen in the illustration), otherwise the trim will look odd and unbalanced. Remember, once the scissors have cut, there is no turning back.

• Comb the individual three sections of hair on the back leg upward and outward, and then allow it to fall or settle naturally. Scissor each section to a smooth, rounded finish.

• Scissor the tail as for the "Lamb" clip (see page 274).

"CONTINENTAL LION" CLIP

Most of the Poodles that are shown in the United States are put into this trim at 12 months of age. It takes less time than the Traditional or Puppy trims, but still there is a lot of work here.

- Clip the feet, face and tail, and bathe, condition and blow the hair dry as for the Puppy trim (page 281).

- Cut in the front end (mane) as for the Lion (page 283), including scissoring to finish.

- For beginners, it is a good idea to place a saucer on the hip joint to define a rosette. Take the scissors and cut around the saucer. Remove the saucer and you will reveal a large rosette. Depending on whether the dog is longer than he should be in the back, or perfectly proportioned, the saucer can be moved backwards or forwards to achieve the best balance before cutting commences.

- With a No. 10 blade, start clipping from a position just above the hock joint and clip up to your newly made rosette. Clip around this, being careful not to clip the rosette itself. Clip the narrow area between the end of the mane and the rosette.

- Lifting the hair with a comb, scissor around the rosette to achieve a stylish, round puff of hair.

- Trim the tail as for the Puppy trim (page 281).

18 DESIGNER DOGS

BACKGROUND

At the beginning of its evolutionary history, it is thought that there were about seven types of dog. Gradually, through selective breeding, humans began to affect the shapes of different breeds. We recognised the benefit of having canine companions that would fetch food for us, guard and protect us and our herds and assist us when hunting. Later, we saw how dogs could perform search and rescue functions, guide the blind and be our faithful lap dogs and loving companions. Different breeds came about to fulfill these needs. The pedigree dog became so popular because people knew exactly what they were buying and the type of look and temperament that they could expect from their chosen breed.

In more recent years the Australian guide dogs for the blind organization Guide Dogs Australia took it upon themselves to try to develop a dog with the intelligence and steadiness of the Labrador and the non-molting coat of the Poodle to help blind people who were allergic to molting dogs. The name Labradoodle was coined as a catchy title to attract pet owners to purchase surplus puppies, and the Designer Dog started to come to public attention.

In any case it was discovered that these did not always turn out as planned. On many occasions they were doubly troublesome in that they shed hair as well as having wool that matted into itself. They often had rather unruly temperaments. However, the catchy name persisted and became such a hot topic in the media that other breeders decided to "jump on the bandwagon" and so a large variety of crosses were created, sometimes for fun and sometimes for profit.

The rights and wrongs of crossbreeding are not the groomer's concern. The trimming and care of the coats of these first, and sometimes second, crosses, famous for the often intriguing names they are given, have recently become a major feature in the grooming salon, particularly in the United States. The following recommendations provide guidelines regarding the coat care and styles to which some of these dogs are best suited. The truth is that any artistic groomers may like to put their own designs and interpretations on these breeds, where the coat so allows, but here we will concentrate on some of the more popular styles that have evolved.

COAT TYPES

As far as the groomer is concerned, we have all seen many different coat types cropping up within a single litter of a first or second cross. No doubt this will continue to be the case as breeders cross all sorts of sometimes obscure pairings with more unusual mixtures of hair on one dog than is normal for a pedigree breed. We can see both molt and matted-wool on one dog with growth of hair varying even across one area of the dog, such as its back. Sometimes we see thick curly coat along the spine and thinner wire-type hair on the side of the body and the legs.

The trimming of many crossbred or Designer Dogs is generally guided by the parent the dog most resembles, such as the Labradoodle with the Poodle-type wool coat, or the Cavapoo with wool hair or the more typical silky coat with a certain amount of wave. Silky type coats would not necessarily need the same amount of trimming, but may still form mats and knots if grooming is not sufficient. More and more work then falls to the professional groomer as these "mixture" coats evolve and they can be far more troublesome to the pet owner than the original pedigree dog coat. Many of the crossbreeds are longcoated with thick, wool-type coats that form mats if neglected. They can be harder work than the individual pedigree breeds that produced them. Some of these coats, as well as forming mats under the front legs, behind the ears and on the breeches. It sometimes seems to the groomer that the coat is constantly changing.

POPULAR CROSSES

Some of the best known designer crosses are the Labradoodle, Goldenpoo, the Cockerpoo, the Bichonpoo, the Lhasapoo, the Cavapoo as well as Yorkiepoo. Then come the terrier crosses in many shapes and forms, as well as the Old English Sheepdog cross, and many others. Certainly there are now many types of crossbreeds available, and sometimes there seems to be no rhyme or reason for the cross. If we look ahead to the next generation, we may see the first cross of two breeds being mated back to one half of the two parent breeds, creating a three-quarter-type cross. Whatever name they are given, these crossbreeds are important as clients and they should be groomed as efficiently as possible to create the best picture possible.

The Cavapoos and Labradoodles are generally the most popular of the crossbred dogs that come into the salon. They range in size and coat. The Labradoodle can be trimmed in full clip with a Poodle head (shaved face and top knot or helmet). They generally look just like a chunky Poodle, but can offer the option of a variety of styles to a creative groomer.

In other regions there are many Cockerpoos, Labradoodles that look like Springerxpoodle, Pokies or Yorkiepoos (Yorkshire Terrier x Poodle), Chorkies (Chihuahua and Yorkshire Terrier), Maltipoos, Sprockers (Springer and Cocker Spaniels), Goldendoodles, Boxerdoodles, Lhasaxmaltese, Bichonxmaltese and so it goes on. For sensible reasons, we will concentrate on the crosses generally most seen in the salon.

Some groomers may not know how to deal with these dogs. Grooming the varied coats that come through the door has been described as a nightmare by some groomers as the coat can differ from dog to dog and does not conform to a general expectation

Above: *This is what can result if basic regular grooming is neglected.*

breeders are just not aware of how much care is required to maintain such a coat, and so they do not pass on this information to their purchaser, much to the dismay of the groomer. They may own short-haired or non-wool-coated breeds and they don't know about coat change. Puppies look cute and can be sold without proper consultation. Only later does the the purchaser realize and then a six-month or year-old comes into the parlor for the groomer to try and sort out the coat. The behavior of the crossbreeds is also sometimes unruly with many groomers reporting that they are more difficult to handle than the pedigree.

the pedigree coat. Indeed several puppies from one litter can have completely different coat types.

The Designer Dog may well have been developed to meet popular demand, or its current popularity may have been boosted by the example of celebrity owners, cute photography and media attention, but for the groomer the only consideration must be the trimming of these dogs and how best to present each animal and take the best care of the individual coat.

We see some of these crosses coming in to the salon absolutely matted from head to toe and tail, with wads of coat connecting the legs and testicles or vulva. You wonder how on earth the animals manage to urinate. Often a skin rash has developed caused by the fluids caught in the felted hair. Here a 7f or 10 blade may need to be used to take the coat as short as possible to get under the felts.

Groomers often remark that when these dogs have a Bichon or Poodle as one parent, the coats shed and get more matted than is the case with the full pedigree. Some of the

Sam Kohl, a professional groomer in the United States, says in his own words, "We do have the same problems here with the designer doodles. There seem to be tons of these crazy crossbreeds. Groomers don't know what to expect from them, the coats and dispositions are never what they're supposed to be. Nor are their breeds near what the owners have been told they are mixed with. What was originally touted to be a smart and 'non-allergic' breeding of a Standard Poodle and a Labrador (which is far from non-allergic) as service dogs, turned out to be a boon for unscrupulous breeders. Since we know there still is no such thing as a 'non-allergic dog', it's been a dreadful hoax on the public and a nightmare for groomers."

We may share his sentiments, but as groomers our task is to cope with all that comes our way.

OLD ENGLISH SHEEPDOG X

The pedigree breed traces its origin to the west of England when a strong dog was required with the capability of defending flocks and herds from wolves. Later they were used to drive cattle and sheep to market. A working dog, their tails had to be docked as proof of their use, a custom that led the breed to be nicknamed the Bobtail.

Seen in the show ring in the late 1800s, the breed became a popular companion, as well as working dog. Media attention has caused quite an explosion in popularity from time to time, which has not always been beneficial to the breed. The modern dog has a profuse coat and is more likely to be kept as a pet or show dog, rather than a working dog.

As a rule the breed has a gentle nature, and is sometimes amusing and playful. but he is quite a home loving dog devoted to his family so is a dog that needs a home life and company, but can sometimes be a bit headstrong. This is a breed that needs plenty of exercise, walking and free running. The Old English Sheepdog is sometimes crossed with other breeds and the resulting dog generally requires a great deal of attention to its coat. **The cross variety** will generally be raised and groomed in much the same way as the pedigree strain (see page 99).

COAT: The coat care of the pedigree or crossbreed needs consideration. The length and depth of coat growth means the dog will need daily brushing and combing and removal of debris collected during walks and in the course of general day-to-day living. The pedigree coat is described as profuse, but not excessive. Often the crossbreed can be much more of a problem depending on the type of coat of the other parent.

In the grooming room we see quite a variety of coat conditions from thick, unkempt, matted, extremely felted to fluffy top coat and matted undercoat. Less commonly, some dogs are nicely groomed out. Most owners of pet dogs are happy to have the coat kept reasonably short once out of puppyhood. Some have them clipped fairly close when the coat is out of control. Some pedigree and crossbreeds need close shaving once the coat is a solid felt. Hard work!

In her breed notes in *Dog World* Sarah Winson tells of an OES featured in her local newspaper that had to undergo a general anaesthetic so that vets and nurses could remove 29 lb (13 kg) of matted hair, clip his 2-inch (5-cm) long claws and remove cysts and grass seeds from his paws and ears.

How sad that any dog should experience this kind of neglect. If we can only get across to all puppy owners that the necessity that grooming must be considered when taking on a long-coated dog, and how important it is to use a professional groomer on a regular basis to prevent this sort of neglect. Unfortunately this appears to be quite a common problem; many groomers say that they wish owners would think more seriously about what they are buying when they take on a cute puppy. How will the adult dog look and what will it cost in grooming expenses?

MAINTENANCE: Ordinarily scissors and clippers are not used on the pedigree coat as we have seen in the section on the pedigree OES. However, pet owners are not always as vigilant as they could be about brushing and combing, or they may find themselves gradually getting lost with the coat for one reason or another. As a result, this is a dog that is frequently seen with considerably shortened hair. Rather than causing any dog

to suffer the consequences of a matted coat, regular professional grooming needs to be considered. Perhaps breeders selling puppies should emphasize this problem. The cross is no different. It generally has a coat that needs high maintenance.

It is always a good idea to get a puppy accustomed to lying on its side on a non-slip mat on a table to be brushed and combed. To me this is an essential training procedure that should be started on day one when bringing a puppy home. This will help to prevent a bad back caused by grooming on the floor, form a bond between dog and owner, and prepare the dog for more thorough grooming as it grows. Puppies like the one-on-one attention and this proves a good time for bonding.

PROCEDURE

Equipment needed: Clipper, 16, 12 or 7 blade, 5 or 10 blade for hygiene areas, scissors, thinners, pin and slicker brushes, medium-toothed comb.

Breed tip: Lift coat to brush close to the skin.

• Firstly the coat is checked for any tangles or felts, and brushed through. A decision is made as to what length of coat will be left. A rough clip or shortening with the scissors,

always going with the lie of coat, can be done to begin with. Then, if the length is acceptable, the dog is bathed and thoroughly dried. A blaster may be used if the dog is not upset by the noise and water is blasted from its coat quickly, before it is dried with a medium-warm drier.

• Once thoroughly dry, the clipper can be put over the coat, or scissors used to ensure a good clean finish. Again clipping is done working with the lie of the coat and never against the grain as this will remove twice as much coat. The clipping should be done from the top of the neck, down to shoulders, along and down the side of the chest and back towards the tail.

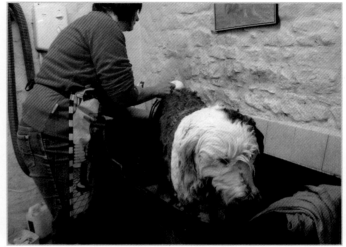

- Our model, Molly, had her coat taken down with an Aesculap 16 clipper blades, before being brushed, bathed in protein shampoo, rinsed, conditioner applied, and rinsed again. Excess water was removed with the blaster before Molly went onto the grooming table to finish drying. The finished clip was done with an Aesculap 12, leaving about 1½ inches (30 mm) of coat. The tummy area and groin region, (or what are known as hygiene areas) are taken down with a 5 or 10 blade for reasons of simple hygiene.

- The back and sides can also be clipped with a 5 blade and the legs and feet scissored short with ears clipped or shortened as the face.

- The feet are tidied to a rounded shape, and hair removed from the under pads with scissors. The ears are trimmed to the shape of the leather. The head is trimmed with the 12 blade and finished to shape with scissors.

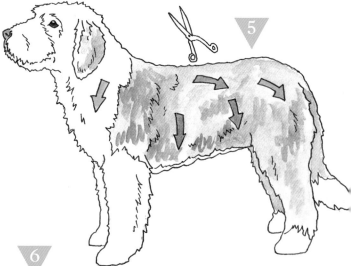

- The inside of the ears are checked for freshness and cleanliness, and the teeth are brushed where necessary using canine toothpaste. Brushing or using a cotton pad with the wonderful Petzlife oral care products on dirty or tartar-stained teeth is a godsend, although owners really need to take this task on at home too. This stuff really works. For anyone not familiar with this product, it is a good idea to get to grips with it, as owners can easily use it and the tartar just melts away. Even very bad teeth can be helped considerably.

- An alternative to clipping the coat is to use thinning scissors all over and remove enough hair as to prevent matting for some time. However, this is extremely time-consuming, and requires a patient dog. Scissoring of the feet and under the pads, as well as clipping the tummy and hygiene areas, is also required.

- The finished dog.

CAVAPOO

COAT: The coat is generally thicker and less silky than that of the pedigree Cavalier with thicker feathering, sometimes woolly in texture, and varying in appearance from flattish to quite fluffy. Generally carries curly wool on the head.

MAINTENANCE: Brush on regular daily basis with pin or slicker. Comb through well especially where feathering is more profuse.

PROCEDURE

Equipment needed: Slicker brush, medium comb, scissors, clippers.

Breed tip: Styling can be varied to suit type and size, and condition of coat.

- Groom through to remove any tangles, using anti-tangle spray or dematter where needed. Scissor to medium length all over, or clip the body with a 5 blade, blending in the legs with scissors.

- Scissor the legs to a tubular shape.

- Tidy around the head leaving whiskers. Cut back the fringe from the eyes.

- Bath in a protein shampoo and then dry, brushing the coat away from the body.

- Tidy loose ends after drying.

- Check nails, ears and teeth.

COCKERPOO

COAT: Varies in degree of thickness and length of growth, usually it is far more profuse, wavy and curly than the pedigree Cocker. Groomers report that Cockerpoos are definitely more consistent in coat than some crosses (which are usually a nightmare!). Some lovely ones come into the salon, but this is a cross that is not properly understood by prospective owners – they are usually pretty manic in temperament with very high-maintenance coats which owners really struggle to look after.

MAINTENANCE: Constant brushing with a slicker and combing through with a medium-toothed comb. When the coat is kept long, regular monthly appointments may be required to keep it in good condition. Oatmeal shampoo with coat conditioner is a popular asset, which many find helpful to deal with tangles and to prevent matting. At about a year old most customers cannot cope with the coat because it mats so easily after exercise; if it gets wet, they cannot dry a dog with so profuse a coat. Most of them come into the grooming salon every eight weeks for a complete clip.

PROCEDURE:

Equipment needed: Clippers, scissors, slicker brush.

Breed tip: Brushing between trims is essential if the coat is to be kept a reasonable length.

- The entire coat can be scissored to a manageable length if it is not matted, or if mats are removable.

- The 7f or 5 blade is often used on the body of the Cockerpoo. Blend legs with scissors to a tubular shape, or clip them down with the 5

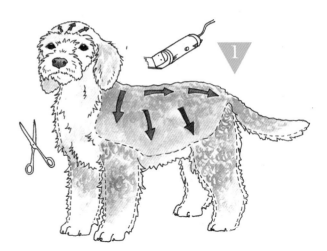

blade. The feet should be scissored to a tidy around finish.

- Some customers like the head clipped with the 5 blade, or it can be scissored to a round shape, leaving whiskers and beard where desired, if not matted.

- Shampoo used is a natural oatmeal product. On the face tearless shampoo is suggested.

- Blow dry, brushing long hair away from the body.

- Tidy any loose ends.

- Check ears, teeth and nails.

GOLDENDOODLE

COAT: The Goldendoodles can have a mixed coat, which is generally thick and wavy. It looks similar to a Golden Retriever but has more of a Poodle texture. The coat can grow a lot longer than the pure-bred Golden but with a curlier texture. It can take quite a while to bath and dry. It is sometimes silky and sheds like the Golden Retriever parent, or it can be thick and woolly like the Poodle parent shedding hair into the coat.

MAINTENANCE: It is essential to brush and comb at least three times weekly to remove shedding hair and keep the wool-dense areas free of felts. Regular trips to the grooming salon are generally the rule.

PROCEDURE:

Equipment needed: Slicker and pin brush, medium-toothed comb, thinners, scissors, clippers.

Breed tip: Try using coat spray when pre-brushing to loosen and remove hair and tangles to aid drying the thick coat.

- Bath in protein-rich or oatmeal shampoo.

- Blast out excess water if dog tolerates the noise and power of this dryer.

- Finish drying with warm air using the slicker.

- Coat Handler detangler spray helps with particularly dense areas of coat as it loosens it to assist a quicker drying time.

- Comb from head to toe after drying.

- The 44-tooth thinning scissors are ideal here, no shears or clipping scissors are needed apart from under the feet to clean out the pads.

- Shape the back legs to angulation, thinning out the breeches.

- Scissor the front leg furnishings or use thinners depending on thickness of the feathering.

- Make a natural foot shape using thinners and texturize the body coat with the thinners.

- Thinners can be used on the chest if the coat is not too thick.

- Edge the ear leather with thinners and where the coat is wispy around the ears fold the ear, angle it slightly towards the center of head (as in shaping a Westie ear) and thin off the coat.

- Tidy the head and face with thinners as well as the throat and neck to blend and flow easily into the body.

- Leave a wispy "skirt" and clip out under the tail (near the bottom) to stop debris gathering in the coat.

- The tail should be flagged as with a retriever.

- Check ears, teeth and nails.

Above: With the more curly, Poodle-like coat the Goldendoodle can be clipped out like a Standard Poodle in Sporting or lamb trim – as shown here.

LABRADOODLE

COAT: There is much variation in the coat of this popular crossbreed. It ranges from short, close, constantly shedding hair to long and flat, wavy, dense, and thick and woolly that sheds coat like a molt as well as sheds into itself to form felts if not groomed regularly.

Such a mixture of coat is also seen on one dog. Rarely – if ever – are they non-shedding as claimed by some breeders. The contrasting coats are often referred to as Fleece (woolly) and Scruffy (wiry).

MAINTENANCE: Includes brushing with slicker and or pin brush, combing with medium-toothed comb, regular trimming, clipping and bathing for most of these dogs. A glove or bristle brush can be used on the short-haired variety. A regular thorough brushing for the Scruffy type.

PROCEDURE

Equipment needed: Slicker and pin brush, medium-toothed comb, clippers, scissors, thinners, glove.

Breed tip: Identify the coat type before deciding whether to thin or clip coat, or to merely bath and brush. The head is important as it can be clipped like the Poodle, scissored to a round shape leaving whiskers, or left Scruffy depending on coat type.

• Having decided on the type of coat, groom through with a slicker.

• If clipping has been decided upon, use a 5 or coarser blade to clip the body from the head down the neck and sides of the body to rear (see OES X profile on page 289). Clip under the tail for hygiene.

• If the coat is silky it may be preferable to scissor to an even length all over.

• When this crossbreed resembles its Poodle parent more closely, the face and feet may be clipped with a 10 blade, and the body shaped into the Lamb trim or clipped into the Sporting trim (see Poodle profile on pages 270–284).

• Bath in tea tree and lavender oil shampoo or

Left: Labradoodle Fleece type coat

oatmeal. Condition if necessary, although often a conditioning spray brushed into coat will suffice, once it is patted dry with a towel or the hair has been blasted dry for a few minutes to remove excess water.

• Dry with warm air, brushing constantly if the coat is of the wool type. Use of a cabinet dryer is up to the preference of the individual – they can save time in a busy salon, but make sure the dog is thoroughly free of tangles and felts first.

• Clip over body to tidy loose hairs, or scissor to required length and the style preferred to suit the coat and the owner's ability to look after it between trims.

• Check ears, teeth and nails.

Above: Labradoodle Scruffy type coat

LHASAPOO

COAT: Usually relatively thick with a tendency to mat and will grow to good length when brushed regularly.

MAINTENANCE: Needs constant brushing and combing with added conditioner when left to grow. Most get matted and are better trimmed to a manageable length.

PROCEDURE

Equipment needed: Slicker brush, medium-toothed comb, clippers, scissors, thinning scissors.

Breed tip: Requires a lot of grooming to keep free of tangles.

- When the dog is matted, the easiest course is to clip all over with an Oster 5 blade, including clipping down the ears and tidying around the edges with scissors.

- The head can be rounded with scissors and the beard blended in if it is possible to comb it free of tangles. Frequently the cheeks of the face are also clipped, leaving whiskers to the side of muzzle and chin.

- The feet are scissored to neaten the outline around the toes and the underside can be clipped or taken out with scissors. The tail is left with a short plume where possible.

- Check nails, ears and teeth.

MALTI X

COAT: Can be silky as the Maltese with much potential for a lot of growth or quite woolly depending on the cross involved.

MAINTENANCE: Where the coat is silky it can be maintained at a decent length if required by brushing with the pin or slicker brush and combing with a wide- to medium-toothed comb.

PROCEDURE

Equipment needed: Slicker brush, scissors, thinning scissors or clippers.

Breed tip: Be sure to groom under the arms and behind the ears to prevent mats forming.

• Groom through removing tangles with anti-tangle spray when required.

• Bath with protein or oatmeal shampoo, using conditioner and warm blow drying the hair away from the body while constantly brushing with slicker or pin brush.

• Tidy around the feet with scissors.

PEKE X

COAT: Very thick and generally dense.

MAINTENANCE: There is a tendency for the coat to knot behind the ears and under body. It needs regular brushing with pin or slicker.

PROCEDURE

Equipment needed: Slicker, clippers, scissors, eye cleaner.

Breed tip: Lift and separate hair when brushing to avoid excess hair forming felts.

• Groom thoroughly, bath in a protein shampoo followed by a conditioner, blow dry.

• This cross is frequently clipped all over with 5 blade for comfort and coolness.

• Clip the face with 7 blade or scissor to a short rounded shape.

• Tidy the feet with scissors.

• Check ears, teeth and nails.

• Trim away hair from around the eyes and remove any tangles left on the face.

• The alternative is to clip all over with a 5 blade tidying face, feet and tail with scissors, or clip face with 10 blade leaving whiskers. Or clip the body with a 5 blade and scissor the legs to blend in.

• Check under the tail and trim hair to keep this area clean and hygienic.

• Check ears, teeth and nails.

• Check any folds in the skin and clean these areas with cotton wool and a solution of eye cleaner.

POOCHON

COAT: The Bichon Frise has a coat that is quite dense and soft and which tends to form corkscrew curls. The Poodle has what is described as a unique and distinguished coat. Other breeds want to take advantage of it so they cross with the Poodle to that end. It rarely works. The Poochon's undercoat is cottony in texture, dense and tending to curl, especially when wet. The top coat can be classed as soft and curly, which will hang in fluffy ringlets and become straight when brushed out. So perhaps these two breeds are not as diverse as some crosses.

MAINTENANCE: Certainly there is scope for artistic licence with a coat that is well groomed. Daily brushing and bathing regularly with added conditioner is essential to keep the coat in good form. Many Poochons are shaped with the scissors to look most like the Bichon and so they will need the constant four to six week grooming maintenance that is typical of this breed.

PROCEDURE

Equipment needed: Pin and slicker brush, scissors, clippers.

Breed tip: Grooming spray will help to remove dead hair, and lift and separate the coat while grooming.

- If the Poochon is to be scissored, it may be advisable to follow the trimming of the Bichon Frise (see pages 252-3). The alternative is to clip the body with a 5 blade.

- Scissor legs as for the Poodle Lamb trim, giving a tubular shape, blending into the body hair.

- Scissor the hair on face to a manageable length in a rounded fashion rather than attempting the far more taxing shaping of the show Bichon.

- Bath in protein shampoo, use a quality conditioner and blow dry the coat away from body while constantly brushing. Blend in all clipped or scissored hair.

- Check ears, teeth and nails.

SPRINGER X

COAT: Unlike the pedigree dog, the coat of a Springer cross can be quite woolly and unruly, growing profusely.

MAINTENANCE: To prevent matting, daily brushing with a pin or slicker brush. These crosses generally need regular trimming.

PROCEDURE

Equipment needed: Slicker and pin brush, clippers, scissors, thinning scissors.

Breed tip: Coat can "run away" to thickness and matting.

- The crossbreed and sometimes the English Springer pedigree whose coat has "run away" is often clipped all over with a 5 or 7 blade including the ears and tail. Bath as usual, with a light blow dry. Under the pads must be checked for wads.

- Where the coat is "groomable", it can be thinned, brushed and combed, with feathering tidied with scissors.

- Check ears, teeth and nails.

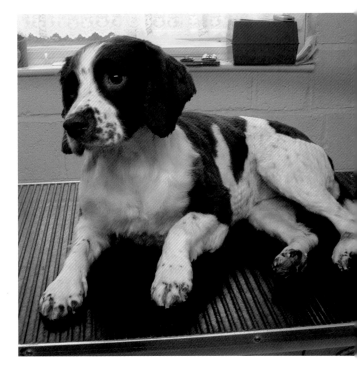

TERRIER X

COAT: These coats are generally wiry to the touch and molt or shed considerably.

MAINTENANCE: Constant brushing to remove dead hairs.

PROCEDURE

Equipment needed: Soft brush or glove, clippers, scissors.

Breed tip: Such variation in coat may be hand-stripped or clipped.

- The coat can be clipped all over with a 5 blade or coarser

- Hand-strip if required or preferred.

- Face and ears should be tidied with scissors.

- Bath and dry with a warm blower.

YORKIE X

COAT: Thick woolly coat or long and silky, or both types of coat combined.

MAINTENANCE: Daily brushing (or at least three times weekly) will keep this crossbreed tangle-free. However, the coat can grow extremely long and will need regular bathing and conditioner to be applied.

PROCEDURE

Equipment needed: Pin and slicker brushes, medium-toothed comb.

Breed tip: Can vary in coat type and size so trimming needs to suit the individual dog taking coat care into consideration.

- Brush through with a pin or slicker brush. Use a medium-toothed comb to check for any resistant tangles. Use groom spray or detangle spray. If trimming is required, clip with a 5 blade or scissor to controllable length.

- Tidy the feet, checking under the pads for excess hair and the formation of wads.

- Bath in a protein or oatmeal shampoo, adding conditioner, rinse out thoroughly. Blow dry brushing the hair away from the body. Tidy any loose hair with scissors.

- Check ears, teeth and nails.

Creative Grooming

Not to everybody's taste, but the art of creative grooming is becoming increasingly popular – admittedly it is designed more for show competitions and fun events than normal everyday life.

What is creative grooming? I asked intrepid creative groomer Su Eld Weaver to explain. "I started creative grooming many moons ago. I was using color to give my black standards a more vibrant color for competition grooming. I had a thing about purple blacks. I did more subtle changes in the past but then I came across the magazine *Groomer to Groomer.*"

Above: *A Chinese Crested struts his stuff.*

Above: *This Poodle sports amazing zebra stripes.*

Su says she loves to paint and sculpt and play with all sorts of media so this was just a new form of art for her. "I started on a white Standard Poodle I had at home, which I was not showing and she seemed to really enjoy the whole process. It was quite a big bonding session and she had my attention one-on-one the whole way through. Needless to say my first trial was a disaster as the colors did not

behave in the way I thought they should."

Clients of Su's saw her work and they asked for creative styles (spirals, Mohawk and pin striping) and then different colors. Some wanted more subtle work and temporary tattoos, so special stencils were created.

Su dreamed of going to the United States to compete and to design a creative piece that would rival the best that American creative groomers could produce. She says "The UK started to put on creative classes, Ireland did the first one three years ago, then an English groomer group started in 2010."

The colors used are mainly vegetable-based dyes and are very kind to the dog's skin. Some permanent colors are used in certain designs but they are only to be used by experienced groomers. Su is qualified as a hairdresser so she understood about the different types of colors and had a good understanding of how to apply coloring. Su felt it was important to have some solid knowledge behind her if she was going to help others and give attention to clients' dogs.

Su performs creative grooming on any breed, saying that the lighter the natural color of the coat, the better the colors actually work, although the darker coats are just as good for pin stripes and shapes. The only limit is your own imagination.

INDEX OF BREEDS

K

L

M

N

O

P